# Corinthian Democracy

# Princeton Theological Monograph Series

K. C. Hanson, Charles M. Collier, D. Christopher Spinks,
and Robin A. Parry, Series Editors

*Recent volumes in the series:*

Koo Dong Yun
*The Holy Spirit and Ch'i (Qi):
A Chiological Approach to Pneumatology*

Stanley S. MacLean
*Resurrection, Apocalypse, and the Kingdom of Christ:
The Eschatology of Thomas F. Torrance*

Brian Neil Peterson
*Ezekiel in Context: Ezekiel's Message Understood in Its Historical
Setting of Covenant Curses and Ancient Near
Eastern Mythological Motifs*

Amy E. Richter
*Enoch and the Gospel of Matthew*

Maeve Louise Heaney
*Music as Theology: What Music Says about the Word*

Eric M. Vail
*Creation and Chaos Talk: Charting a Way Forward*

David L. Reinhart
*Prayer as Memory: Toward the Comparative Study of Prayer
as Apocalyptic Language and Thought*

Peter D. Neumann
*Pentecostal Experience: An Ecumenical Encounter*

Ashish J. Naidu
*Transformed in Christ:
Christology and the Christian Life in John Chrysostom*

# Corinthian Democracy
*Democratic Discourse in 1 Corinthians*

ANNA C. MILLER

◆PICKWICK *Publications* · Eugene, Oregon

CORINTHIAN DEMOCRACY
Democratic Discourse in 1 Corinthians

Princeton Theological Monograph Series 220

Copyright © 2015 Anna C. Miller. All rights reserved. Except for brief quotations in critical publications or reviews, no part of this book may be reproduced in any manner without prior written permission from the publisher. Write: Permissions, Wipf and Stock Publishers, 199 W. 8th Ave., Suite 3, Eugene, OR 97401.

Pickwick Publications
An Imprint of Wipf and Stock Publishers
199 W. 8th Ave., Suite 3
Eugene, OR 97401

www.wipfandstock.com

ISBN 13: 978-1-62032-905-4

*Cataloging-in-Publication data:*

Miller, Anna C.

Corinthian democracy : democratic discourse in 1 Corinthians / Anna C. Miller.

xii + 204 p. ; 23 cm. —Includes bibliographical references and index(es).

Princeton Theological Monograph Series 220

ISBN 13: 978-1-62032-905-4

1. Bible. Corinthians, 1st—Criticism, interpretation, etc. 2. Paul, the Apostle, Saint—Political and social views. 3. Corinth (Greece)—Church history. I. Title. II. Series.

BS2675.2 M55 2015

Manufactured in the U.S.A.  04/30/2015

For Chad, Ben and Mary Martha—
You have lived this book with me

"This is freedom: 'Who is willing, having good counsel, to bring it before the People?'" τοὐλεύθερον δ' ἐκεῖνο· Τίς θέλει πόλει χρηστόν τι βούλευμ' εἰς μέσον φέρειν ἔχων; (Euripides, Suppl. 435).

# Contents

*Acknowledgments*   ix
*Abbreviations*   x

Introduction   1

1   The *Ekklēsia* in Greek Education   14

2   The First-Century *Ekklēsia* in the Writings of Dio and Plutarch   40

3   Moses in the *Ekklēsia*: Josephus' Use of Democratic Discourse   68

4   Speech and Wisdom of the Corinthian *Ekklēsia*   90

5   The Gendering of Democratic Participation   115

6   "As in all the *Ekklēsiai* of the Saints": 1 Cor 12–14   154

Conclusion   187

*Bibliography*   191
*Ancient Sources Index*   205
*Subject Index*   215

# Acknowledgments

I OFFER MY MOST SINCERE THANKS TO THOSE WHO HAVE OFFERED THEIR support and critical feedback for different elements of this study. First, I want to thank Elisabeth Schüssler Fiorenza for her unstinting support for this project since its inception. She has been exceptionally generous with her time and advice, while her own work has been essential to the success of this project—providing both critical methodology as well as inspiration for my own writing. I also want to thank Karen King and Laura Nasrallah for their attentive reading to earlier versions of this project. Both provided illuminating critiques that challenged and advanced my thinking. At Xavier University, I give many thanks to my colleagues Art Dewey and Sarah Melcher for their friendship, critical reading, and intellectual stimulation. Likewise, I want to thank my colleagues and friends Carly Daniel-Hughes and Katherine Shaner who have helped and challenged me more than I can say over these many years. Mary Martha Miles deserves my gratitude for sharing her editing skills through many drafts. Finally, my husband Chad Clark has never wavered in his belief in me and in the project, a faith that sustained me through the many highs and lows of creating this book.

# Abbreviations

| | |
|---|---|
| 1 Cor | 1 Corinthians |
| 1 Sam | 1 Samuel |
| 1 Thess | 1 Thessalonians |
| 2 Chron | 2 Chronicles |
| 2 Cor | 2 Corinthians |
| Ael. | Aelius Aristides |
| Aeschin. | Aeschines |
| Aristophanes | |
|   *Eccl.* | *Ecclesiazusae* |
|   *Lys.* | *Lysistrata* |
| Aristotle | |
|   *Ath. Pol.* | *Athenian Politics* |
|   *Pol.* | *Politics* |
|   *Rhet.* | *Rhetoric* |
| Chrys. | John Chrysostom |
|   *Hom. in 1 Cor.* | *Homily in 1 Corinthians* |
| Dem. | Demosthenes |
|   *Ex.* | *Exordia* |
| Deut. | Deuteronomy |
| Dio | Dio Chrysostom |
|   *Or.* | *Oration* |
| Dion. Hal. | Dionysius Halicarnassus |
| Eph | Ephesians |
| Epictetus | |
|   *Diatr.* | *Dissertationes* |
| Euripides | |
|   *Heracl.* | *Children of Hercules* |
|   *Hipp.* | *Hippolytus* |
|   *Phoen.* | *Phoenissae (Phoenician Women)* |
|   *Suppl.* | *Suppliant Women* |

| | | |
|---|---|---|
| | TDNT | *Theological Dictionary of the New Testament* |
| | THKNT | *Theologischer Kommentar zum Neuen Testament* |
| | Thuc. | Thucydides |
| | Xen. | Xenophon |
| | *Symp.* | *Symposium* |
| | Ps.- Xen | Pseudo-Xenophon |
| | [*Ath.*] | *Anthenaion Politeia* |
| | ZPE | *Zeitschrift für Papyrologie und Epigraphik* |

| | |
|---|---|
| Ex | Exodus |
| Hdt. | Herodotus |
| Homer | |
|   *Il.* | *Iliad* |
| Ignatius | |
|   *Eph.* | *To the Ephesians* |
| Isoc. | Isocrates |
| Josephus | Flavius Josephus |
|   *Ant.* | *Antiquities of the Jews* |
|   *War* | *Jewish War* |
| JRA | Journal of Roman Archaeology |
| JSOT | Journal for the Study of the New Testament |
| Judg | Judges |
| LCL | Loeb Classical Library |
| Lib. | Libanius |
| Lys. | Lysias |
| Num. | Numbers |
| PCPS | *Proceedings of the Cambridge Philological Society* |
| Phil | Philippians |
| Philo | Philo of Alexandria |
|   *Praem.* | *On Rewards and Punishments* |
|   *Somn.* | *On Dreams* |
| Plato | |
|   *Menex.* | *Menexenus* |
|   *Phd.* | *Phaedo* |
|   *Phdr.* | *Phaedrus* |
|   *Prt.* | *Protagoras* |
|   *Resp.* | *Respublica* |
| Plutarch | |
|   *An seni* | *Old Men in Political Affairs* |
|   *Conj. praec.* | *Advice to the Bride and Groom* |
|   *Cons. ux.* | *A Consolation to His Wife* |
|   *Exil.* | *On Exile* |
|   *Praec. ger. rei publ.* | *Political Advice* |
|   *Pyth. orac.* | *On the Pythian Oracles* |
|   *Quaest. conv.* | *Quastionum convivalium* |
|   *Sept. sap. conv.* | *The Dinner of the Seven Wise Men* |
|   *Vit. aere al.* | *De vitando aere alieno* |
| Quint. | Quintillian |
|   *Inst.* | *Institutio oratoria* |
| REG | *Revue des Études Greques* |

# Introduction

## Introductory Considerations

IN THE FIRST CENTURY CE, THE APOSTLE PAUL WROTE TO MEMBERS OF THE Corinthian *ekklēsia* in the letter 1 Corinthians, accusing them of fostering division and injustice in their construction of community. New Testament scholars have long debated the nature of the community Paul depicts in this letter, alternately theorizing the Corinthians as hopeless libertines, extreme ascetics, or inspired charismatics. This book will suggest that previous research on 1 Corinthians has largely failed to recognize the deeper struggle over leadership and freedom that characterizes the debates between Paul and the Christians at Corinth. In fact, Paul's unflattering presentation of the Corinthians' interaction as divisive does not necessarily indicate a truly fractious community. Instead, Paul's rhetorical aim in this letter seems to be convincing the Corinthians of his vision of communal practice while shoring up particular modes of authority. Toward this aim, 1 Corinthians is marked by rhetorical tactics drawn from a robust discourse of democracy— what I term "*ekklēsia* discourse"—a discourse pervasive in the eastern Roman Empire and within the Corinthian community. I argue that Paul's rhetoric is inscribed with this *ekklēsia* discourse in order to make his own leadership legitimate in a context where the same discourse was being mobilized to construct a community around the actions of empowered, free citizens.

Michel Foucault defines discourse as "practices that systematically form the objects of which they speak."[1] Discourses never exist apart from power relations but in fact sustain and are sustained by them. Yet discourses also contain within them "a plurality of resistances"[2] that provide the

---

1. Foucault, *The Archaeology of Knowledge*, 49.
2. Foucault, *The History of Sexuality*, 96.

possibility of undermining those very same power structures from within the same discursive space. Indeed, it is precisely the discontinuous nature of *ekklēsia* discourse that led to its deployment in a host of ancient contexts. Through the course of the book, I trace a persuasive ancient discourse of democracy that emerged out of the Greek civic institution composed of the body of free citizens,[3] the *ekklēsia*. Moreover, my research shows that this discourse expanded into other fields of the Greco-Roman world to constitute a prevalent kind of social knowledge and cultural logics that defined debates over civic power and authority in a variety of contexts. I will map the contours of this discourse, tracing various sites in the first century where "democracy" could be deployed in the service of different social and political agendas.

My examination of these sources leads me into a treatment of the debates and struggles in Corinth. I argue that an analysis of Paul's rhetoric reveals that this ancient Christian community was constructed, at least rhetorically, as a civic and political body. Informed by the rhetorical-critical model articulated by Elisabeth Schüssler Fiorenza, my aim is to problematize readings that simply reiterate Paul's logic or his rhetorical presentation of the Corinthian community. Examining the competing deployments of *ekklēsia* discourse between Paul and the Corinthians in this letter will reveal that disparate community members at Corinth took a vocal role in deliberative decision-making within this Christian community.

## History of Scholarship

In the late nineteenth century, I. Lévy set the tone for subsequent scholarship on the Greek civic *ekklēsia*, or assembly, under the Roman Empire, writing:

> The *ekklēsia* endured everywhere . . . However, changes had altered its composition, restrained its competence, limited its powers, modified to its detriment the relations with other civic leaders, so that, in fact, only the name remained of the ancient sovereign assembly.[4]

Following Lévy's lead, scholars of ancient history have largely dismissed the possibility that the assembly, and by extension, democracy itself, continued

---

3. Traditionally, these citizens of the Greek city were both free and male, and part of this study investigates the gendered nature of democratic discourse.

4. My translation. Lévy, "Études sur la vie municipale de l'Aie Mineure sous les Antonins," 218.

to take a vital role in Greek cities under the Roman Empire.⁵ Through a fresh reading of first-century Greek texts, my project challenges this tradition, showing that this period knew an *ekklēsia* active both in practice, and in its role as a compelling cultural motif connecting people with an ideal of citizen equality. Reassessing the vitality of the assembly compels us to entertain a new paradigm for first-century community dynamics that emphasizes speech and collective judgment. In particular, this reassessment calls for a new interpretation of the early Christian letter 1 Corinthians, a text distinguished in the New Testament for its focus on community interaction within a group labeled *ekklēsia*. Read through the lens of democratic discourse, 1 Corinthians becomes a forum of active negotiation over issues such as leadership, freedom, and gender. This very negotiation places the letter in conversation with diverse genres of first-century literature. Recognizing this letter's democratic political valence allows us to explore the significance of the Corinthians coming together as a whole to engage in discussion and contest over the shape of their community.

The argument that *ekklēsia* discourse was both common and lively in the first-century Roman Empire, and in turn, that it impacted early Christian communities, requires a reassessment of accepted trends of scholarship both in classics and in New Testament studies. Scholars of antiquity have proven that the cultural legacy of classical Athens remained strong in Greek cities during the first centuries of the Roman Empire. In fact, scholars like Simon Swain have carefully mapped out the intensification of Greek culture and Greek identity in the eastern empire during the period of the Second Sophistic, a period beginning in the first century CE.⁶ During the Second Sophistic, this Greek identity and culture stood in a complicated relationship with Roman authority since it could be associated with differentiation and resistance to the empire, even as Roman rule itself "drew on Greek language, incorporated Greek political ideas and fostered Greek literature."⁷ While scholars have acknowledged both this intensification of Greek culture and its tension with the empire in the first century, few have

---

5. Ste Croix, *The Class Struggle in the Ancient Greek World*, 527ff.; Jones, *The Greek City from Alexander to Justinian*, 170; Millar, "The Greek City in the Roman Period," 241.

6. Swain notes that a "cultural confidence" runs through this period for elites of the Greek East that related directly to their perceived closeness with the classical past. Swain, *Hellenism and Empire*, 6–10. For a further in-depth study of this period, see Anderson, *The Second Sophistic*.

7. Rajak, "Judaism and Hellenism Revisited," 3–4.

recognized the democratic *ekklēsia* as a robust element of Hellenistic culture and identity in this time.⁸

A preoccupation with changes resulting from Roman rule has dominated scholarship directed toward political thought and practice in the early empire. In these terms, the continued meeting of assemblies has been largely ignored or described as meaningless in light of eroding civic power and democracy.⁹ This approach has obscured the fact that *topoi* familiar from classical literature, such as idealization of an empowered citizen body and the speech of the assembly, continued to fill Greek texts circulating in the early Roman Empire. Further, these themes were applied not only to historical assemblies of the past or to theoretical assemblies of the imagination but also to the assemblies that were meeting in Greek cities of the first century. Drawing upon Greek educational and political literature, my study establishes the survival of language and dynamics associated with the classical *ekklēsia*. In the process, this project also reveals the complexity of democratic practice under Roman domination.

Recognition of first-century democratic discourse also signals a departure in analyzing Paul's interaction with the Corinthian community, a group taking the title *ekklēsia* in common with other early Christian communities coming together in cities around the Mediterranean during this time. Following the lead of classics, scholars of the New Testament have largely dismissed the civic *ekklēsia* as an institution that retained real authority or discursive power in the first century. In turn, these scholars tend to eliminate the civic *ekklēsia* as a possible source for the title taken by early Christian communities or as an influence on the organization these communities assumed.

The scholarly consensus in New Testament studies locates the emergence of *ekklēsia* as a community title in its Septuagint usage, suggesting that early Christians chose the title for its "particular religious significance."¹⁰ Meanwhile, scholars of recent decades have often looked to other social

---

8. Ma's article on the *Euboicus* provides a helpful exception. Ma, "Public Speech and Community."

9. Ste Croix, *Class Struggle*, 527–533; Jones, *The Greek City*, 170; Millar, "The Greek City in the Roman Period," 241. To see this perspective reflected in New Testament scholarship, see Horsley, "Rhetoric and Empire- and 1 Corinthians," 79; Blumenfeld, *The Political Paul*, 103. Unlike Horsley, Blumenfeld does acknowledge that however emasculated he sees it to be, the *ekklēsia* did continue "to express the old ideal of self-government" (113).

10. McCready, "*Ekklēsia* and Voluntary Association," 47. Schmidt writes on this matter, "Constitutive for the Christian ἐκκλησία within Greek usage is the line from the Septuagint to the NT. Only on this line does the word take on its particular significance." Schmidt, "*Ekklēsia*," 514. See also: Meeks, *The First Urban Christians*, 108.

groups active in the first-century to explain the form and interaction of these early Christian *ekklēsiai*. In this pursuit, Wayne Meeks' identification of four ancient "models" to compare and contrast the Christian *ekklēsia* has been highly influential.[11] My own study will demonstrate that locating the origin of the Christian title *ekklēsia* in select aspects of its Septuagint usage obscures the full application of the term in the Septuagint. This explanation for the Christian title also neglects the widest and most persistent use of the word from the classical period into the first century: the designation for the civic, political assembly of citizens.[12] I trace a discourse centered on that *ekklēsia* in the first century, which explains some of the significant similarities Meeks has highlighted between the Christian assembly and other ancient organizations like the synagogue or voluntary association. These similarities betray a common participation in a wider discourse of *ekklēsia* democracy that belongs not to a classical past, but to the first-century presence of these groups.[13]

---

11. Meeks, *The First Urban Christians*. Some of the most extensive recent work on ancient institutions as a model for early Christians centers on what Meeks designates "the voluntary association." For a sample of this work, see Kloppenborg and Wilson, *Voluntary Associations in the Graeco-Roman World*; Ascough, *Paul's Macedonian Associations*; Harland, *Associations, Synagogues and Congregations*. For examples of Meeks influence on theories of organization in the ancient world, see Kloppenborg, "Edwin Hatch, Churches and Collegia"; McCready, "*Ekklēsia* and Voluntary Association," 62ff. For a critique of Meeks' failure to include sanctuary space among these models, see Økland, *Women in Their Place*, 141.

12. I would suggest that the reluctance to fully consider the civic *ekklēsia* as the source of the Christian title or as a model for the form of early Christian communities may result in part from the common separation in modern discussions of "secular" and "religious" realms. While often an artificial division even in the present, I would argue that this kind of separation fails to capture, and even does a disservice to, the complexity of ancient practice. Certainly Dio Chrysostom can identify his speech before the assembly as divinely inspired (*Or.* 34.5), while Plutarch describes those speaking in the assembly as "servants of Zeus, god of the Council, the Market-Place, and the State" (*An seni* 789 D). As I will show, Josephus' presentation of Moses and the Israelite community in the assembly setting helps to further break down any idea of such division, as does the way that both Paul and the Corinthians draw on *ekklēsia* discourse even as they appeal to the divine.

13. In these terms, Schüssler Fiorenza explains with regard to synagogues, voluntary associations, professional clubs, religious cults, and funeral societies, "These 'private' organizations did not adopt the structures of the patriarchal household, however, but utilized rules and offices of the democratic assembly, i.e., the *ekklēsia* of the polis." Schüssler Fiorenza, *The Power of the Word*, 108. Meeks suggests the classical polis as the model for democracy practiced within voluntary associations. Meeks, *The First Urban Christians*, 78.

With regard to 1 Corinthians, the scholarly approach of those investigating the letter as a piece of rhetoric has come closer to recognizing the influence of the civic sphere on Christian communities in general, and the Corinthians in particular. Scholars such as Hans Dieter Betz and Margaret Mitchell have offered generous evidence that Paul uses political terms and *topoi* throughout 1 Corinthians, including those associated with leadership and citizenship.[14] Betz, Mitchell, and others provide invaluable analysis in tracing the symmetry between the rhetoric and internal logic of Paul's arguments and those found in ancient Greek speeches and rhetorical handbooks. These scholars focus primarily on Paul as author of the letter when they establish stylistic similarities between Paul's work and ancient rhetoric, proceeding in a project of "listing and labeling rhetorical figures of speech and figures of thought."[15] However, this approach has rarely addressed the democratic context of Paul's rhetorical conventions. Thus, these scholars often reinforce Paul's view as normative for the Corinthian community because their approach is designed to draw out the author's rhetorical agenda without seriously considering the audience. J. David Amador Hester concisely explains the methodology and goals of this project as discerning the "rhetorical historical situation of the community from the perspective of the (implied) author of a particular text."[16] In other words, they offer an intensive examination of Paul's rhetoric with little consideration of what, to use the words of Elisabeth Schüssler Fiorenza, is the "rhetorical situation" inside Corinth that solicited Paul's response.[17]

In contrast, this study employs a rhetorical analysis that is informed by Elisabeth Schüssler Fiorenza's rhetorical criticism, a model which destabilizes Paul's voice as normative. Schüssler Fiorenza is less interested in exploring Paul's use of technical rhetoric than in drawing out the "letter's rhetorical functions."[18] She characterizes all rhetoric, both ancient and modern, as an act that "seeks to instigate a change of attitudes and motivations, and it strives to persuade, to teach, and to engage the hearer/reader by eliciting reactions, emotions, convictions, and identifications."[19] Bringing together "discourse theory and reader-response criticism as well as the insight into

---

14. Mitchell, *Paul and the Rhetoric of Reconciliation*; Betz, "The Problem of Rhetoric and Theology."

15. Amador, *Academic Constraints in Rhetorical Criticism*, 89.

16. Ibid., 156.

17. Schüssler Fiorenza, *Rhetoric and Ethic*, 115.

18. Ibid., 107.

19. Ibid., 108.

the linguisticality and rhetorical character of all historiography,"[20] Schüssler Fiorenza's model assesses the complex relationship between speaker and audience, author and reader, in order to come to an understanding in the final stages of its process of the "common historical situation and symbolic universe" they share. This model decenters Paul as a normative authority by recognizing his voice "as one among many actual and potential perspectives upon a particular setting or situation."[21] Moreover, the model also emphasizes the relationship between speaker and audience as it delves into the rhetorical strategies used to persuade, the nature of the audience, and rhetorical occasion that frames a piece of rhetoric.

My work builds on Schüssler Fiorenza's model specifically by considering how an analysis of Paul's rhetorical strategies—as inscribed with the discourse of democracy—might illuminate the struggles and debates over authority and identity inside this community. In fact, Schüssler Fiorenza has already indicated such connections when she notes that 1 Corinthians is an instance of deliberative rhetoric—that ancient type of rhetoric at home in the *ekklēsia* as "the voting assembly of freeborn men."[22] Thus, by interrogating Paul's rhetorical strategies in 1 Corinthians, I intend to show that Paul, in common with the speakers in the civic *ekklēsia*, must use both persuasive speech and negotiation to attain the community's judgment in favor of his own leadership and his goals for the group. Paul's own rhetorical strategies and persuasion, in turn, reveal the decision-making authority that the Corinthians wield in the role of *ekklēsia* audience.

## Mapping *Ekklēsia* Discourse

Michel Foucault's concept of discourse is critical for this project in allowing me to trace what is at stake in Paul's particular rhetorical strategies in 1 Corinthians. Indeed, I suggest that scholars have not fully developed an understanding of Paul and various members of the Corinthian *ekklēsia* as participating in differing articulations and contestations of communal and individual authority. More specifically, I argue that these issues were being negotiated through differing deployments of *ekklēsia* discourse—the logic and *topoi* that marked constructions of "democracy" in the first century of the Roman Empire. Thus, Foucault's conception of discourse allows me to frame Paul's letter inside a particular rhetorical and discursive space where his construction of *ekklēsia* in 1 Corinthians is but one possible vision that

20. Ibid.
21. Amador, *Academic Constraints in Rhetorical Criticism*, 256.
22. Schüssler Fiorenza, *Rhetoric and Ethic*, 121.

had to compete with other visions that were offered up within the Corinthian community. Foucault's understanding of discourse allows that a discourse, as a kind of practice and social knowledge, can enforce and resist particular power relations. Discourse, then, is helpful for my analysis as a means to constantly destabilize Paul's voice by illuminating the possible resistances or counter-deployments his rhetoric aims to mask or reject.

Foucault explains, "[D]iscourse can be both an instrument and an effect of power, but also a hindrance, a stumbling-block, a point of resistance . . . Discourse transmits and produces power; it reinforces it, but it also undermines and exposes it, renders it fragile and makes it possible to thwart it."[23] Tracing *ekklēsia* discourse broadly in the ancient world, I use Foucault's conception to draw out how this particular discourse intervened in the struggle between elite interests and the principles of political equality and free participation that make possible both democratic government and resistance to elite domination. Yet these negotiations extend beyond the contexts of local governance as a means for Greek authors to articulate meaningful social and political identities in the face of Roman domination. Here again Foucault's conception of discourse proves useful because he argues that such practices and modes of knowledge are sustained through, but not limited to, particular institutions.[24] While I show that civic *ekklēsiai* continued to meet and function democratically in Greek cities of the Roman Empire, I also confirm that a variety of practices maintained *ekklēsia* discourse as a vital part of the Greek cultural context. These practices included education, historical reconstruction, the practice of rhetoric, and the reading of a canon of Greek literature deriving primarily from classical Athens.

A major goal of this book is to map this *ekklēsia* discourse in various sites in the first century in order to draw out more exactly how Paul and the members of the Corinthian community variously mobilized its logic and *topoi*. Constituted in the ancient civic *ekklēsia*, "democracy" concerned itself with the rights and responsibilities of citizen participants in the assembly, as well as the interaction between this citizen body and its leaders. The actions of speech and judgment took a central place in this discourse since they constituted the decision-making process of democratic government. Moreover, these actions of speech and judgment came to define the freedom and equality of the democratic citizen, the actions that realized that citizenship. Freedom and equality were themselves major *topoi* in the discourse, joined by the common conversation over the relationship of rich

---

23. Foucault, *The History of Sexuality*, 101.
24. Foucault, *The Archaeology of Knowledge*, 45.

and poor, elite and non-elite within the democratic city, and protecting political—but not economic—parity.[25] This last conversation cut to the heart of *ekklēsia* participation and of democracy itself. Finally, this discourse embraced *ekklēsia* dynamics that touched on the role and extent of debate in the *ekklēsia*, as well as the constant negotiation between those who led in the *ekklēsia* through persuasive speech, and the powerful audience who held final decision-making authority.

Ultimately, the goal of this brief, and in no way exhaustive, mapping of *ekklēsia* discourse is to place 1 Corinthians inside a discursive space of contestation over the nature of communal authority and leadership. Thus, my analysis of Paul's own rhetorical strategies demonstrates that he employs *topoi* indicative of this pervasive discourse—*topoi* including freedom, equality and modes of communal speech and discernment. Indeed I will suggest that Paul's rhetoric demonstrates that he deploys these *topoi* precisely because the Corinthians themselves were using *ekklēsia* discourse to envisage legitimate modes of speech and leadership. In this light, I argue that for Paul's claims of leadership to be sensible to this community, he must construct them according to this discourse. Nevertheless, a struggle remains visible in the text between Paul's mobilization of the discourse and that of the Corinthians. This struggle appears most dramatically in Paul's attempt to reinforce his authority through the institution of a communal hierarchy and through his gendering of speech so as to foreclose the full participation, the full citizenship of women in the Corinthian assembly. Meanwhile, some in the Corinthian community mobilize this same discourse to promote extensive freedom and *ekklēsia* participation—participation encompassing women and men from across the economic and social strata of the assembly at Corinth.

## The Argument of the Chapters

The book opens with a chapter on Greek education in the first century. In the Greek system, advanced education was characterized primarily by the study of rhetoric[26]—a practice long marked by *ekklēsia* discourse. I contend in this chapter that Greek education at all levels exposed students to literature that reinforced ideals associated with the democracy of the *ekklēsia*. Greek education used a canon of authors, primarily authors from

---

25. Ober, *Mass and Elite*. See chapter 5.

26. As Schüssler Fiorenza notes, "in antiquity the 'science' of rhetoric was practically identical with advanced education and conceived of as public discourse." Schüssler Fiorenza, *Rhetoric and Ethic*, 107.

classical, democratic Athens, as the vehicle for a variety of exercises that guided students through early reading and writing and into the complex advanced work of rhetoric. This educational practice introduced students to core values of Athenian democracy, including the association of free speech with the equality of democratic citizenship. Indeed, I contend that Greek education formed students as citizens of the democratic *polis*. For beginning students, an emphasis on speech as the currency of democratic citizenship might be gained from the most pervasive authors throughout the educational process, Euripides and Homer. This foundation in *ekklēsia* discourse prepared a more select group of students for the most popular form of advanced education: training in rhetoric.

Theon's first-century *progymnasmata* handbook proves a valuable resource for exploring educational practice during this period. The *progymnasmata* exercises themselves illustrate the progression of Greek education, providing a link between the grammar exercises of early education and the advanced work of rhetoric to follow. Both the reading list and exercises Theon prescribes in his handbook furthered student immersion in *ekklēsia* discourse. In working through this handbook, students would not only imaginatively come to inhabit a Greek city featuring the democratic *ekklēsia* but would also gain familiarity with the classical literature most concerned with the democratic assembly. Such a program of instruction prepared the future citizen for the *ekklēsia* as one critical sphere of civic action and responsibility. At the same time, Greek *paideia* socialized students into a citizenship based in free speech and discernment.

The second chapter pursues *ekklēsia* discourse in the political writings of Dio Chrysostom and Plutarch, two influential, elite authors in the first-century Greek East. Together, Dio and Plutarch introduce the reader to the intricacies of democratic practice under the early Roman Empire. Both hailing from cities of the Greek East, Dio and Plutarch evince a loyalty to the Romans that reveals the connection between provincial elite interests and the fortunes of the empire. At the same time, they both advocate enduring, if limited, liberty for Greek cities realized in the self-government of the *ekklēsia*. Dio's public speeches and Plutarch's political writings expose their own first-hand familiarity with the civic *ekklēsia*, including the negotiation between speaker and assembly audience. In these terms, Dio and Plutarch witness the authority of *ekklēsia* audiences to make binding decisions for the city on many topics familiar from the classical period. For Dio and Plutarch the civic *ekklēsia* remains not only an authoritative civic institution but also an enduring site for debate over topics such as citizen equality and civic harmony.

The third chapter considers Josephus' mobilization of *ekklēsia* discourse in a context that parts ways with the more traditional location of this discourse in education or contemporary civic politics. I examine his use of democratic discourse in the exegesis and re-writing of a key biblical scene, the rebellion of Korah from Numbers 16. Within the Antiquities, Josephus reimagines the gathered Israelites of this episode as a democratic *ekklēsia* coming together over perceived abuses of power by their leadership. Josephus portrays Moses' own excellence as a leader in this narrative as an orator who is able to calm the people's fears over tyranny as he assures them of his commitment to democratic equality in the *ekklēsia* context. Josephus' choice to reimagine Moses, his biblical hero, with the values and talents of a Pericles attests to the continued resonance of democratic discourse for Josephus' Greco-Roman audience. Likewise, this choice suggests that democratic discourse remained a powerful element of the first-century Hellenism negotiated by Jews of the eastern empire. Josephus' use of both the title and dynamics of the democratic *ekklēsia* to "translate" scenes from the biblical narrative helps to undermine a firm differentiation between a biblical or religious meaning for the term *ekklēsia* and its civic, political connotations. Josephus' inclusion of democratic discourse also engenders a tension between divine sovereignty and democracy in the narrative that may speak not only to the negotiation of first-century Jews with their wider cultural context but also to the tension experienced by residents of the Greek East between democracy and the sovereignty of the empire.

My argument concludes with three chapters that interpret 1 Corinthians in light of the vitality of first-century democratic discourse. In the fourth chapter, I note that Paul not only addresses the Corinthian community with the title *ekklēsia* but also that he includes *topoi* serving as the hallmarks of *ekklēsia* discourse in other contexts. Foremost among these are the *topoi* of speech and wisdom that dominate the first four chapters of 1 Corinthians. Paul appeals to the Corinthians as a group gifted in speech and wisdom. Moreover, his rhetoric signals their expectations for leadership in persuasive speech, along with their desire for communal debate and decision. In this way, Paul's rhetoric attests to Corinthian identity as an authoritative *ekklēsia* composed of "citizens," each possessing the power of speech and decision. However, Paul also challenges Corinthian collective speech and wisdom in the early chapters of this letter in a bid to assert his own leadership and vision for the community. Toward this end, Paul constructs a division of speech and wisdom into divine and earthly types. Paul's argument that the Corinthians possess inferior, earthly wisdom and speech works to destabilize authority of the Corinthian *ekklēsia* based—as in the case of its civic counterparts—in productive speech and wise discernment. Meanwhile,

Paul's own claims to superior, divine speech and wisdom are bolstered by his self-presentation as an unskilled speaker—another common *topos* from the democratic *ekklēsia*. An awareness of democratic discourse in this letter not only clarifies Paul's rhetorical strategies but also locates those strategies as part of larger debates between Paul and the Corinthians over the nature of authority and community formation in this particular group.

The fifth chapter of the book further explores the nature of community and citizenship in Paul's first letter to the Corinthians. This chapter offers an exegesis of 1 Cor 11:2–16, a passage centered on women's speech. In preparation for that exegesis, I consider the way in which speech was gendered in democratic discourse as part of the maintenance of the boundary between citizens and non-citizens in the ancient democratic polis. In democratic discourse, free speech and discernment of the *ekklēsia* defined citizenship. However, only the free, native-born male possessed this full, political citizenship. In this chapter, I trace justifications for the exclusion of women from full citizenship in the democratic polis. Authors from the classical period forward portrayed women and slaves as lacking in the inherent wisdom and virtue necessary for public, political speech. In this construct, women's virtue manifested instead in their public silence, while their public speech was portrayed as disorderly and even dangerous. I argue that this very concern, this tension around women's speech in democratic discourse, attests to the possibility of transgressing the citizen boundary—a possibility facilitated by the liberative claims of democracy itself. In the exegesis of 1 Cor 11:2–16, I part ways with scholarship explaining Paul's rhetoric as responding to the Corinthian women's disregard for gender norms in dress or hairstyle. Instead, Paul's rhetoric participates in democratic discourse with a portrayal of women's speech as lacking in reason and control. Toward this end, Paul draws on the *topoi* of hair and veiling as a way of naturalizing the danger, the disorder that women pose through their speech. Moreover, Paul gives this construct a theological foundation with an appeal to cosmology and an exegesis of Genesis that renders woman the secondary product of creation, naturally subordinate to man. I argue that in this passage Paul responds to a differing interpretation of community and citizenship from the one he seeks to impose. I contend that this community, influenced by democratic discourse and their understanding of the baptismal transformation recorded in Gal 3:27–28, defined citizenship to include women as speaking subjects.

Chapter six, the last chapter of the book, examines 1 Cor 12–14, ending with consideration of the difficult verses of 1 Cor 14:33–36. Far from seeing these verses as an interpolation, I argue that Paul has carefully prepared the rhetorical ground for this command demanding women's *ekklēsia* silence. This preparation includes Paul's work in gendering speech in 1 Cor 11:2–16. In 1 Cor 12–14, Paul then creates a hierarchy of speech and speakers that builds toward the ideal *ekklēsia* Paul constructs in chapter 14. Both the hierarchy and ideal *ekklēsia* Paul describes owe much to democratic discourse. Specifically, Paul holds forth an ideal of *ekklēsia* speech guided by self-control and the mind. In the earlier verses of 1 Cor 11:2–16, Paul has already gendered women's speech as lacking in these very qualities. Together, the gendering of speech in chapter 11 and Paul's definition in 1 Cor 12–14 of correct *ekklēsia* speech make sensible Paul's command that women's voices be excluded from the *ekklēsia* context. As I argue in this chapter, such a command has profound implications for women's status—and the status of slaves—as full citizens in the community. As in the preceding chapter, I contend that Paul's rhetoric indicates a different construction of community and citizenship boundaries within his Corinthian audience. Paul's rhetoric suggests that the liberative potential of democratic discourse, together with the baptismal promise of Gal 3:28, empowers some within that audience to conceive of an *ekklēsia* in which men, women and slaves all have the freedom and equality of speech.

# I

# The *Ekklēsia* in Greek Education

## Introduction

MUCH RECENT SCHOLARSHIP HAS ADDRESSED THE INFLUENCE THAT ROMAN imperial politics had on the early communities the Apostle Paul addresses in his letters. However, little attention has been given to another concurrent, political expression in the cradle of early Christianity. Despite Roman imperial rule in the first century CE, Greek democratic thought and practice in the eastern Roman Empire flourished. In fact, democratic discourse in the eastern empire bridged an earlier classical period dominated by a powerful, democratic Athens to the first century. Cultural and political continuity in Greek democratic thought centered on the citizen assembly or *ekklēsia*, historically one of the key institutions for democratic city-states. In the model of classical Athens, such an *ekklēsia* was open to all citizens and made the key decisions determining the city's welfare. Citizenship in a democratic city like Athens was tied closely to this institution, with the ideal of each citizen having both a voice as a potential speaker and a vote as a deciding member of the assembly. While the classical discussion over the relationship of audiences to speakers and elites to non-elites within the assembly was extremely complex, it became even more so with the shift of time and empires that compromised the independence of any first-century *polis*. *Ekklēsia* discourse in the first century is remarkable not just for this complexity, but for its very survival in a time and political landscape so distant from fifth- or fourth-century BCE Athens. To understand democratic discourse in the first-century empire, one must examine specific practices and institutions that continued to give *ekklēsia* discourse life in the Greek East.

Education served as one such institution responsible for transmitting and replicating the democratic discourse of the *ekklēsia*. Greek education engaged students across the eastern empire in a widespread and remarkably stable practice. While elites dominated the upper levels of this educational practice, students from all economic backgrounds pursued lower levels of instruction. For all these students, Greek education developed an intellectual and cultural continuity between fifth-century Athens and the first-century Greek East.

From earliest writing exercises to advanced rhetorical training, students in the East encountered a culturally Greek and overwhelmingly classical canon of literature. This canon and process of education foregrounded public, political speech. Such an emphasis on speech contributed to the place of rhetoric as the most common, advanced course of study and the implied goal of the earlier levels. In turn, as Joy Connolly argues with regard to the early imperial period, "The survival of a rhetorical pedagogy, designed to train students for civic participation through public speech, insures by its face to face, communicative nature that education retains a direct connection to citizenship and politics. Rhetorical education reminds its practitioners to ask what sort of citizen education should produce."[1]

Within this chapter, I will contend that this educational process trained students, at least in part, as future democratic citizens, empowered and limited by a discourse centered on the civic *ekklēsia*. Further, it will be my argument that students from the earliest levels of education encountered political values at the core of democratic discourse and practice. Certainly students would encounter the foundational values of equality, freedom, and security—as well as their place in debates over the nature of citizen participation and economic inequality.

# Part I

## Greek Education: An Overview

Education in the first-century eastern Roman Empire immersed students[2] in literature of the past. Greek education remained consistent over a remark-

---

1. Connolly, "Problems of the Past," 342.
2. There remains great debate as to just what percentage of the population in the ancient world was literate and therefore would have been educated. Harris asserts that Greek education, especially at the elementary levels, reached its height during the Hellenistic period when cities and private donors took the greatest active interest in education. He posits a 20–30 percent literacy rate during this period. By contrast he suggests that literacy went down in the Greek East during the imperial period, with a

able sweep of history, with educational content relatively static between the Hellenistic and Byzantine periods.[3] Without a standard curriculum across regions, or even within the same city, this educational path was nevertheless very similar throughout the Greek East.[4] In preliminary exercises, teachers used snippets of Greek classics to move the student gradually from learning letters to copying sentences, to memorization, grammar study, and eventually toward writing their own compositions. More advanced study was also predicated on students' engagement with a canon of ancient writers, as students drew heavily on these authors for models, topics, and background for compositions. In contrast to the Roman Latin educational process which incorporated both Latin and Greek writers, Greek education virtually ignored writers of Latin. With several exceptions, the most notable being Homer, this educational process drew on Athenian literature of the fourth and fifth centuries BCE—literature written during the height of democratic Athens' power and prestige.

Recent scholarship on ancient Greek education has helped to integrate the information about education provided by ancient writers from the early empire, like Plutarch and Dio Chrysostom, with the first-hand evidence of papyri fragments from elementary school exercises and the rhetorical handbooks that guided more advanced study.[5] This research demonstrates that classical authors, such as Euripides and Isocrates, accompanied students through all levels of education. The detailed and often imaginative work that students performed with this canon meant that the ideas permeating centuries-old literature became a present experience of the learner. As students used this material to copy, to memorize, to explore grammar, and eventually to argue for or against certain points in the text, an immersion

---

corresponding drop in education. His arguments directly contradict the earlier work of Henri Marrou who contends that there was near universal elementary education in the Hellenistic period that incorporated both boys and girls, with only a slight drop during the imperial age. Harris, *Ancient Literacy*, 141; Marrou, *A History of Education in Antiquity*, 221. While Harris's arguments have gained wide acceptance among scholars, there are certainly those who fault him for being overly pessimistic and not complex enough in his presentation of literacy in the ancient world. For one example, see Horsfall, "Statistics or States of Mind?," 573.

3. Morgan, *Literate Education*, 3–7; Cribiore, *Gymnastics*, 3.

4. Morgan, *Literate Education*, 25, 45–46. Morgan stresses in her work on Greek education, "the continuity of literate education across place, time and to a significant extent between social groups" in the ancient world (46).

5. Morgan and Cribiore have done some of the most intensive work with the school text papyri. While Cribiore's book focuses more on the papyri, Morgan has gone further toward integrating the papyri with other ancient sources on education. Cribiore, *Writing, Teachers and Students*; Morgan, *Literate Education*.

took place in "a transferable body of cultural knowledge" that allowed students from all over the Eastern Roman Empire to claim not just literacy but a certain "Greekness."[6] I suggest that democratic discourse formed part of this cultural knowledge—part of this Greekness. Authors like Homer and Euripides might shadow students throughout their education emphasizing for students a public, political speech corresponding to the rights of citizenship within a particular type of Greek *polis*.

In her discussion of ancient schools, specifically the philosophical schools,[7] Loveday Alexander describes this education as "public" in many ways. Instruction often took place in the open air or in spaces which belonged to the city and thus attracted two tiers of students: those devoted to (and paying) a certain teacher as an inner circle, and an outer circle from the urban context who joined in the scholarly conversation for varying amounts of time as constructive or critical participants.[8] Further, Alexander argues, "For most of the philosophical schools . . . the public arena was the *polis* itself. The city provided both a social matrix and a physical location for their teaching activity."[9] A similar argument can be advanced for other educational instruction in the Greek East. While we have evidence for education at various levels as a visible and audible part of the urban landscape,[10] the political and social construction of the "*polis*" gave coherence to this educational pursuit.

---

6. Morgan, *Literate Education*, 23.

7. Alexander conjectures that "[m]any of the structural features that we associate with the philosophical schools are in fact found across a wide range of subjects and disciplines." Alexander, *Paul and the Hellenistic Schools*, 67.

8. Ibid., 76.

9. Ibid., 79.

10. As Morgan points out, our knowledge about locations for educational practice are limited by the "the infrequency, the vagueness, and the inconsistency of our references" to such schooling locations. Morgan, *Literate Education*, 32. Cribiore posits a variety of locations in which education took place including public buildings, private homes, temples, gymnasia and various open air settings, including the colonnades of cities like Alexandria. Cribiore, *Gymnastics*, 21–34. Nevertheless, amid this variety we get strong evidence that the open air setting was one of the most common for educational instruction. For instance, Dio uses elementary teachers who instruct their students in the streets as an example of professionals who do their jobs in the midst of chaos. Dio, *Or.* 20.9–10. In Pompeii, graffiti under one of the arcades of the *Forum* and one under the *Campus* has led scholars to posit these sites as school locations. Murals in the first location show students being observed by those passing by. Della Corte, "Scuole e maestri," 621–24. This type of open-air instruction seems to form a continuity with classical Athens, which left Attic vases often defining a school "by the presence of a tree beside school objects." Cribiore, *Gymnastics*, 27.

The literature that dominated Greek education meant that this *polis* often remained, at least in imagination, the democratic *polis* represented by the classical Athenian ideal. Students encountered the values and political practice of this *polis* at all levels of education. Moreover, rhetorical work from the initial *progymnasmata* exercises to the pinnacle of rhetorical education, the declamation, asked students to imaginatively inhabit this city in various roles, notably in the person of the most famous classical defender of democracy, the orator Demosthenes.[11] Indeed, such declamations performed by famous rhetorical teachers of the imperial period provided popular entertainment at civic venues like the theater, odeion, or even the temple.[12] Here audiences engaged the classical, democratic past along with performers by calling out themes for the rhetor to enact, and by signalling their appreciation or disappointment of speeches through their own vocal participation.[13]

Scholarship in the last decades has shown that the many significant question marks about ancient education—namely location of schools, methods of teaching, and the nature of the school day itself—must be contrasted with the "precise and consistent information we have about the content of education."[14] Teresa Morgan suggests this contrast may itself be informative, demonstrating that content rather than method took precedence in ancient educational practice.[15] In the next sections, I investigate certain aspects of this content, including the place of central authors and pieces of literature in Greek education as students progressed from elementary exercises and into the preliminary rhetorical work of the *Progymnasmata*. This focus on content will draw out the significant democratic values and discourse within Greek educational practice.

---

11. I will talk about Demosthenes' place in the *Progymnasmata* in the following part of the chapter. Regarding declamations, Whitmarsh explains that the majority of those that survive consisted of *meletai*, a speech given in the person of, or addressed to, a famous figure from myth or ancient history. Whitmarsh, *The Second Sophistic*, 20. Swain includes the calculation that 36 percent of the identifiable historical declamations in Philostratus are imitations of Demosthenes. Swain, *Hellenism and Empire*, 96.

12. For examples of performance locations for declamations, see Russell, *Greek Declamation*, 76–77; Korenjak, *Publikum und Redner*, 27–33; Whitmarsh, *The Second Sophistic*, 20.

13. Whitmarsh, *The Second Sophistic*, 24–25; Korenjak, *Publikum und Redner*, 68–95.

14. Morgan, *Literate Education*, 32.

15. Ibid.

## Homer and Euripides

For the most part, modern scholars have explained ancient education as a matter of exercises and texts in a set order encountered by all pupils, with those pupils "diverging at the end to become orators and philosophers."[16] Teresa Morgan critiques this curricular model for failing to account for the diversity of texts and exercises in the evidence that remains to us. Instead, she sets forth a "core" and "periphery" model to make sense of this practice. In her model, ancient education possessed a "core" accounting for what the "most people learned, what they learned first and, in the case of reading, what they went on practicing longest."[17] The "periphery" then includes everything outside of the "core"—though Morgan cautions that some authors and texts would be much closer to the core, and some more peripheral than others. The "core" of Greek education involving the greatest number of students was the practice of learning to read and write, accomplished most often using various gnomic sayings and passages from Homer. By contrast, a much smaller group of students proceeded into grammar, and an even smaller group into the most advanced work of rhetorical practice that began with the *progymnasmata* exercises. If we work with the "core" and "periphery" model, Homer and Euripides stand out as those authors encountered by the greatest number of ancient students, and the two authors who would accompany an ever dwindling number of learners into advanced academic work. In Greek *paideia*, these authors also took a central role in socializing students into Greek identity and an ideal of citizenship.

In the first century CE, Dio Chrysostom attests to Homer's popularity at all levels of study when he writes, "For Homer comes first and in the middle and last, giving of himself to every child and adult and old man as much as each of them can take."[18] Ancient literature and surviving school texts indicate that Dio did not exaggerate Homer's educational role. Of all the ancient writers pressed into educational service, Homer is the one most likely to be encountered by all students no matter how briefly they were educated, thus dominating the "core" of Greek education.[19] For instance, Homer takes the lead by a wide margin in the papyri, only to be followed by Euripides as a distant second. Plutarch by contrast quotes Homer only

---

16. Ibid., 67.
17. Morgan, *Literate Education*, 71.
18. *Or.* 18.8. Ὅμηρος δὲ καὶ πρῶτος καὶ μέσος καὶ ὕστατος, παντὶ παιδὶ καὶ ἀνδρὶ καὶ γέροντι τοσοῦτον ἀφ᾽ αὑτοῦ διδοὺς ὅσον ἕκαστος δύναται λαβεῖν. My translation. For Dio Chrysostom's works, I have used the edition of *Dio Chrysostom* (trans. Cohoon and Crosby, LCL) in consultation with that of *Dionis Prusaensis* (trans. Arnim).
19. Morgan, *Literate Education*, 71–82.

slightly less than Plato (889 to 915 instances), while Euripides is the next most popular after Homer.[20]

Homer's widespread dissemination becomes especially significant if he is recognized not only as a Greek writer but also, as Teresa Morgan explains, *the* quintessential Greek writer.[21] Morgan writes:

> Reading Homer is, among other things, a statement of Greek identity, and more precisely of identity with those in a society who are reading Homer in any particular period . . . The fact that Homer was so prominent in education suggests that it was accepted that education would result in the entry of some non-Greeks to some degree of Greekness.[22]

As Homer may bear some responsibility for the creation of overarching panhellenism in archaic Greece, so he also had a role in the early Roman Empire in forging common, Greek cultural territory.[23] Indeed, Homer took pride of place in a construction of Greek identity determined by Greek *paideia*, an identity that could be assumed by diverse groups of people far beyond the physical or ethnic boundaries of Greece. Isocrates first elaborated this assumption of Greek identity through education, defining both according to the ideal of democratic Athens. At *Panegyricus* 51 he claims, "Our city has left the rest of mankind so far behind in thought and speech that her pupils have become the teachers of others, and the name 'Greek' no longer refers to a race but to a way of thinking, and those who share our education are called 'Greeks' rather than those who share our nature." In this formulation, Athens defines for all who want to be Greek an educational and political practice associated with speech and wisdom in the public setting.[24]

---

20. Ibid., 318–19.

21. Ibid., 75.

22. Ibid.

23. Beginning most notably with Isocrates' *Panegyricus*, the idea that it was possible to become Greek through education becomes common, desirable on the basis of claims to a superior culture that includes in Isocrates' rendering the democratic government of Athens based in free speech. Ibid., 20.

24. Livingstone suggests that the main point of this passage is the "potential *of paideia*." He argues that Isocrates, "claims for his own profession of paideia the ability to not merely to define Greekness, but also to extend it." At the same time, Livingstone also observes the diversity of political viewpoint in Isocrates' speeches. While the *Panegyricus* along with *Panathenaicus*, and *Antidosis*, all speak in praise of democratic Athens and its hegemony, other speeches like *Philip* and *To Niocles* strongly favor the rule of monarchs. Livingstone, "The Voice of Isocrates," 273–75.

Part of Homer's usefulness in passing along the "Greekness" Isocrates describes involved the extent and quality of speeches in his epic poetry.[25] The lengthy speeches Homer crafted for his various characters became a critical model for the Greek practice of *mimesis* of speech in literature, both in epic and history. Moreover, this influence remained strong as this practice was expanded with the first systematic teaching of rhetoric in late fifth-century BCE Athens. Certainly Homer would become central to the later educational practice of declamation.[26] In earlier levels of education, Raffaella Cribiore's catalogue of school exercises from Greco-Roman Egypt shows that nearly half of the papyri with Homer quotations include speeches given by various characters.[27] For instance, one of these papyri features part of Thersites' memorable speech before the assembled army—a speech that is the focus of a *progymnasmata* exercise I will discuss at the end of this chapter.[28]

Authors of the first century CE, such as Dio Chrysostom and Aelius Theon, demonstrate that Homer's extensive speeches earned him a reputation as an expert in oratory. In Theon's handbook of preliminary exercises for rhetoric students, Homer is repeatedly cited as the author that students should consult for προσωποποιία, or personification, since Homer "attributes suitable words to each of the characters he introduces."[29] In his *Second Discourse on Kingship*, Dio Chrysostom, too, weighs in on Homer's rhetorical skills with a staged conversation between Philip of Macedonia and his son Alexander.[30] In this passage, Alexander seeks to persuade his father of Homer's greatness and utility for understanding rhetoric by claiming that Homer portrayed key figures like Nestor and Odysseus as counselors using rhetoric with discernment and persuasiveness. As one of several examples, Alexander cites Odysseus's actions to keep the Greeks from departing after Thersites had induced anger and panic in the assembly.[31] Dio's discussion is

---

25. While there are a few passages of the *Odyssey* in the school text papyri, the overwhelming majority of examples from Homer are drawn from the *Iliad*. Ibid., 105.

26. Russell, *Greek Declamation*, 15–16.

27. For representative examples, see Cribiore, *Writing, Teachers and Students*, 33, 259.

28. P. Oslo III 66. Cribiore includes a plate of this papyri: *Writing, Teachers and Students*, plate XXX.

29. Theon, *Progymnasmata*, 60.27–29; 68.22–24. ὅτι οἱ κείους λόγους περιτέθεικεν ἑκάστῳ τῶν εἰσαγομένων προσώπων. For the Greek text established by Patillon, see Patillon and Bolognesi, *Theon, Progymnasmata*. For a translation of this and the other Greek handbooks, see Kennedy, *Progymnasmata*.

30. *Or.* 2.18–24.

31. *Il.* 2.245ff.

remarkable for its assumption that Homer is familiar with formal rhetoric of a much later period. In this case, Dio's Alexander highlights the value of rhetoric in Homer by invoking the abilities of Philip's great opponent in the Athenian *ekklēsia*, Demosthenes.[32] This passage was certainly not unique in assigning anachronistic knowledge or values to Homer. Dio and other Greek writers easily telescoped time between the *Iliad* and later Greek literature.[33] This allowed Homer's archaic narrative to be used to great effect, as I will show later in the chapter, in a meditation over values and debates essential to Greek democracy.

Second only to Homer in the school text papyri, Euripides likewise commanded an exceptional place in education and beyond, based in part on his emphasis on public speech. Euripides, like Homer, may be singled out from other writers in his genre[34] for the exceptional, polished speeches he provides for his characters. Nevertheless, Euripides must also be distinguished from Homer as an author steeped in democratic discourse and the debates of classical Athens. Scholars have long known Euripides as "the most democratic of the ancient playwrights . . . the spokesman for democratic egalitarianism."[35] Certainly Euripides writes eloquently about speech in the democratic *polis*, invoking its associations with freedom and citizenship. The presence of this discussion in Euripides' most prominent play within the school papyri gives some insight into this author's utility in transmitting *ekklēsia* discourse.

Among the school text papyri, the play *Phoenissae*, or the *Phoenician Women*, accounts by a wide margin for the most extant passages from Euripidean plays.[36] Plutarch again corroborates popularity of school texts with the use of those texts in a post-educational context, giving more quotations from *Phoenissae* than from any other Euripidean work.[37] The play's reca-

32. *Or.* 2.18–19.

33. Anderson, *The Second Sophistic*, 83. Anderson writes of the intellectual world inhabited by members of the Second Sophistic, "It is not so much the world of the fifth century, however, as a world in which the fifth century has been relocated somewhere in the vicinity of the Trojan War, since we still find Homer cheek by jowl with Socrates."

34. In this, he is the most "rhetorical" of the Greek tragic poets and well suited for his weighty place in an educational process that was structured toward the goal of rhetorical instruction. Conacher, "Rhetoric and Relevance in Euripidean Drama," 82.

35. Saxonhouse, "Another Antigone," 476.

36. Cribiore, "The Grammarian's Choice."

37. Helmbold and O'Neil, *Plutarch's Quotations*, 31. Of the identified Euripidean plays that Plutarch quotes, *Phoenissae* has more than twenty-five mentions with only fifteen from *Orestes* as the nearest competitor. Dunn explains that Euripides' *Phoenician Women* and his *Orestes* were the most well quoted and read classical works except

pitulation of the entire Theban cycle surely contributed to its long-standing prominence in the ancient world. However, Cribiore suggests that the play's educational utility is also based on the initial conversations between Jocasta and her sons, conversations including various pithy statements well suited for writing exercises.[38] In turn, these pithy statements include some of Euripides' most memorable assertions regarding the relationship of speech, freedom, and citizenship.

In the initial conversations of *Phoenissae*, Euripides defines slavery and freedom, exile and citizenship, according to one's right to speech. Early on, Jocasta meets with her son Polyneices who has become an exile after his brother Eteocles robbed him of his birthright to rule. Jocasta asks Polyneices to name the most terrible experience of exile, to which he replies, "One is greatest, not to have freedom of speech."[39] Jocasta agrees, saying, "Not to speak openly is a slave's life."[40] Polyneices further elaborates the nature of this slavery when he says that in this state, "One must endure the ignorance of rulers."[41] As Arlene Saxonhouse points out, the action in *Phoenissae* does not take place in a democratic *polis* featuring the "communal decision-making" of the *ekklēsia*.[42] Nevertheless, Euripides uses these lines to explore *parrhēsia* as that freedom guaranteeing the empowerment and equality of citizens under Athenian democracy. Here, *parrhēsia* grants each citizen a voice, a visibility that allows them to critique those policies and leaders they find lacking in wisdom. By contrast, all those without *parrhēsia*—slaves, foreigners, and women—are rendered politically invisible. As Saxonhouse explains, this group experiences disempowerment related to "the necessity of hiding one's thoughts, of having to cover or veil what one believes or knows to be true before another who is less wise," even as one is "denied the opportunity to criticize the absence of wisdom in others."[43] Thus, in these lines, Euripides describes slavery as the inability to speak freely regarding political policy. Meanwhile, freedom within the Greek city means having

---

for Homer through all antiquity. Dunn, *Tragedy's End*, 180.

38. Cribiore, "The Grammarian's Choice." This argument is buttressed by numerous quotations that later authors incorporate into their own works. Plutarch, for instance, mostly quotes from the early part of this play. Helmbold and O'Neil, *Plutarch's Quotations*, 31.

39. Phoen. 390–94 (Way, LCL). ἓν μὲν μέγιστον, οὐκ ἔχει παρρησίαν.

40. Ibid. δούλου τόδ' εἶπας, μὴ λέγειν ἅ τις φρονεῖ.

41. Ibid. τὰς τῶν κρατούντων ἀμαθίας φέρειν χρεών.

42. Saxonhouse, "Another Antigone," 477.

43. Ibid., 482.

a "share in the critique of others without the fear of reprisals."[44] Euripides' support for equality based in *parrhēsia* and his own critique of the exclusions of certain groups from that equality may be represented in one of Jocasta's most memorable lines in which she argues the givenness of equality by stating that, "nature gave men the law of equality."[45]

The maxims taken from these passages in *Phoenissae* fail to touch on some of the most popular topics in other educational maxims known to us.[46] This play has little discussion over the benefits or downfall of wealth, fate or misogynic passages about women. Instead, the early speeches of Jocasta, Polyneices, and Eteocles address more complex political concepts, fostering "a student's understanding of larger themes" with regard to the civic context.[47] If *Phoenissae* is, as Cribiore hypothesizes, the "school text par excellence," it is worth considering what values and understanding regarding politics and citizenship are imparted by the passages I have discussed. One can debate whether students could come away from the earliest exercises in writing or reading with any nuanced understanding of the ideas included in maxims such as these. Nevertheless, such literature would at the least introduce students to the intertwined values most foundational to Athenian democratic culture.

Josiah Ober names the foundational values of Athenian democracy as equality, freedom, and security—all values implicated in the condition of citizenship. As he explains, equality in this culture translates into equal legal and political rights, equal vote, and equal opportunity for political speech. Freedom concerns both the "positive" freedom to participate in political life as well as the "negative" freedom to, within limits, do what one wishes in private life. Finally, security encompasses the immunity of the weaker citizen, whether physically or economically weaker, from physical assault or other arbitrary exercise of power by citizens with greater physical, economic or political clout.[48] All three of these values are associated with the *parrhēsia* Euripides considers in *Phoenissae*. Free speech defined political participation and equality between citizens, even as the security of those citizens depended on their ability to speak without fear of repercussions. The popularity of *Phoenissae* in school texts and advanced literature alike suggests that Euripides' construct of democratic citizenship would be one students might encounter at each level of academic work, and a construct

---

44. Ibid., 483.
45. *Phoen.* 538 (Way, LCL). τὸ γὰρ ἴσον νόμιμον ἀνθρώποις ἔφυ.
46. Cribiore, "The Grammarian's Choice," 249.
47. Ibid., 250.
48. Ober, *Mass and Elite*, 293–307.

that would lead them to conceive both "Greekness" and citizenship within the political valence of Athenian democracy.

This popularity of *Phoenissae* speaks to one of the critical functions of Greek *paideia*: to form students as citizens. I earlier quoted Joy Connolly in her assertion that, "Rhetorical education reminds its practitioners to ask what sort of citizen education should produce." Here, I suggest that a text like *Phoenissae*, encountered in rhetorical education and in the earlier levels of instruction, forms students toward the ideal of democratic citizenship realized in free speech. In the passage I have examined, the *Phoenissae* also demonstrates how much the meaning and value of this citizenship was defined through the exclusions of democracy. In this vein, Euripides explains the ability to act and to speak as a citizen in comparison with those lacking this ultimate right of democratic citizenship. Classical texts like the *Phoenissae* had a critical role in a Greek *paideia* designed to train free, male students to take up the role of citizen in the Greek *polis*. However, this educational process formed that citizen against the non-citizen of slave, foreigner, and woman. Certainly, the Greek education I discuss here was highly gendered, with particular tension around speech, the very act *Phoenissae* identifies as the mark of the citizen.[49] While women's literacy and participation in earlier levels of education is well attested, Cribiore points out that the study of rhetoric was closed to women.[50] The significance of the tension over women's speech within democratic discourse will occupy much of Chapter Five later in this book.

Dio Chrysostom's "Reply to Diodorus" gives one instructive example of the way that *Phoenissae*, perhaps first approached through the early educational process, might be applied by the fully formed citizen within a first-century political context. Dio's oration appears to be one that was actually performed in the civic *ekklēsia* of Prusa, his home town. Accusing a citizen who has just spoken of acting with self-interest rather than honesty in their praise of a third party, Dio quotes Jocasta's line, "Not to speak openly is a slave's life."[51] Dio uses this line both to critique another citizen speaker and to praise frank, honest speech that works to the benefit of both audience and the speaker. In this oration, Dio invokes the democratic Athenian context not only by quoting from the *Phoenissae* discussion over *parrhēsia* but also

---

49. For a discussion over the significance of gender and voice in rhetorical training, see Gleason, *Making Men*, 82–102. In discussing the resistance to women's education in the Greek East, Morgan writes, "The characteristics of power, speech and literacy go together and it is essential- even natural- that men should have them all and women none." Morgan, *Literate Education*, 137.

50. Cribiore, *Gymnastics*, 78–100.

51. Dio Chrysostom, *Or.* 51.1 (Crosby, LCL). *Phoen.* 392.

by holding up the great Athenian leader Pericles as a model citizen who improved his audience through such honest speech.[52] Partly by drawing on the *Phoenissae*, Dio makes a strong connection between free, citizen speech in classical Athens and the concept of free speech associated with the assembly of his own time and place. This quotation by Dio not only shows that maxims characterizing early education could make their way into the "end product" of finished rhetoric but also demonstrates the resonance that this part of the play still had in the first century for political speech in an assembly setting.

Understanding Homer's and Euripides' influence in configuring public speech for early students in Greek education becomes valuable when the discussion turns to higher levels of study. Homer and Euripides might introduce students to an association between Greek culture and civic public speech and help students to construct an ideal of citizenship based on the practice of *parrhēsia*. However, more advanced study would allow students to locate these concepts within democratic institutions such as the *ekklēsia* or the court. In part, such development in advanced study grew out of increasing familiarity with authors like Demosthenes about whom most students in earliest education learned little more than their names.[53] Furthermore, we can speculate that the political contexts of public speaking would become ever more vivid for those who were themselves being trained in the skills designed to produce competency in those very contexts.

# Part II

## *Theon's Progymnasmata*

Morgan's "core" and "periphery" model of ancient education indicates that a much smaller and more elite group of students would proceed out of the "core" of learning to read, write, and practice grammar, and into more the more advanced study of rhetoric. In turn, this smaller group of students could be expected to gain a much more thorough understanding of the history and political ideas included in the classical literature that animated all levels of education. For those students who embarked upon the study of rhetoric, the *progymnasmata* exercises introduced a range of tasks that

---

52. *Or.* 51.7–8.

53. Demosthenes, Isocrates, and Menander were encountered by younger students primarily in the context of *chreia* and gnomic sayings that would have allowed the students some name recognition, but little chance to engage much political thought in these authors. Morgan, *Literate Education*, 117.

prepared the ground for sophisticated rhetorical work. The *progymnasmata* thus bridged different levels of education, with some of the earliest exercises just out of the grammarian's purview and some of the later ones sharing themes and methods with advanced rhetorical study. For a study of democratic discourse in the first century, the *progymnasmata* are useful in helping to chart the more complex and intense nature of this discourse for students as they moved into higher levels of education. Moreover, one of the most valuable ancient educational texts we possess dates from the first century. In his *progymnasmata* handbook, Aelius Theon produced one of the most extensive and earliest surviving manuals on rhetorical training in the ancient world.[54] When examined in conjunction with the sample *progymnasmata* exercises written by the famous educator Libanius in the fourth century CE, Theon's handbook provides a particularly valuable tool for understanding the dissemination of democratic discourse in higher levels of education.

As a transition between learning grammar and more advanced rhetorical exercises of declamation, *progymnasmata* were designed to help students write their own compositions based on a number of simpler exercises such as expanding *chreia*, composing a speech fitting to some historical or mythical character (*prosopopoeia*) or more advanced exercises such as crafting a thesis.[55] Ruth Webb argues convincingly that the *progymnasmata* must not be seen in isolation as arcane and pointless exercises for their own sake but rather as an integral part of a greater pedagogical and cultural program.[56] The poets like Homer and Euripides whom most students would have used earlier, now became the material for a range of exercises requiring varying levels of ingenuity and imagination. Authors like Isocrates and Demosthenes that a student in lower levels would have had some likelihood of encountering primarily in gnomic sayings or in *chreia*, here stand as examples for varied exercises throughout the manual. Predicated on classical examples, the *progymnasmata* exercises provided students with "a store of techniques of presentation and argumentation, with flexible patterns on which to model their own compositions, and a set of common narratives, personae and values to appeal to."[57] In contrast to the elementary levels of education, students studying first *progymnasmata* and then more advanced forms of rhetoric like declamation were reading and creatively working with

---

54. The earliest date that Theon can have been writing is determined by the latest authors he refers to such as Dionysius of Halicarnassus, while Quintillian's reference to Theon on stasis theory suggest he wrote before Quintilian published his *Institutio Oratoria* in 95 CE. Kennedy, *Progymnasmata*, 1.

55. Webb, "The *Progymnasmata* as Practice," 289–90.

56. Ibid., 289–92.

57. Ibid., 290.

much larger amounts of material, thus investing students and teachers alike in what Ruth Webb calls, "a shared code."[58]

Theon's *progymnasmata*, like many Greek declamations, manifests such a shared code by locating the exercises within a specific urban environment. Donald Russell gives a now classic description of the city serving as the implicit context for Greek declamations in the Roman Empire. Drawn from literature of and about the sophists, Russell named his composite city "Sophistopolis."[59] For Russell, "most important" to understanding this city is its democratic government in the model of ancient Athens. Indeed, he explains, "That democracy is the right form of government, no one ever doubts."[60] Sophistopolis, like Athens, is defined by the civic institutions of assembly and court. Meanwhile, the city is inhabited by stock characters such as the rich and poor man, the tyrant and the tyrannicide that all contributed to the values and debates of classical democratic discourse. Like Sophistopolis, the city in which Theon's students are asked to place themselves is a democratic Greek city with a similar cast of stock characters. While Theon's text does not closely examine the democratic institution of the assembly, nevertheless, as with Russell's Sophistopolis, the *ekklēsia* does provide a critical arena of action for the student rhetor.

Theon mentions the *ekklēsia* first in exercises in which the student must either specify the setting for a story or be clear as to their own (imaginary) context in making a speech. The exercise of narrative (*diēgēma*) provides the occasion for one appearance of the *ekklēsia* as Theon directs the student to be clear in describing not only the time frame and the people performing the action but also the place it occurs. One must be able to specify not only time of day and year for this action but also if it was performed at the assembly, a feast or procession, "ἐκκλησίας οὔσης ἐγένετο τὸ πρᾶγμα ἢ πομπῆς ἢ ἑορτῆς"[61] Likewise, in the exercise of *prosopopoeia*, where the student attempts to craft a speech imagined in the character of someone else, Theon suggests that for the speech to be successful, the student must be aware not only of the imagined character speaking but also of the circumstances in which the speech is delivered. Different words are suited to different events, and Theon argues the same words would not fit both army camp and *ekklēsia*.[62]

---

58. Ibid., 292.

59. For Russell's vision of this city, see Russell, *Greek Declamation*, 21–39. Webb makes this connection as well: Webb, "The *Progymnasmata* as Practice," 304.

60. Russell, *Greek Declamation*, 22.

61. Theon, *Progymnasmata* 79.4; Patillon, 39.

62. 116.9–10; Patillon, 71. Πρέπουσι δὲ λόγοι καὶ τόποις καὶ καῖρος, οὐ γὰρ ἐπὶ τοῦ

Theon further specifies the significance of the *ekklēsia* context for the rhetor in his explanation of the *thesis* exercise. He uses a comparison with the exercise of *topos* to guide the student in crafting a *thesis*. These exercises differ according to the contrasting goals of each speech. According to Theon, the *thesis* concerns a matter in doubt and aims to persuade (τέλος ἐστὶ τὸ πεῖσαι), while the *topos* assumes a point of agreement and strives for retribution (τὸ τιμωρίαν).[63] Each exercise also calls for a different context and audience. The setting of the *topos* is the law-court (ἐν δικαστηρίῳ), and those who hear the speech are the jurors (δικασταί). However, the *thesis* takes place in the *ekklēsia*, and Theon names its audience "plainly" or "absolutely" made up of citizens (ἁπλῶς πολῖται). In this description of the *thesis*, Theon grants a balance of power to the citizen *ekklēsia* audience endowed with authority of decision over whatever matter the speaker presents. With this definition of *thesis*, Theon voices the connection of the *ekklēsia* with speech and citizen decision that dominated democratic discourse in classical Athens[64] and continued to be a critical element of *ekklēsia* discourse under the Roman Empire.

In his *progymnasmata* examples, Libanius further elaborates the place of the assembly in the imaginative exercise of education. In expanding upon a *chreia* from Isocrates about the fruits of education, Libanius names the greatest of these benefits to be the future political involvement of the student. As he explains, "For when the young man has been sufficiently educated, he is invited to the Council, he is invited to the Assembly, the whole People looks toward his opinion, and they obey his proposals as if they were oracles."[65] Libanius imagines the student as young, male, and clearly a citizen. Moreover, this is a citizen destined for leadership through the persuasive speech of the democratic assembly. Indeed, a number of Libanius' exercises reveal that the civic context for which he trains students. His very definition of a city is shaped by the democratic institutions of *ekklēsia*, court, and council. For instance, Libanius' argues the necessity for marriage based on the production of citizens, without whom, "What sort of sacrifices

---

στρατοπέδου οἱ αὐτοὶ καὶ ἐν ἐκκλησίᾳ.

63. 120.21–24; Patillon, 83.

64. Ober has done extensive work on this topic. For representative work, see Ober, *The Athenian Revolution*; *Mass and Elite*.

65. Libanius, *Progymnasmata, Anecdotes* 3, 13. For Libanius' *Progymnasmata* exercises, I use Craig Gibson's edition with translation and notes (Gibson, *Libanius's Progymnasmata: Model Exercises in Greek Prose Composition and Rhetoric*). Gibson, *Progymnasmata*, 68–69. ἐπειδὰν γὰρ ὁ νέος ἱκανῶς ἔχῃ τοῦ παιδεύεσθαι, καλεῖται μὲν εἰς βουλήν, καλεῖται δὲ εἰς ἐκκλησίαν, δῆμος δὲ ὅλος εἰς τὴν ἐκείνου γνώμην ὁρᾷ, καὶ καθάπερ χρησμοῖς πείθονται ταῖς εἰσηγήσεσι.

to the gods could there be in the future? What sort of councils? What sort of assemblies?"⁶⁶

*Progymnasmata* not only ask students to inhabit the democratic *ekklēsia* and court but also require that they conjure stock characters familiar from classical literature. These characters illustrate the debates and struggles over democracy that a student might learn to bring to the context of the *ekklēsia*. The *topos* exercise⁶⁷ most directly addresses these stock characters, placing the tyrant among the traitor, murderer, and profligate as figures to be condemned. Meanwhile, the tyrannicide shares the company of the hero and lawgiver. This list of "good" and "bad" characters gives us important cultural information. In this formulation, the tyrant, recognizable in classical literature as someone abusing power at the expense of the *dēmos*, becomes the equal of a murderer or traitor. By the same token, the tyrannicide⁶⁸ shares ultimate honor with a lawgiver like Solon or a hero like Achilles. These two figures of tyrant and tyrannicide, ubiquitous in both *progymnasmata* and declamations, reveal a bias toward democracy, along with a palpable sense that this democracy is in constant need of defense. In the early Roman Empire, Ruth Webb suggests that the anti-tyrannical tradition represented in these exercises is more than "an unreal nostalgia for a long lost democratic past."⁶⁹ Instead, this tradition must be seen as part of the current political conversation of the early empire in which such a tradition "provided a stock of arguments against the misuse of power which inform Greek responses to Roman imperial rule."⁷⁰

Within his *progymnasmata* examples, Libanius' *topos* exercise against the tyrant shows that this subject could occasion a full-fledged defense of democratic practice, values, and institutions. In turn, such a defense is highly informative about the place of democratic discourse in educational practice. In this exercise, Libanius describes the characteristics of democratic government as a way to explain the gravity of the tyrant's crimes against the people. Libanius' democracy plays out in council, court, and the meeting of the *dēmos* in the assembly. Offices are held by "only those to whom an

---

66. Libanius, *Progymnasmata*, Thesis 1, 11 (Gibson, *Progymnasmata*, 512–13). Ποῖαι μὲν γὰρ θυσίαι θεοῖς ἔτι; ποῖα δὲ βουλευτήρια; ποῖαι δὲ ἐκκλησίαι;

67. Theon defines the *topos* exercise as, τόπος ἐστὶ λόγος αὐξητικός ὁμολογουμένου πράγματος ἤτοι ἁμαρτήματος ἢ ἀνδραγαθήματος. *Progymnasmata*, 106.5–6; Patillon, 62.

68. It is a point of interest that Theon mentions not only the apparently male tyrannicide but also a woman who kills the tyrant. *Progymnasmata*, 106.14–15.

69. Webb, "The *Progymnasmata* as Practice," 303

70. Ibid.

allotment or a vote of the People (*dēmos*) grants it."[71] Beyond such offices, leadership is provided by those who speak persuasively in the *ekklēsia* setting, since "the rostrum is open to anyone who wishes to speak."[72] Such leadership is carefully monitored and assessed after its performance as "nothing in a democracy should go unexamined."[73]

Libanius names clear benefits of the democratic system he defends in the face of tyranny. Democracy means freedom, even as it "respects equality, honors justice, punishes excess, and rejects the opposite, putting forth the benefits derived from it to be shared by everyone."[74] In contrast to tyranny, democracy makes it possible for people to live together—rich and poor—without fear of violence since this type of governance instills self-control. In this full *topos* exercise, the democratic values only alluded to in Theon's handbook are fully elaborated and located within the civic context, most visibly within the citizen *ekklēsia*.

The rich man and the poor man also feature as common characters both in *progymnasmata* and in declamation. As with the tyrant/tyrannicide, this pair speaks to a tension or struggle within democratic discourse. In this case, these figures are often used to explore the ideal of political equality in tension with the acceptance of economic inequality. The value of "security" in this pairing applies both to the protection the poor citizen enjoys from the abuse of the wealthy, even as the wealthy are assured security of property and person within a demos dominated by "the many." Both Theon and Libanius use this pair in their *progymnasmata* training to elaborate these very principles of democratic government. In his *topos* exercise condemning the tyrant, Libanius praises democracy for its ability to include both poor and rich without violence on either side, a contrast to the government of the tyrant who uses his wealth to abuse the poor and deny them their rights. Meanwhile, Theon claims that a law must apply equally to all to be acceptable. In explaining the exercise for "introduction of a law," he illustrates this principle with a theoretical law that either fines those who are guilty of inflicting physical wounds 10,000 drachmas or deprives them of their civil rights.[75] According to Theon, the student should argue this law as unfair

---

71. Libanius, *Progymnasmata, Common Topics*, 4, 5 (Gibson, *Progymnasmata*, 180–81). ἀλλ' ὅτῳ τοῦτο δίδωσιν ὁ κλῆρος ἢ χειροτονία τοῦ δήμου.

72. Ibid. τὸ βῆμα δὲ ἀνέῳκται τοῖς βουλομένοις λέγειν.

73. Ibid.

74. Ibid., 4, 7. δημοκρατία δὲ τὸ ἴσον νέμει καὶ τὸ δίκαιον τιμᾷ καὶ τὸ πλέον κολάζει καὶ τοὐναντίον ἐκβάλλει κοινὰ πᾶσι τὰ παρ' αὑτῆς ἀγαθὰ προτιθεῖσα.

75. Here I am dependent on Michel Patillon's and Giancarlo Golognesi's French translation of the Armenian text that alone preserves this part of Theon's manual. Theon, *Progymnasmata*, 101.

since the poor and rich will be affected in vastly different ways: For the rich, such a fine is easily paid, but the poor will pay a much larger price in losing their rights.

These examples from Theon and Libanius carry forward classical democratic ideals in which the law must act to create a level playing field for both rich and poor as citizens, even as economic status is not fundamentally altered by the democratic system.[76] Elite students training in such *progymnasmata* exercises would thus encounter a construction of democratic citizenship that did not necessarily threaten their own wealth but did insist on the protection for the poor and their equality within the political realm.

## *The Ekklēsia in Student Reading*

For students working through the *progymnasmata* exercises, the most direct path to understanding the values and practice of the democratic *ekklēsia* would have been the classical literature accompanying all phases of this instruction. Theon's handbook advises the teacher to guide students through each exercise in a program of listening to classical examples, reading them aloud, and finally writing their own compositions in imitation. For Theon, the activities of reading aloud and listening to this literature were intensely interactive. The student listener was expected to cultivate an appropriate state of mind for each piece of literature,[77] and in reading, worked to "think himself into the speaker's situation, using the appropriate gestures and acting out the text as an utterance in a past time and place."[78] Such practice was intended to "imprint" a set of examples that would allow students to create their own compositions in worthy imitation of lofty classical models. In the process, students could strongly identify and internalize such classical models—especially the most well-known and revered.[79] Among these classical models, one of those best suited for transmitting ideals of *ekklēsia* leadership and audience participation is the great champion of Athenian democracy, Demosthenes. He is also the ancient author and speaker most visible, and certainly most revered, within Theon's handbook.

---

76. Thuc. 2.37. This portion of Pericles' famous funeral oration describes the Athenian democracy in light of the laws that allow equality and protection of the oppressed. For Demosthenes formulation of equality and voice in the civic setting, see Dem. 21.124–127.

77. Webb, "The *Progymnasmata* as Practice," 308.

78. Ibid.

79. Ibid., 309.

Throughout his manual, Theon highlights key authors in the literary construction of classical Athenian democracy—intellectuals that include Lysias,[80] Thucydides,[81] and Isocrates.[82] In this august company, Demosthenes takes pride of place for the frequency with which he is mentioned, the range of exercises he illustrates, and the importance Theon accords him as a model. Theon predictably names Demosthenes as an example for oratory regarding the introduction or protest of a law[83] but he also cites him as a skillful model to follow in crafting exercises such as the narrative or paraphrase.[84] Further, Theon makes Demosthenes the ultimate model for students by describing him as the orator with the best preparation to speak on matters both large and small—a preparation Theon urges his students to develop for themselves.[85] The intensity of Demosthenes' example in Theon's handbook does not seem to be an anomaly. Indeed, Libanius' educational literature and orations share this focus while 36 percent of the historical declamations attested by Philostratus have Demosthenic themes. Aelius Aristides epitomizes the thorough identification with Demosthenes that could result from such rhetorical training and practice when he records a dream that he is himself Demosthenes addressing the Athenian *dēmos*.[86]

Three of Demosthenes' speeches most frequently cited by Theon offer a vision of how this influential author might shape students' understanding of *ekklēsia* dynamics and leadership. Of the three orations—*On the Crown, False Legation, and the Second Olynthiac*—*On the Crown* is the speech that Theon mentions most frequently and it acts as an especially valuable resource for explaining the replication of *ekklēsia* discourse through Greek education. While only one of these speeches, the *Second Olynthiac*, is directed to the assembly,[87] all three are deeply concerned with the action taking place in that context. These speeches all incorporate significant consideration of the relationship between speaker and audience, and in the process they provide insight into the process and debates of the assembly.

---

80. Lys. 2; Theon, *Progymnasmata*, 68.27.
81. Thuc. 2.35–46; Theon, *Progymnasmata*, 68.26.
82. Isoc. 4; Theon, *Progymnasmata*, 63.27–28
83. Theon suggests that Demosthenes' best speeches are in this category. 61.15–16.
84. 63.3–7; 92.5–15.
85. *Progymnasmata*, 72.24–25.
86. Aristides, *Hieroi logoi* I.16.
87. The others are court speeches of Demosthenes, one in his own defense (*On the Crown*) and one in prosecution (*False Legation*). For these speeches, I use the edition of *Demosthenes* (trans. C.A. and J.H. Vince et al.; LCL).

Demosthenes depicts an assembly with complex speaker-audience interaction even as he conveys the responsibility of both speakers and audience for making the democratic system successful. Demosthenes' assembly—the *ekklēsia* first-century students imaginatively entered through his speeches—is the democratic state's most visible and powerful institution, responsible for making momentous decisions affecting not only Athens but also much of the Greek-speaking world. In *On the Crown*, Demosthenes explains that the best orator approaches this assembly with the goal of always crafting his persuasive speech to the advantage of the citizens.[88] Demosthenes' ideal speaker acts as a counselor who puts the good of the city before his own interests. In fact, Demosthenes implies this speaker should be willing to suffer for this steadfast loyalty as Demosthenes himself has suffered at the hands of his enemies.[89]

The speech *On the Crown* also exposes a tension between competition and citizen equality that was an important current in classical democratic discourse in the *ekklēsia* context.[90] Demosthenes argues his own excellence as a speaker based on his ability to provide the best policies for Athens when there was true competition among speakers in the assembly.[91] In this competition, each speaker courts the approval, or persuasion, of the *dēmos* as it sits in assembly and court. Demosthenes' claims of success in this competition[92] are matched, however, by a portrayal of himself as a champion of the citizen equality that creates a level playing field for this contest.

In Demosthenes's rhetoric, this level playing field includes a respect for the political equality between rich and poor, even as it means guarding the *parrhēsia* of Athenian citizenship. In defending his own leadership, Demosthenes explains that his actions in pushing the wealthy to more equally share the burden of funding the navy[93] represent his long-standing policy that, "Within the city, I never preferred the gratitude of the rich to the claims of the poor."[94] Likewise, Demosthenes asserts both in *On the Crown* and the *Second Olynthiac* that the *dēmos* must honor the equal right of each citizen

---

88. 18.278; 321.

89. 18.322.

90. Ober, "The Debate Over Civic Education in Classical Athens."

91. 18.320.

92. 18.86.

93. 18.102.

94. 18.109 (Vince, LCL). Οὔτε γὰρ ἐν τῇ πόλει τὰς παρὰ τῶν πλουσίων χάριτας μᾶλλον ἢ τὰ τῶν πολλῶν δίκαι' εἱλόμην . . .

"to counsel, to speak and to act"[95] in order to guard citizen equality more broadly.

Demosthenes includes his expectations for the assembly audience alongside his description of an ideal speaker. For Demosthenes, the *ekklēsia* audience itself has a responsibility to allow each citizen to raise his voice in the assembly. This responsibility ties into the assembly's primary duty of choosing the best advice for the city based on all the options presented by citizen advisors. Demosthenes lays out the correct course of events for the assembly in *False Legation*: first, the assembly receives the facts of each case, these facts are followed by a decision, and then come the execution of the determined action.[96] In a passage concerning the assembly, Demosthenes contends that it is always the policy for the Athenians to put forward matters publicly in order to determine the common good.[97] While responsibility lies with speakers to provide the information necessary to make decisions about this common good, the assembly itself must make these decisions fairly and conscientiously. Demosthenes chides the Athenians for often failing in this very task. He accuses them of preferring the entertainment provided by attacks against those leaders offering good advice to the good advice itself.[98]

Demosthenes discusses another hindrance to the effective functioning of the assembly in the *Second Olynthiac* oration. He argues that the Athenians have been dividing themselves politically into large groups. This practice endangers the state since the warring parties distract from the external and internal demands on the city. In these circumstances, the Athenians have permitted individual leaders of the factions to rule over them tyrannically while executing unfair divisions of labor among the wider population. Demosthenes suggests that the state can only function effectively if the factions are broken down and each citizen present has a chance to speak, because only in these circumstances can the assembly choose the best advice and the state prosper.

## A *Progymnasmata* Example

Although the fourth-century Libanius falls by a wide margin outside the first-century time frame I seek to impose on this study, his *progymnasmata*

---

95. 2.30 (Vince, LCL) νῦν γενομένους κοινὸν καὶ τὸ βουλεύεσθαι καὶ τὸ λέγειν καὶ τὸ πράττειν ποιῆσαι.

96. 19.34.

97. 18.273 (Vince, LCL) ἀεὶ δ' ἐν κοινῷ τὸ συμφέρον ἡ πόλις προυτίθει σκοπεῖν.

98. 18.138.

examples are the most complete left to us, and thus help to illuminate more broadly Theon's first-century handbook as well as the ancient study of rhetoric. A number of Libanius' exercises quite compellingly deploy elements of democratic *ekklēsia* discourse examined throughout this chapter. One of the most interesting examples, an *encomium* for Thersites, bridges Morgan's "core" and "periphery" levels of Greek education, even as it applies the values and practice of the democratic *ekklēsia* to the construction of an ideal citizen leader in that setting. This chapter concludes with a brief examination of this *encomium*, Libanius' reframing of one of Homer's most maligned characters.

In this *encomium*, Libanius transforms a key scene from early in the *Iliad* that figures significantly in the school text papyri. Homer reserves special vitriol for Thersites in the *Iliad*,[99] elaborating his lameness and physical deficiency in legs, shoulders, chest, skull, and even his hair in order to mark Thersites as a contemptible figure.[100] Libanius reimagines and names the meeting in which Thersites speaks out as an "*ekklēsia*" gathering, even as he paints Thersites as a heroic orator courageously addressing that assembly. In transforming this character so thoroughly, Libanius makes a startling departure from Homer's own description of Thersites—a departure he acknowledges by asking Homer's pardon at the beginning of his *encomium*.[101] In the *Iliad*, Thersites' physical shortcomings combine with his "disorderly words,"[102] which are "in no orderly wise"[103] and uttered with "shrill cries."[104] When this repulsive character speaks against Agamemnon, his speech is met with Odysseus' derision and, ultimately, violence.[105] In Libanius' encomium, the thoroughly unsympathetic character Thersites becomes such a paragon of democratic virtues that Webb names him a "proto-democrat"[106] in this speech.

Libanius suggests that Thersites did not critique Agamemnon in order to cause trouble but instead only comes forward in the *ekklēsia* when he

99. Libanius, *Progymnasmata*, Encomium 4,1 (Gibson, *Progymnasmata*, 229ff.).

100. *Il.* 2.215–20 (Murray, LCL).

101. Theon describes the *encomium* as, "language revealing the greatness or virtuous actions and other good qualities belonging to a particular person." Theon, *Progymnasmata*, 109.1–2.

102. Ibid. 2.214.

103. Ibid., 2.215.

104. Ibid., 2.222.

105. *Il.* 2.245–325. Homer targets his legs, a handicapped foot, his shoulders, chest, skull, and even his hair as marking Thersites to be a contemptible figure!

106. Webb, "The *Progymnasmata* as Practice," 301.

recognizes a failure of the leadership and sees the "need of someone with wisdom and a beneficial frankness of speech."[107] In this rendering, Thersites acts as a thoughtful speaker who risks his own welfare for the common good. Libanius compares Thersites to Demosthenes in this selflessness and in his willingness to tell the assembly the things that they need, rather than wish, to hear.[108] By likening Thersites to Demosthenes, Libanius cues the reader that the changes he has wrought in Thersites can only be understood in terms of a larger revisioning of the scene. In Libanius' description, the *ekklēsia* in which the characters meet is not a gathering of soldiers dominated by aristocratic leaders but rather an assembly that better matches Demosthenes' time and place—a democratic assembly where *parrhēsia* and equality are virtues to be commended.

Libanius' Thersites possesses further virtues recognizable from classical democratic discourse. In common with Demosthenes' self-presentation, Thersites not only practices courageous free speech but he also does so in part to curb the free rein of power given to the wealthy.[109] Libanius writes about this character, "He did not fear the status of some, and he did not flatter those in power while being harsh to men of the people, foully abusing and persecuting those who were weaker."[110] Thersites' stand against the powerful is accentuated by his own refusal to elevate himself over others based on his impressive ancestry. Thersites' value as a speaker on behalf of equality and the common good is demonstrated by the discerning assembly audience, which allows him to complete his speech and does not punish him for telling the truth.[111] In this *encomium*, Thersites appears in the mold of an ideal democratic leader, promoting the common good through his frank speech at the same time he stands for that essential value of democracy—equality.

Finally, Libanius makes Odysseus Thersites' foil, not as the hero but as the citizen who uses violence rather than reason to accomplish his goals. Far from applauding Odysseus' beating of Thersites, Libanius claims that Thersites was attacked because Odysseus could neither contest what he said nor compare with him as an orator. Libanius accuses Odysseus in this situation

---

107. Libanius, *Progymnasmata*, *Encomium* 4,7 (Gibson, *Progymnasmata*, 233). δεῖ τινος ἔχοντος φρόνημα καὶ παρρησίαν συμφέρουσαν.

108. Ibid., 4,8 (Gibson, *Progymnasmata*, 232–33). Οἷον ὕστερον συνέβη γενέσθαι παρ' Ἀθηναίοις τὸν Δημοσθένην, ᾧ τὸ κοινῇ συμφέρον πρὸ τῶν αὐτῷ λυσιτελούντων ἐκέκριτο καὶ λέγων οἷς ᾔδει τὸν δῆμον ἀνιάσων μᾶλλον ᾑρεῖτο λυπεῖν ἢ χαρίζεσθαι κακῶς.

109. Ibid., 4,6–7.

110. Ibid., 4, 6 (Gibson, *Progymnasmata*, 232–33). Οὐ δεδιὼς τὰς τύχας ἐνίων οὐδὲ τοὺς μὲν δυναστείαν ἔχοντας κολακεύων, τοῖς δὲ τοῦ δήμου χαλεπὸς ὢν καὶ προπηλακίζων καὶ ἐλαύνων ἕκαστον τῶν ἀσθενεστέρων.

111. Ibid., 4,17.

of breaking laws regarding assault, while he praises Thersites for remaining loyal in spite of his ill treatment. Here, Thersites' handicap is not a reason to reject him but rather a testament to his own heroism in earlier wars, a courage reinforced for the reader by his willingness to exercise παρρησία. Moreover, his handicap highlights Odysseus' wrong in using violence to silence a physically weaker opponent, thus betraying equality based in *parrhēsia* in a similar way to that arch-enemy of democracy—the tyrant.

## Conclusion

Greek education was a particularly important vehicle for the dissemination of *ekklēsia* discourse in the eastern Roman Empire of Paul's time. In their earliest exposure to education, students were introduced to a canon of important Greek writers from the past that allowed students to claim a certain cultural "Greekness." At all levels of education, this canon featured an emphasis on public, political speech, which younger students might first experience with authors like Homer or Euripides, and students who continued into advanced levels would more fully develop in their own rhetorical training. As Joy Connolly explains, this emphasis on public speech had its origin in democratic cities that oriented students toward a citizenship bound up with communication in assembly and court.[112] As the school texts drawn from Euripides' *Phoenissae* show, students from their earliest school exercises might well encounter authors that would reinforce the association of citizenship with free speech.

In this chapter, I have shown that the *paideia* of Greek education formed students not simply as citizens, but as citizens of the democratic *polis*. This process of *paideia* greatly intensified for those students pursuing even the earliest stages of rhetorical training. Theon's first-century *Progymnasmata* handbook allows us a valuable window on students' exposure to democratic discourse in the context of that training. Theon retains the democratic *ekklēsia* as one of the critical contexts for which students train. Theon's description of various exercises also features key figures and themes from classical democratic literature—including an insistence on political equality based in free speech.

As a fully realized example of the exercises Theon proscribes, the *progymnasmata* composition of Libanius on Thersites demonstrates how the building blocks of Greek education could come together in a full throated defense of democratic ideals and practice. Echoing Demosthenes, Libanius suggests that a speaker must provide an equalizing effect both by keeping

---

112. Connolly, "Problems of the Past," 342.

the wealthy from exercising undue influence and by protecting the rights of the poor. While courage in battle is not absent from this picture, the greater courage means exercising παρρησία in the interest of fellow citizens and telling them the truth even if it is unpleasant. Deliberation thus has high value, and violence is deplored as the exercise of unfair and uncivil advantage. For generations of students in the early empire, Greek education disseminated this vision of correct political practice. Moreover, this vision—this discourse—was literally in the air of Greek cities as teachers and students pursued this *paideia* together in civic public spaces. In the following chapters, I will show that democratic discourse was not limited to the educational or theoretical realms. Instead, the first-century authors Dio Chysostom and Plutarch show the prevalent place of this discourse both in political discussion and in the practice of the Greek *polis*.

# 2

# The First-Century *Ekklēsia* in the Writings of Dio and Plutarch

## Introduction

THE DISCOURSE OF THE DEMOCRATIC *EKKLĒSIA* RAN AS A THREAD THROUGH all levels of Greek education. As I have shown, first-century students would encounter the civic *ekklēsia* in a range of classical texts—an encounter socializing these students into a discourse that included both ideals and debates at the core of ancient democracy. In this chapter, I ask, "How might those first-century students—and those adults like the apostle Paul who lived and worked in Greek cities throughout the Mediterranean—have envisioned this civic *ekklēsia*? In what way would these denizens of the Greek East have expected debates and ideals alike to play out in the relationships, the rhetoric, and the discourse that characterized the citizen assembly?"

Classical texts do not supply the best answers to these questions. Better resources lie closer to hand in first-century texts that address *polis* democracy in the *ekklēsia* context. This chapter begins by visiting a scene from Dio Chrysostom's *Euboicus*, one of our most vivid—if fictional—accounts of a civic *ekklēsia* enthusiastically carrying out the business of democracy. This account encourages a reexamination of scholarly assertions that the *ekklēsia* and civic democracy ceased to be a meaningful presence in Greek cities of the early Empire. Indeed, I argue that the wider corpus of Dio Chrysostom himself, and his first-century counterpart Plutarch, substantiate the vitality of practice and democratic discourse manifest in the *Euboicus* passage. The works of Dio Chrysostom and Plutarch reveal provincial elites deeply engaged in civic life and institutions, including the *ekklēsia*. While both show a commitment to the *ekklēsia* as a mark of continuing, if limited civic independence, Plutarch and Dio also convey an ambivalence toward this institution that reveals their own delicate placement as elites within the wider context of the Roman Empire. With materials ranging from political treatises to speeches performed in civic settings, these authors demonstrate that many issues connected with democracy and the citizen assembly remained a concern for people in Greek city-states under the Roman Empire. Together, Dio Chrysostom and Plutarch paint a vivid image of Greek politics in which the nature of citizen equality, civic harmony, the exercise of power by the elites, and democracy itself are all still being debated. For asserting the survival of *ekklēsia* discourse in the first century, the correlation of debate with the public assembly context is nearly as important as the issues under discussion by the assembly. Plutarch and Dio make clear that the tumultuous reciprocity characterizing the relationship of audiences and speakers in the democratic assembly was not merely an artifact of the past.

## The Euboicus

Dio Chrysostom's *Euboicus* tells a thrilling story of the author's shipwreck and rescue by a rustic hunter living in the countryside at a distance from the nearest city. The narrative of the *Euboicus* is a series of nested stories in which Dio's rescue provides the occasion for the hunter to tell his own life story. In these stories, Dio's own life may have provided some elements for the narrative. However, D. A. Russell explains of this text, "What we have here is a carefully-structured narrative, using many pastoral topics but directed at specific moral ends . . . that poverty is no bar to hospitality, nor, in general, to a good and happy life."[1] Within this fictional narrative, the poor hunter relates his first introduction to the urban context and, specifically, his first encounter with the civic assembly. In this way, the hunter's first-person account brings the civic *ekklēsia* to life. As readers, we borrow the hunter's eyes to see the *ekklēsia* as an institution with customs strange and even frightening for someone not versed in the ways of the city. The pastoral hunter's meticulous account of the assembly meeting thus reads almost like an anthropologist's description of foreign ritual—valuable description for modern readers standing at a distance of many centuries from the first-century context.

The circumstances that bring the hunter to the assembly explain some of the inherent drama in the *Euboicus*' *ekklēsia* scene. A citizen of the local city accuses the hunter of becoming wealthy by living on public lands.

---

1. Russell, *Dio Chrysostom Orations*, 9. For the *Euboicus*, I use Cohoon's (LCL) text in consultation with that of Russell in this volume.

Though settled at a distance from the city proper, the hunter lives on lands owned by the city and as a citizen must account for his failure to contribute money to the *polis*. Although he offers his accuser what limited resources he has, the hunter finds himself brought before the assembly for examination and judgment by the civic body.

In his first contact with the citizen *ekklēsia*, the hunter experiences a scene of noisy chaos. Shortly after arriving in the city, the hunter approaches the theater where he sees a large group of people congregating. They are so loud with their shouting that at first he thinks they are "all fighting with one another."[2] As Dio portrays them, the deliberations of the assembly are full of disorder and characterized by passionate speech and shouting most of the time.[3] The crowd drives the action in the hunter's narrative, interacting with each speaker and weighing each item of business as it expresses pleasure or displeasure with shouting, applause or laughter. The power and noise of the crowd, especially when angry, overwhelms the hunter who describes it as a wave or thunderstorm that nearly knocks him down when it washes over him.[4] The speakers, some speaking for a short time and others for an extended period, either address the crowd from the front or simply speak from their seats. The time allotted for each speaker depends on the will of the audience which cuts some short before they even get started.[5]

With Dio's rustic hunter as narrator, we thus encounter a vibrant civic assembly engaged with the noisy, colorful business of democratic politics. As the ancient history scholar John Ma observes, this depiction of a first-century assembly parallels the classical democratic *ekklēsia* in notable respects.[6] The procedural structure in which the examination of a citizen is followed by debate, proposed decrees, and a subsequent vote recall Athenian practices, as does the close involvement of the crowd demonstrating approval or disapproval of various speakers.[7] As in Athens, speech is the primary political tool and means of participation, wielded by citizens with varying levels of formality. Citizenship means a voice, a stake in this assembly, even for our hunter who has never lived within the city's walls. In

---

2. 7.23 (Cohoon, LCL).... ὥστε ἐμοὶ ἐδόκουν πάντες μάχεσθαι ἀλλήλοις.

3. 7.25.

4. 7.25–26 (Cohoon, LCL). ἐγὼ δὲ καὶ αὐτὸς ἅπαξ ὀλίγου κατέπεσον ὑπὸ τῆς κραυγῆς, ὥσπερ κλύδωνος ἐξαίφνης ἢ βροντῆς ἐπιρραγείσης.

5. Ibid.

6. Ma, "Public Speech and Community," 108.

7. Ibid. Ober, *Mass and Elite*, 104. Hansen provides an overview of the interaction between speakers and audiences in the Athenian assembly: Hansen, *The Athenian Democracy*, 142–47.

the assembly of the *Euboicus*, lively, even raucous debate seems expected by everyone except the politically inexperienced hunter. The citizens freely argue various issues, with the debate over the hunter receiving the fullest description. Each speaker must compete to lead the assembly by persuading the crowd to their point of view.

As readers of this account, what connections can we draw between the assembly in the narrative and wider first-century practice and discourse characterizing Greek cities? Many aspects of the *Euboicus* show Dio's active borrowing from diverse genres of Greek literature that include New Comedy, the Greek novel, and rhetorical training exercises.[8] For his part, Graham Anderson asserts that in the *Euboicus* we see various *progymnasmata* exercises brought together in an ensemble work.[9] Should we thus regard the *ekklēsia* scene of the *Euboicus* as wholly an imaginative exercise in "the conventions of rhetoric and declamation"[10] by which Dio Chrysostom relocates classical democratic practice to his own first-century context? Or—as John Ma contends—can we see in this tale a reflection of "sociopolitical realities and ideologies current in the contemporary *polis*"?[11] The scholarship devoted to the first-century *polis* and its political practices gives a range of responses to these questions. Although past consensus ruled civic democracy a dead letter in the first century, recent analysis encourages reconsideration of vibrant democratic discourse and practice centered on the assembly in this era.[12]

## An Argument for Democratic Continuity

The prevailing scholarship from the last century and a half inclines one to see the democratic practice of the *Euboicus*' *ekklēsia* as fiction—stirring fiction, but fiction nonetheless. In no uncertain terms, this body of scholarship has posited the demise of both the active assembly and democracy itself in the early empire. Scholars like G.E.M. de Ste Croix, following the lead of I. Levy writing more than a century ago,[13] have posited an increasingly orna-

---

8. Ma, "Public Speech and Community," 110.
9. Anderson, *The Second Sophistic*, 53.
10. Ma, "Public Speech and Community," 121.
11. Ibid.
12. Ibid.
13. Lévy describes an assembly isolated from any serious decision making, writing, "Mais, si l'*ekklēsia* est associée, au moins nominalement, au vote des décisions générales, la boulè statue seule sur tout ce qui a pratiquement une importance réelle" (215). Further, Lévy describes this weakening of the assembly in terms of the

mental assembly during this time period manipulated by elite councilmen and magistrates serving as Rome's chosen representatives in each district.[14] Ste Croix suggests that the assembly became increasingly powerless, falling into complete political insignificance by the beginning of the Principate in Greece and by the mid-second century CE in Asia Minor.[15] Meanwhile A. H. M. Jones claims that democracy itself had ceased to exist in any meaningful sense for Greek cities even by the beginning of the second century BCE.[16] In this portrayal of the Greek city, the fortunes of the civic council rise in direct proportion to the disenfranchisement of the assembly.[17] In the classical Athenian system, the council was "the executive and preparatory body for the decision making organ, the assembly."[18] This Athenian council took on an administrative role and set the agenda for the assembly. By contrast, the assembly ideally included all citizens as the sovereign power of the democratic state. Jones argues that in the first century, the assembly was only "still in theory the sovereign body, electing the magistrates and passing decrees," while the council now conducted all the real business. In these terms, the acclamation of the assembly became a formality in endorsing the candidates and decrees of the council.[19]

Only recently have scholars begun to debate with some rigor the conclusion that real democracy ceased to exist under the Roman Empire. For instance, Philippe Gauthier has gone far in demonstrating that the Hellenistic city assembly bears many resemblances in form and function to the classical democratic assembly—a direct contrast to Jones' picture of a decisive break with democratic tradition.[20] Meanwhile, Stephen Mitchell has questioned the argument that the Romans were closely, and universally, involved with the administration of cities by sponsoring hereditary councils and imposing property qualifications for assembly membership. Instead, Mitchell asserts that there are only a small number of specific instances that

---

city government: "L'affaiblissement de l'*ekklēsia*, ou plutôt son annihilation, tel est, à l'époque Antonine, le phénomène capital de la vie constitutionnelle de la cite grecque." Lévy, "Études sur la vie municipale," 218.

14. Ste Croix, *Class Struggle*, 531–32.
15. Ibid., 527–32.
16. Jones, *The Greek City*, 170.
17. Millar, "The Greek City in the Roman Period," 241.
18. Hansen, *The Athenian Democracy*, 246.
19. Jones, *The Greek City*, 177.
20. Gauthier assigns an active continuing role in "les cinq sujets de délibération qu'Aristote jugeait être les plus importants pour toute assemblée de citoyens," including finance, international relations, and defense. Gauthier, "Les cités hellénistiques," 219ff.

evidence this kind of direct involvement. In the main, the Romans seemed content to let the cities determine the "shape" of their own governments.²¹

With scholars like John Ma and Giovanni Salmeri, I contend that the continuation of democratic practice extended into the Roman period—that the *Euboicus*' assembly can be convincingly located as part of the countervailing culture and ideology of Dio Chrysostom's own time. In this chapter, I will argue that democratic discourse and behavior associated with an active, influential assembly existed into the late first and early second century CE. To do so, I will investigate the dynamics and function that Dio and Plutarch describe for assemblies during their time period and, more specifically, the relationship between speakers and audiences in this setting. In part, I will substantiate that the dynamics and ideology Dio Chrysostom describes in the *Euboicus* find a correspondence in the way these authors elsewhere discuss the *ekklēsia*. The way that speakers and audiences interact not only illuminates the way assemblies functioned but also in a larger sense helps to explain the power relations characterizing Greek citizenry in the first century. While evidence of democratic dynamics may also be investigated through the epigraphic record,²² the writings of Dio and Plutarch access a certain level of complexity in interaction between speakers and audiences that inscriptions do not often provide. The rhetorical engagement of these authors with *ekklēsia* discourse reveals the varied types of authority still associated with the assembly and ways in which this discourse is deployed in a mediation between assembly power and elite interests.

---

21. Mitchell, *Anatolia*, 1:210.

22. While suggesting that the assembly is no longer vital, Jones does point out his research into the epigraphic remains suggest that the civic governments of Greek cities well into the second century continued to require that motions be approved by both council and assembly. Only very rarely is there a case of a decree passed only by the council. Jones, *The Greek City*, 177. Mitchell addresses the epigraphic record regarding the assembly at least briefly in his work, concluding that the vast majority of remains mentioning the assembly are honorific decrees. He argues that this makes sense since negative decisions would have been put in the city archives. Mitchell, *Anatolia*, 1:201. For further engagement with documentary evidence related to the activity of both *ekklēsia* and democracy in the first century, see Ma, "Public Speech and Community"; Salmeri, "Dio, Rome, and the Civic Life," 71; Rhodes and Lewis, *The Decrees of the Greek States*.

## Dio of Prusa and Plutarch of Chaeronea: Greek Citizens/Roman Subjects

Giovanni Salmeri declares of the first-century authors Dio Chrysostom and Plutarch, "It is above all the writings of Plutarch and Dio that show the *ekklēsia* as a far from negligible element in the political life of the *polis* during the imperial age."[23] Two of the most significant intellectuals of the early empire,[24] Dio and Plutarch's own civic engagement make them particularly well-suited for interrogating the nature of first-century *ekklēsia* discourse and practice. Plutarch and Dio betray this civic involvement in many of their works, notably in extensive political treatises and assembly speeches.[25] While both men enjoyed influence in the politics of the wider empire by offering advice to prominent friends and even cities,[26] their

---

23. Salmeri, "Dio, Rome, and the Civic Life," 71–72.

24. Ibid., 61.

25. In the case of Dio, there remain a number of speeches that he gave before the *ekklēsiai* of various cities, including eight before the assembly in his home city of Prusa. These speeches help to establish the types of concerns that might have been brought before a civic assembly, but also demonstrate how these issues would have been discussed and ultimately settled. Although we retain no speeches that Plutarch may have actually delivered in an *ekklēsia*, we do have several political treatises, most notably *Political Advice* and *Old Men in Political Affairs*, that dwell at length on the relationship of statesmen to an active civic assembly. These texts contain wonderful descriptions of the functioning first-century *ekklēsia* that strongly suggest Plutarch himself had considerable experience in the arena of the assembly during his public career. In their focus on political involvement rather than rhetorical teaching, they provide a contrast to some members of the Second Sophistic. Salmeri suggests that Philostratus presents influential figures of the Second Sophistic as primarily involved in such teaching, in contrast to Plutarch and Dio's more varied interests. Salmeri, "Dio, Rome, and the Civic Life," 66. Anderson argues that Philostratus' working definition of the sophist as "a specialist teacher and a specialist in ornamental oratory," might be traced back to the Athens of Isocrates, but would come to be personified by figures of the Second Sophistic like Hermagoras and Dionysius Atticus. Anderson, *The Second Sophistic*, 18–19.

26. Dio not only offered advice in public speeches to cities like Alexandria (*Or.* 32) but received honorary citizenship at several cities where he also delivered speeches, including Nicomedia (*Or.* 38) and Apamea (*Or.* 41). The reason for Dio's exile under Domitian is a matter for some debate (see Jones, *The Roman World of Dio Chrysostom*, 45ff.), but he seemed to have returned to prominence afterwards with a successful embassy to Trajan, during which he may presented to the new emperor one of his orations on kingship. Jones, *The Roman World of Dio Chrysostom*, 53. Dio certainly uses correspondence between himself and the emperor to effect in his speeches. See: *Or.* 40.5, 44.12, 47.13. Swain, *Hellenism and Empire*, 195. Plutarch likewise held citizenship elsewhere, notably in Athens. Plutarch, *Quaest. conv.* 628 A. Plutarch was

dedication to local politics manifested itself in service in their respective city assemblies of Prusa and Chaerona. In fact, the very detail with which Dio and Plutarch describe the dynamics of the civic assembly substantiates their intimate involvement with the politics of the Greek city. As members of the elite in their respective communities, both appear to have accepted prestigious honors and offices,[27] as well as more mundane civic responsibilities.[28] These authors represent involvement in local politics featuring an active *ekklēsia* as both a duty and an honor that citizens, especially elite citizens, owe to their cities. Moreover, both assign local political participation an equal, if not greater, value than serving the Roman Empire.[29] For

---

made procurator of Greece by Hadrian and received the *ornamenta* from Trajan. Jones, *Plutarch and Rome*, 34. Lamberton, *Plutarch*. He also seems to have served on the Amphictyonic council as its "executive officer" (Plutarch, *Vit. aere al.* 829 A).

27. A member of an influential family, Dio served as member of Prusa's council as well as one of it chief magistrates, a post his son would also assume. For a discussion of his family, see *Or.* 46.2–6. On his undertaking city offices: *Or.* 49.15; 50.10. Dio also undertook an embassy to Rome when Trajan became emperor and pressed for various concessions for Prusa. Salmeri argues that this embassy resulted not only in the increase in the number of councilors for the city but its elevation to an assize-district in which the Roman governor would hold judicial sessions. For the embassy to Trajan, see *Or.* 40.13–15. Salmeri, "Dio, Rome, and the Civic Life," 68–9. For the changes in the council, see *Or.* 45.3–7. In the case of Plutarch, we know that he served as an ambassador to the proconsul of Achaea (*Praec, ger. rei publ.* 816 C) and perhaps also participated in embassies to Rome. Unfortunately, much about Plutarch's public career can only be conjectured. Based on the mention Plutarch makes of embassies to Rome as important for a politician's career (*Praec, ger. rei publ.* 805 A; *Exil.* 602 C), Jones hypothesizes that Plutarch himself may well have taken part in such activity: Jones, *Plutarch and Rome*, 21. This in contrast to Russell who argues that Plutarch's political influence outside of Chaeronea was limited. Russell, "On Reading Plutarch's *Moralia*," 130. In another hypothesis, Jones suggests that offices Plutarch mentions such as Boetotian magistrate, and superintendent of public games, may refer to offices that Plutarch has actually held. Jones, *Plutarch and Rome*, 26. We do know Plutarch also served at the shrine at Delphi, eventually holding one of the most prestigious positions as a permanent priest. Plutarch, *Quaest. conv.* 700 E. For more discussion of this role, see Lamberton, *Plutarch*, 52ff.

28. Plutarch's claim that he is not ashamed to monitor tile and the delivery of stone for the city is matched by Dio's involvement in various building projects and his fierce loyalty to his native Prusa. Plutarch argues that unimportant or even demeaning tasks are noble when performed as service to one's native city. Plutarch, *Praec, ger. rei publ.* 811 C.

29. Dio states his preference for living and participating in his home city over all the honors and wealth he might have gained through currying favor with the emperor (Trajan). *Or.* 44.6–7. Moreover, Dio asserts that he has only worked for the interests of Prusa rather than for his own gain in meeting with the emperor. *Dio, Or.* 45.3; Swain, *Hellenism and Empire*, 229.

these men, the *polis* remains the primary political forum,[30] and they define citizenship itself in terms of political activities centered on the city. Coming from different areas of the eastern empire, these figures nevertheless attest to a certain common political heritage and practice in the Greek-speaking world that remained vital into the first century and beyond.[31]

## Speech as an Essential Political Tool

In the *Euboicus*, speech and its reception determine the course of events in the civic assembly. Certainly *ekklēsia* speech shapes the hunter's own experience, and ultimately, his fate. The *Euboicus*' assembly scene portrays a complex interaction between citizens acting out leadership through persuasive speech and the citizen audience responsible for assessing this vocal leadership. In this animated *ekklēsia* setting, speakers address the assembly by coming to the front of the assembly or simply rising to speak from their seats. The varied location and procedure in addressing the gathering indicates the access each assembly member has to their own speech, and by extension, to leadership. Enthusiastic audience participation means that assessment of this leadership registers immediately. Within this loud and chaotic setting, it is the persuasive power of each speaker's rhetoric that secures—or fails to secure—the policies they propose.

The dynamics of this scene strongly recalls the democratic Athenian *ekklēsia* as it is represented in classical literature. In democratic Athens, the right to public, political speech delineated the nature of freedom and equality promised to the citizen by the state.[32] The extraordinary freedom

---

30. Ma, "Public Speech and Community," 123. Aalders points out that even when dealing with Roman political examples, Plutarch consistently uses the framework of the Greek *polis*. Aalders, *Plutarch's Political Thought*, 27. Dio, by contrast, associates freedom and law with the city, and the life of a barbarian and exile to life in a village in a speech to Prusa: *Or.* 47.10. This passage in turn supports Bowie's contention that, "The Greek's natural unit of organization is the *polis*." Bowie, "Hellenism in the Writers of the Early Second Sophistic," 197.

31. In fact, Desideri claims that Dio and Plutarch witness a renewed focus during this period on one's native city as a political sphere in which the "Greek intellectual" could exercise their talents, "reviving the tradition of the political life of their city." Desideri, "City and Country in Dio," 105–6. Salmeri claims a direct connection of this focus on one's native city to a shared Hellenistic heritage, arguing that writings of both Dio and Plutarch, "give full expression to the classical Greek point of view, according to which political engagement in one's city should not be seen as a *Beruf*, and should afford no concrete gains, but must appear a natural activity of men, and virtually their primary duty." Salmeri, "Dio, Rome, and the Civic Life," 63.

32. Hansen, *The Athenian Democracy*, 85; Ober, *Mass and Elite*; Saxonhouse, *Free*

and equality that democracy granted to its male citizens[33] crystallized in the ability to stand and speak persuasively to the gathered *dēmos*.[34] Ancient authors alternately described this freedom of speech with the words *isēgoria* and *parrhēsia*.[35] Not every citizen might make use of this right. However, Josiah Ober contends that the emphasis on *isēgoria* in the fifth century BCE—this radical right to political speech for each citizen—meant an equally radical impact for the majority of Athenian citizens attending the assembly. He explains, "*Isēgoria* changed the nature of mass experience from one of passive approval (or rejection) of measures presented, to one of actively listening to and judging the merits of complex, competing arguments."[36] In these terms, an active, discerning assembly audience decided matters of the state based on the speech brought before them. As *isēgoria* defined the status of citizenship, it also circumscribed the exercise of political authority. "Direct public communication" was the foundation of whatever leadership someone might offer in the democratic *polis*, a leadership always in a complicated negotiation with the power of the *dēmos*.[37]

In the *Euboicus* assembly—as in the classical Athenian *ekklēsia*—each citizens' equality and freedom manifests in the political involvement of παρρησία. Elite speakers have a prominent place in this setting, but their authority is circumscribed, and ultimately decided, by a powerful *dēmos*.[38]

---

*Speech and Democracy.*

33. It is critical to note that the male citizen subject was realized through a constant redefining of that subject over and against those that could not claim this status: women, slaves, children, and resident aliens. For an analysis of this process, see Hedrick, "The Zero Degree of Society."

34. Because fourth- and fifth-century BCE literature offers little systematic endorsement of democracy, Euripides, in his play *Suppliant Women*, stands out with his lucid definition of free speech and its relationship with democratic citizenship. In this play, Euripides explains freedom by quoting the formula used to open the assembly, "This is freedom: 'Who is willing, having good counsel, to bring it before the people?'" τοὐλεύθερον δ' ἐκεῖνο· Τίς θέλει πόλει χρηστόν τι βούλευμ' εἰς μέσον φέρειν ἔχων; (Euripides, *Suppl.* 435; my translation, in consultation with Saxonhouse, *Free Speech and Democracy*, 132).

35. Saxonhouse provides a helpful survey of the literature regarding these two terms and the subtle differences in their use regarding free speech within democracy. Saxonhouse, *Free Speech and Democracy*, 94–95.

36. Ober, *Mass and Elite*, 79.

37. Ibid., 107.

38. In addressing terms used to describe politicians in Athens, including the title of "advisor" and "rhetor," Ober notes, "The vocabulary of political activism in Athens reveals that direct public communication was the primary locus of whatever power, authority, or influence the Athenian rhetor might hope to exercise." Ober, *Mass and Elite*, 107ff.

As John Ma points out, this narrative description also manifests ideology "reminiscent of that of classical Athens."[39] In this ideology, the citizen right to equality and freedom in speech matches the citizen responsibility to foster "the common good." In Dio's account, the citizens' responsibility to contribute to the city according to their resources is unquestioned. Likewise, "Establishing credibility entails savaging rivals and perceived public enemies as a matter of course."[40]

The hunter's own speech in the assembly context realizes key elements of the ideology woven into classical Greek democracy. He demonstrates his claim to citizenship through his own surprisingly eloquent *ekklēsia* speech and through his willingness to serve the popular welfare of the city. However, he also echoes Euripides in *Phoenissae* by defining his citizenship and its attendant rights through the exclusions of democracy. He claims that as a citizen he is exempt from physical violence because he is neither a foreigner nor a criminal. The hunter thus evokes the value of security which Ober places alongside freedom and equality as a fundamental value of democracy.[41] The hunter explains this security for citizens through the contrast with those who do not have, or deserve, this protection—thus indicating an essential difference between citizens and those beyond the circle of citizenship.

The wider corpus of Dio and Plutarch's works show that the ideology and dynamics of the *Euboicus* assembly scene—the democratic discourse that permeates this scene—are not isolated to this particular, fictional writing. Instead, democratic discourse colors some of their most substantive speeches and treatises on politics within the Greek city. Each deploys this discourse in works in which they present persuasive, public speech as the action determining ideal civic leadership and circumscribing the experience of citizenship. Moreover, each locates such speech in the governing institutions of the Greek city, most notably in the *ekklēsia* context itself.

39. Ma, "Public Speech and Community," 114.

40. Ibid.

41. Lysias gives one of the most eloquent summations of Athenian democracy in the classical canon when he explains of those responsible for creating democracy, "They considered that it was the act of wild beasts to be subdued by each other with force, but it is appropriate for men to define justice by law, to convince by reason, and to serve these two in action, being ruled by law, and taught by reason." Lys. 2.19 (Lamb, LCL). ἡγησάμενοι θηρίων μὲν ἔργον εἶναι ὑπ' ἀλλήλων βίᾳ κρατεῖσθαι, ἀνθρώποις δὲ προσήκειν νόμῳ μὲν ὁρίσαι τὸ δίκαιον, λόγῳ δὲ πεῖσαι, ἔργῳ δὲ τούτοις ὑπηρετεῖν, ὑπὸ νόμου μὲν βασιλευομένους, ὑπὸ λόγου δὲ διδασκομένους.

Plutarch's treatise *Political Advice* is a guidebook for the elite young man desiring to enter politics within a Greek city of the Roman Empire.[42] Much of this treatise constructs an ideal of elite leadership in negotiation with the various challenges of this Greek civic context,[43] including—as I will show—the role of Roman power. Plutarch lists many necessary skills and qualities to be cultivated by the statesman. Among these, wise, persuasive speech stands out as the politician's most valuable tool. Plutarch describes the necessity for this skill by juxtaposing leadership of the people (δῆμος) or city (πόλις) with attempting to influence the mob (ὄχλος). Plutarch likens the mob, or crowd, to irrational beasts that a leader may try to bribe with banquets and other amusements. However, Plutarch argues that there is a difference when one tries to lead the *dēmos*. He suggests, "It is necessary to lead a people (δῆμος) or a city mostly by the ears ... For leadership of a people is leadership of those who are persuaded by speech."[44] He continues that "the charm and power of speech" (τῆς περὶ τὸν λόγον χάριτος καὶ δυνάμεως) must be combined with a superior character in order to persuade.[45] Plutarch's hypothetical statesman achieves political aims by engaging the *dēmos* with persuasive speech. In this equation, the *dēmos* has the power to judge the statesman not only by his rhetoric but also by his character.

Dio is no less constrained and enabled by a model of persuasive speech, as evidenced by the persuasion woven through many of his civic speeches. Whether he is arguing his own commitment to Prusa,[46] or calling for the assembly to create an impression of harmony,[47] Dio acknowledges that the

---

42. This work is addressed to a young man named Menemachus who appears to belong to an elite family in Sardis. *Praec. ger. rei publ.* 798 A-B. Jones says that this work deserves a special place among Plutarch's political treatises, and that together these treatises are critical resources for understanding Plutarch's political thought and the relationship between Greece and Rome. Jones, *Plutarch and Rome*, 110–11.

43. Plutarch includes some Roman illustrations, but uses mainly Greek classical models for different conversations within the treatise. Ma points out that in this treatise, "the terms of the debate, and the assumptions that city politics are defined by interaction with the people (*hoi polloi*), are identical to those of the classical period he draws his examples from." Ma, "Public Speech and Community," 123.

44. Plut., *Praec, ger. rei publ.* 802 D (Fowler, LCL). (For Plutarch's *Political Advice* and *Old Men in Political Affairs*, I consult the text of Plutarch, *Moralia* [Fowler, LCL], in consultation with that of *Plutarque Oevres Morales* [Cuvigny]). Δῆμον δὲ καὶ πόλιν ἐκ τῶν ὤτων ἄγειν δεῖ μάλιστα . . . δημαγωγία γὰρ ἡ διὰ λόγου πειθομένων ἐστίν . . . Also see *Praec, ger. rei publ.* 801 E.

45. 801 C.

46. Dio, *Or.* 45.

47. *Or.* 48.1–2.

*ekklēsia* audience must be convinced, rather than ordered, to follow his advice or adopt his viewpoint. While this act of persuasion is implicitly played out in many of his speeches, in several instances Dio explicitly names his task as one of exercising leadership through persuasive speech. In a speech before the assembly in Prusa, he urges the people to achieve civil harmony before they lose their rights to assembly, rights only recently regained from the Roman authorities. On his own role as counselor to this assembly, Dio asks, "What would be the advantage of my presence here, if I should not lead you in such matters by persuasion, having constantly engaged with you in discussions of concord and friendship. . ."[48] In another *ekklēsia* speech, this time to the Nicodemians who have recently granted him citizenship, Dio theorizes that he has been honored precisely due to the quality of his council,[49] and suggests, "If you will patiently endure my council, I am very confident you will be persuaded by me concerning the matters about which I am here to advise you."[50]

Dio and Plutarch's focus on speech and persuasion within the context of civic politics and, more specifically, in the arena of the assembly, attests to a complex relationship between elite statesmen and the assembled *dēmos*. The need to convince the assembly to accept certain policies or to take action on particular issues suggests that the *ekklēsia* retained decision-making power that statesmen, even those from powerful, elite backgrounds, would have to take into account.[51] Certainly Dio's fictional *Euboicus* presents the gathered *ekklēsia* as a powerful, corporate actor engaged with the business of governing the city. John Ma reads in that account evidence of political negotiation in the first-century *ekklēsia* as part of the "interaction between elite and community."[52] In the larger corpus of their works, both Dio and Plutarch substantiate such political negotiation between elite orators and a *dēmos* possessing the power to pass judgment not only on the policies determining civic life but also on the leaders who propose such policies. While both express negative aspects of the assembly's powerful role, they also suggest that assembly discernment could foster democratic ideals, notably free speech and equality. A more thorough exploration of Dio and

---

48. *Or.* 48.6 (Crosby, LCL). Τί γὰρ ἂν εἴη τῆς ἡμετέρας ἐπιδημίας ὄφελος, εἰ μὴ πρὸς τὰ τοιαῦτα πειθομένους ὑμᾶς ἄγοιμεν, λόγων ἀεὶ συναγωγῶν ὁμονοίας καὶ φιλίας συναράμενοι . . .

49. *Or.* 38.2

50. *Or.* 38.4 (Fowler, LCL). ὅτι μὲν οὖν, ἐὰν ὑπομείνητε τὴν συμβουλίαν, πεισθήσεσθέ μοι περὶ ὧν συμβουλεύων πάρειμι, καὶ δὴ σφόδρα θαρρῶ.

51. Dio utilizes his illustrious family tree as part of his rhetorical persuasion in several speeches: *Or.* 46.2–6; 44.3–5.

52. Ma, "Public Speech and Community," 122.

Plutarch's description of the *ekklēsia* and its authority as a corporate actor gives a clearer vision of the way each deploys *ekklēsia* discourse, even as it fosters a more thorough interrogation of such elite descriptions of the first-century *ekklēsia*.

## The "Sovereign" Dēmos

Both Plutarch and Dio convey to their readers the great strength of the *dēmos* in relation to its citizen advisors. Speaking before a gathering of the Alexandrian assembly,[53] Dio compares the *dēmos* to a powerful, single ruler that at its best acts like a wise sovereign, but at its worst like a tyrant. The "best" in this case means an assembly that welcomes frankness, or freedom, of speech (παρρησία), and acts fairly, carefully measuring advice from those who admonish and teach.[54] Dio claims that the assembly more commonly acts like the worst kind of ruler, the tyrant, with unpredictable rage and a susceptibility to flattery rather than truthful words.[55] According to Dio, the deficiencies of this second kind of system are much worse than they could ever be in a single person, since the *dēmos* can draw on the faults of all the citizens that are part of its corporate nature.[56] Dio's move of comparing the *dēmos* to the tyrant and king allows several fruitful observations. While his comparisons may partly speak to an elite agenda promoting a passive and peaceful assembly,[57] this passage also shows an appreciation of the *ekklēsia* as a powerful force that can still be represented as the sovereign of the *polis*. At its best, the *ekklēsia* will foster the free speech essential to positive portrayals of democracy, while at its worst the *dēmos* can be unfair and even violent. However, whether the assembly is good or bad, a tyrant or benevolent monarch, the city's leaders must still appeal to this powerful *dēmos* with persuasive speech to achieve their political goals.

Dio's own speeches for his hometown assembly and gatherings in other cities reveal that the *dēmos'* power extended to assessing prominent civic leaders in the public assembly setting. In a discourse to the Apameians, Dio,

---

53. In *Or.* 32, Dio addresses a gathering of Alexandrians in the theater. This seems to suggest an assembly gathering, as does the focus in Dio's speech on the behavior of civic assemblies: for example, Dio, *Or.* 32.25. Jones suggests it was a speech before the Alexandrian assembly during the reign of Vespasian. Jones, *The Roman World of Dio Chrysostom*, 36.

54. *Or.* 32.26–27.

55. Ibid.

56. Ibid.

57. Salmeri, "Dio, Rome, and the Civic Life," 74.

as an adopted citizen, claims that he accepts criticism from other citizens as a natural aspect of *polis* politics.[58] Dio writes, "For it is not the nature of democracies, nor is it reasonable, that they should not allow anyone in the city either to speak against a single person or to find fault with him, even when that person shows himself to be doing everything well, but such immunity from criticism is more likely to be accorded to tyrants than to benefactors."[59] Note that Dio presents himself as unworthy of criticism, even as he acknowledges that he is participating in a system that empowers citizens to judge those who come before them as advisers. Dio, like Euripides' *Phoenissae*, defines democracy according to the positive right of citizen voice and critique. Moreover, Dio elaborates this positive right of democratic citizenship through a contrast with tyranny as a system allowing no outlet for citizens to critique their leaders.

Dio' own self-defense in several of his speeches takes assembly critique of citizen leaders out of the hypothetical realm. While assemblies may no longer be the location for political trials as they were during part of the classical period in Athens,[60] they still provide the opportunity for citizens to express their opinions and to influence the way that leaders are serving their city. Dio fields such critique in speeches to his hometown assembly. This criticism includes accusations of tyranny, a watchword in the Greek world for someone usurping undue civic influence to the detriment of citizen equality. Speaking before the assembly of Prusa in *Or*. 43, Dio defends himself against a charge that he had consorted with an unjust Roman official, thereby supporting tyranny against his own city and compromising its democratic government.[61] Dio crafts a rhetorical defense requesting that he be given a full hearing in refuting these charges. In this defense, he compares himself to Socrates who was given a full hearing before he was sentenced.[62] Dio's invocation of Socrates as the ultimate "martyr" to

---

58. It is worth noting that Dio's tone seems much more accommodating in his speeches to a foreign city here than in a number of speeches to his own city of Prusa, where he often seems to be on the defensive. For examples of such defensiveness, see *Or*. 43; 46.

59. *Or*. 41.3 (Crosby, LCL). τὸ γὰρ μηδένα ἐν πόλει μήτε ἀντιλέγειν ἑνὶ μήτε μέμφεσθαι κἂν ἅπαντα φαίνηται ποιῶν καλῶς, οὐ δήμων ἐστὶν οὐδὲ ἐπιεικές, ἀλλὰ μᾶλλον φιλεῖ τὸ τοιοῦτον συμβαίνειν τοῖς τυράννοις ἢ τοῖς εὐεργέταις.

60. Hansen shows that the assembly in Athens had ceased to act as political court after 362 BCE. Hansen, *The Athenian Democracy*, 158–59.

61. *Or*. 43.11.

62. *Or*. 43.12. For questions concerning the extent to which Dio may be exaggerating his "bill of indictment in order to render the case against him ridiculous," see Jones, *The Roman World of Dio Chrysostom*, 102.

the democratic *polis* illustrates the perceived authority of the contemporary assembly. While it is a negative comparison highlighting the injustices possible under a democratic assembly, it is also a comparison that substantiates the strength of the assembly to judge citizen leaders. Dio also implicitly acknowledges the assembly's authority by requesting to mount a self-defense that will open him to its authoritative judgment. Dio makes another such request in a speech before the Prusan council where Dio says that making a defense before fair-minded fellow-citizens is reasonable, even if demeaning before a tyrant.[63] In these speeches, Dio upholds a political system in which the *dēmos*' right to examine the speaker is matched by the speaker's responsibility to submit to examination.

Yet another speech before the Prusan assembly shows that Dio was not only associated with Roman tyranny but also could be accused of being a tyrant in his own right. In *Or.* 50, Dio vigorously defends his efforts to promote the common good through public works against those that accuse him of using these works for self-aggrandizement and of pursuing his agenda to the point of tyranny.[64] Dio says to the assembled citizens, "For now, if I undertake this matter and hasten to get the work done, some say I am acting as a tyrant and demolishing the city and all its shrines."[65] While Dio presents himself as much maligned in these circumstances, his very act of rhetorical defense before the assembly attests to a certain accountability public servants owed the larger citizen body. At the same, this speech also foregrounds citizen vigilance in safeguarding their interests and in interrogating decisions affecting the public welfare. In itself, these charges of tyranny mark a defense of democratic participation, especially when voiced in the context of the civic assembly. As I have demonstrated in earlier passages, Dio himself repeatedly associates tyranny with suppression of citizen speech, including speech critiquing leadership.

Plutarch too portrays a powerful assembly wielding influence over individual politicians. In his *Political Advice*, Plutarch insists that an elite politician must live up to the intense scrutiny of the people. At the same time, such a leader should also make the effort to determine the character of the *dēmos* he intends to lead through his speeches. Plutarch argues that the politician will earn the people's trust only if he is shown to be a moral person with the interests of the *dēmos* in mind both in his public and private life.

---

63. 50.9.

64. 47.18, 23.

65. 47.18 (Crosby, LCL). νῦν γὰρ ἐὰν ἅπτωμαι τοῦ πράγματος καὶ σπουδάζω γίγνεσθαι τὸ ἔργον, τυραννεῖν μέ φασί τινες καὶ κατασκάπτειν τὴν πόλιν καὶ τὰ ἱερὰ πάντα.

In fact, all aspects of the statesman's life will eventually be revealed since the people monitor such figures in both their private and public activities, and "they love and admire one man and dislike and despise another not less for his private than for his public practices."[66]

As the politician is subject to the scrutiny of the *dēmos*, so Plutarch suggests that the very power of the assembly requires that the successful statesman must strive to understand it. Plutarch counsels the prospective politician to carefully scrutinize the character of the city's inhabitants upon deciding to enter public life. Like Dio, he also describes the *dēmos* as a composite of its members. Plutarch writes that the citizens' character "shows itself very much blended from the character of all and is powerful."[67] That this citizen's character relates not just to all inhabitants of the city but more specifically to the assembly, can be supported in part with the classical examples Plutarch provides following this statement. He asserts that one must know the people's character as a prerequisite for successfully speaking before them, and attests to the experience of figures like Cleon[68] and Epaminondas[69] in their civic assemblies. With these examples as background, Plutarch contends that only when the politician has recognized the specific expectations of the city he addresses, can he gradually begin to lead these people in a positive direction.[70]

Plutarch presents a delicate power balance between the speaker and the people composing the assembly audience. While the speaker must first acknowledge the strength of the people and learn its character, he does so in order to shift gradually the *dēmos* in the directions he desires.[71] The ultimate goal in this case is for the politician to be judged worthy by the people, who only then will give their trust. Plutarch suggests that this trust will be a tremendous and lasting asset to the statesman. Such trust allows someone to establish himself in public life in the first place, and once there, this trust protects the moral politician against the envious and wicked who might

---

66. Plut., *Praec, ger. rei publ.* 801 A (Fowler, LCL). . . . οὐχ ἧττον ἀπὸ τῶν ἰδίων ἢ τῶν δημοσίων ἐπιτηδευμάτων τὸν μὲν φιλοῦντες καὶ θαυμάζοντες τὸν δὲ δυσχεραίνοντες καὶ καταφρονοῦντες.

67. 799 B (Fowler; LCL). . . . ὃ μάλιστα συγκραθὲν ἐκ πάντων ἐπιφαίνεται καὶ ἰσχύει.

68. 799 D.

69. 799 F.

70. 799 C.

71. 800 A.

threaten their position.⁷² However, the goodwill of the people is capable of doing even more.

For Plutarch, the people's trust creates nothing less than the equality that allows citizens to be judged on their merits rather than on wealth or birth. Plutarch describes this trust as having potential, "in the matter of power raising the low-born to the level of the nobles, the poor to the rich, and the private citizen to the office-holders."⁷³ When combined with virtue (ἀρετῆς) of the leader, the faith of the people levels the playing field between those who are poor and the wealthy who benefit the city by providing public entertainments and exhibitions. Each can thus have equal opportunity for freedom of speech (παρρησία).⁷⁴ Ultimately, the power of the people acts as a safeguard for the freedom of the city. In this vein, Plutarch writes that Demosthenes was correct⁷⁵ when he suggested that the greatest protection for the state against tyrants was the distrust of the people.⁷⁶

## Debate: Chaos or Productive Practice?

The assembly scene in Dio's *Euboicus* manifests yet another parallel with classical literature. Dio's own elite voice expresses a critique of democracy and "the many" that closely resembles elite criticism of popular government in the fifth and fourth centuries BC. Dio's description of the crowd as noisy, disorderly, and frightening in its wrath conforms to negative elite portrayals of the *dēmos* that date back to the mid-fifth century with the anonymous author known as Pseudo- Xenophon, or the "Old Oligarch." In a rhetorical move adopted by later critics of democracy, Ps.-Xenophon's *Political Regime of the Athenians* portrays democracy as a system in which the morally and intellectually inferior majority rules over elites with greater wisdom and self-control but vastly smaller numbers. Indeed, Ps.-Xenophon indicates that the disorderly behavior of the *dēmos*, together with its ignorance and

---

72. 821 C.

73. Ibid. ἡ παρὰ τῶν πολλῶν εὔνοια . . . πρὸς τὰς δυνάμεις ἐπανισοῦσα τὸν ἀγεννῆ τοῖς εὐπατρίδαις καὶ τὸν πένητα τοῖς πλουσίοις καὶ τὸν ἰδιώτην τοῖς ἄρχουσι.

74. 822 F (Fowler, LCL). Οὕτως οὔτ᾽ ἀγεννές ἐστι πενίαν ὁμολογεῖν, οὔτε λείπονται πρὸς δύναμιν ἐν πόλεσι τῶν ἑστιώντων καὶ χορηγούντων οἱ πένητες, ἂν παρρησίαν ἀπ᾽ ἀρετῆς καὶ πίστιν ἔχωσι.

75. The passage that Plutarch quotes here from Demosthenes is striking as it upholds freedom and law over and against the threats Philip of Macedonia presents as a "tyrant." Dem. 6.24.

76. Plut., *Praec, ger. rei publ.* 821 B (Fowler, LCL). ᾗ καὶ Δημοσθένης ὀρθῶς μέγιστον ἀποφαίνεται πρὸς τοὺς τυράννους φυλακτήριον ἀπιστίαν ταῖς πόλεσι.

lack of culture, marks the many as "wicked."[77] As in Ps.-Xenophon's critique of the Athenian people, Dio's description of the assembly as chaotic, selfish, and easily manipulated questions the ability of this citizen body to carry out the rational decision-making necessary for good government.

Likewise, Dio's portrayal of leadership in the *Euboicus* assembly contributes to an oligarchic critique of democracy. In this scene, the reader encounters two models of leadership, the one embodied by the hunter's opponent and the other by his defender in the *ekklēsia*. Speaking without any factual basis, the first rhetor accuses the hunter of becoming wealthy at the expense of the *dēmos*, even as he contends the hunter poses a danger to the sailors he leads to ruin on the rocks near his house. This speaker seems intent on inflaming the crowd, and by the end of his speech, the hunter reports that the audience had become "very noisy"[78] and even "savage"[79] to the point that the hunter fears for his safety. The next speaker's demeanor and method of address poses a striking contrast to the first. He begins by calming the audience, and only when they are silent does he himself begin to speak in a quiet voice. He questions the first speaker's conclusions, asserting that those taming the public lands distant from the city do a favor to the *polis* even as they are saved from their own idleness and poverty. He establishes his own credibility, and coincidentally his own elite status, when he claims he would welcome people like the hunter to cultivate those parts of his own extensive estates now lying fallow. Dio's portrayal of a fickle and sometimes savage crowd easily moved by the first demagogic speaker betrays what Ma calls, "standard oligarchic positions."[80] Like Isocrates' fourth-century *Antidosis*, Dio here indicts the *dēmos* for being easily led astray by sycophants, especially when such flatterers attack the wealthy. Meanwhile, Dio, like Isocrates, offers a superior alternative to the demagogic flatterer in an elite leader graced with "practical wisdom"[81] and "eloquence"[82]—a leader that bends the people to his will rather than the opposite.

---

77. Indeed this author explains that "among the people there is a maximum of ignorance, disorder, and wickedness" (ἐν δὲ τῷ δήμῳ ἀμαθία τε πλείστη καὶ ἀταξία καὶ πονηρία). [*Ath.*] I.5 (Bowersock, LCL). Ober, *Political Dissent*, 17

78. *Or.* 7.30. τὸ δὲ πλῆθος . . . ἐθορύβουν.

79. Ibid. 7.33. ὁ μὲν ὄχλος ἠγριοῦτο; my translation.

80. Ma, "Public Speech and Community," 116.

81. Isocrates speaks of Athens accomplishing greatness through the wisdom of one man (διὰ δὲ φρόνησιν ἀνδρὸς). Ober supports this reading of a difficult text. This may be a reference to Pericles. Ober, *Political Dissent*, 266.

82. In an exposition on ideal leaders of the past, Isocrates suggests that both Solon and Pericles were themselves educated in rhetorical practice and theory. Isoc. *Antid* 235. Ober, *Political Dissent*, 266.

In his work on political dissent within democratic Athens, Josiah Ober contends that democracy "had exposed the possibility of a human condition (freedom for the many) so profoundly desirable that it threatened to overwhelm all competing values."[83] In this environment, elite critics of democracy faced a difficult task, especially since notions of equality and freedom tied to the exercise of citizenship became such a central aspect of Athenian male identity.[84] Even as they sought to undermine or question aspects of democratic discourse, classical critics were themselves constrained and shaped by the same discourse which dominated public rhetoric and political practice.[85] Dio and Plutarch fit this model of elite interrogators of democracy who critique an ideology with which they are intimately familiar, an ideology whose very prevalence shapes their worldview and the kind of critique they are able to level.[86] Their critique and negotiation of democratic ideology comes into focus precisely with texts, like the *Euboicus*, that consider debate and contest within an *ekklēsia* context. As classical texts show, *ekklēsia* debate provided particularly fertile ground for critiques and defense of democracy alike since this debate manifested both the *dēmos*' power and the location for elite leadership. While Dio and Plutarch use this debate to carry out their own construction of leadership and the role of the *dēmos*, their first-century context means that *ekklēsia* debate also becomes a site of negotiation regarding Rome and the freedom possible in the Greek *polis*. In what follows, I will briefly consider their commentary on debate, leadership, and Rome's place in their political horizon.

Plutarch and Dio both recognize, and even assume, that contest and debate will characterize the political life of elites who lead in the *ekklēsia*. Nevertheless, each in his own way tries to limit such debate, which they

---

83. Ober, *Political Dissent*, 29. Ober argues that in these terms, debate over democracy was "occasioned by the success not the failure of democracy."

84. Ibid., 31.

85. Ober acknowledges with the earlier work of A.H.M. Jones (*The Athenian Democracy*, 41–72) the issues facing the historian sympathetic to classical democracy. The lack of sustained, formal defenses of democracy from that period is matched by a relative wealth of carefully reasoned critiques to democracy. Ober's own work has drawn on public rhetoric to reconstruct the ideology and practice of Athenian democracy. (Especially, see Ober, *Mass and Elite*.) However, Ober argues that the critics of democracy are also extremely informative for understanding classical, democratic discourse. He contends that these critics must be read as "interventions in an ongoing debate about politics . . . The elite authors of critical political texts were, therefore, responding not only to one another but also to the tenets of democratic popular ideology as expressed in public speech." Ober, *Political Dissent*, 33.

86. Ma draws this conclusion with regard to the political writings of both Dio and Plutarch. Ma, "Public Speech and Community," 123.

suggest can be a dangerous practice for elites and for the continuing freedom of individual cities. In his advice to both young and old men who are considering involvement in public affairs,[87] Plutarch describes participation in the public sphere, notably the assembly, in terms of contest or competition. In his *Old Men in Political Affairs*, he calls on elder statesmen to compare themselves to the older men from classical history like Sophocles who could claim impressive accomplishments in their advanced years. If older men of his time period eschew politics, Plutarch says they will compare especially badly with the accomplishments of past leaders, since his own era features cities free from war, siege, and tyranny.[88] In light of this, he urges that these elder statesmen not avoid "unwarlike struggles and rivalries most of which are concluded with justice by law and speech."[89] Later, comparing classical poets, playwrights, and elder statesmen—"old men of the speaking platform" (γερόντων τοὺς ἀπὸ τοῦ βήματος)[90]—Plutarch implies a parallel between drama and poetry contests and the contest of politics. He suggests there will be great dishonor to the politicians if they are found less noble than the playwrights because they avoid the truly sacred contests (τῶν ἱερῶν ὡς ἀληθῶς ἐξισταμένους ἀγώνων)[91] of politics.

If Plutarch tells older statesmen that they should be ashamed of themselves for avoiding a contest that is tame in comparison to that of the classical past, he also advises a younger man that the current contest of politics requires a specific type of strength. His *Political Advice* to Menemachus depicts politics as a contest "not trivial, but all consuming."[92] Again, Plutarch

---

87. Plutarch addresses his *Political Advice* to Menemachus, who seems to be a wealthy man from Sardis. *Praec, ger. rei publ.* 798 A–B. For more, see Stein, "Menemachos," 837–38. His *Old Men in Political Affairs* is dedicated to an Athenian named Euphranes. *An seni* 783 B. For more, see Ziegler, "Plutarckos von Chaironeia," 674. Jones discusses both of these figures briefly: Jones, *Plutarch and Rome*, 110–11.

88. *An seni* 784 F—785 A. This description of his own time may be a statement of the benefits inherent in Roman rule, though Plutarch does not actually mention Rome by name. Swain suggests that Rome may well be implied in this passage. Swain, *Hellenism and Empire*, 180.

89. *An seni* 785 A (Fowler, LCL). ἡμεῖς δ' οἱ νῦν τρυφῶντες ἐν πολιτείαις, μὴ τυραννίδα μὴ πόλεμόν τινα μὴ πολιορκίαν ἐχούσαις, ἀπολέμους δ'ἁμίλλας καὶ φιλοτιμίας νόμῳ τὰ πολλὰ καὶ λόγῳ μετὰ δίκης περαινομένας ἀποδειλιῶμεν;

90. 785 A–C. Sophocles and Simonides are among the examples of classical artists that Plutarch mentions here.

91. Plutarch refers to politics in these same terms as a sacred contest also in *Praec, ger. rei publ.* 820 D.

92. *Praec, ger. rei publ.* 804 C (Fowler, LCL). Δεῖ δὲ καὶ φωνῆς εὐεξία καὶ πνεύματος ῥώμη πρὸς οὐ φαῦλον ἀλλὰ πάμμαχον ἀγῶνα τὸν τῆς πολιτείας ἠθληκότα κομίζειν τὸν λόγον, ὡς μὴ πολλάκις ἀπαγορεύοντα καὶ σβεννύμενον ὑπερβάλλοι τις αὐτὸν . . .

makes clear that politics in the Greek city revolve around speech as it is the key determinant for who will prevail and who will be defeated in the political contest. He counsels the reader that to succeed at this political contest one must train one's ability to speak so that one's strength of breath and voice will be enough to overcome opponents.[93]

Plutarch portrays an assembly audience that expects, and even requires, that struggle and contest be played out publicly in the midst of the assembly. However, the elite leader, Plutarch's ideal, uses manipulation to reach harmonious agreement over the most important city matters. According to Plutarch, all democracies have a critical orientation regarding politicians that leads the people to suspect that there is a conspiracy if measures pass that have no "dissent or resistance" (ἂν μὴ στάσιν ἔχῃ μηδ᾽ ἀντιλογίαν).[94] Plutarch advises elite politicians to avoid "this problem" by engaging in a theatrical exercise meant to deceive their audience. Politicians should agree on important measures for the city, yet be prepared to offer the semblance of disagreement to reassure the assembly. Several friends should collude to disagree and then pretend to have been convinced to the policy previously agreed upon, thus making the people think that they were only "led by the public advantage" (ὑπὸ τοῦ συμφέροντος ἄγεσθαι δόξαντες).[95] What room there is for disagreement must be found in small, relatively unimportant matters over which political friends can indulge in furious argumentation without serious consequences.[96] The display of such real disagreement over the trivial will in turn make their accord in important matters less suspect.

By advising elite speakers to feign debate, Plutarch offers one solution to the classical critique of democracy that some civic matters were too important to be left to the many who did not possess the wisdom, foresight or self-control to make the best decisions for the *polis*.[97] However, this very strategy reveals first-century, democratic citizens who view debate as a prerequisite for making those decisions determining the "public good." This view implies the close involvement of citizens as judges who make decisions through carefully weighing different options presented to them.[98] This pas-

93. Ibid.
94. 813 A.
95. 813 B.
96. 813 C.
97. In the person of Cleon, Thucydides records one such critique. Thuc. 3.37–38.
98. Thuc. 3.37–48. In a passage representing one of the few sustained discussions over participatory democracy in classical literature, Thucydides offers one debate from the Athenian assembly that helps to flesh out this dynamic. In this debate, one speaker, Cleon, argues that the contests among speakers to determine policy actually has the potential to harm the city and that further debate should be discontinued after

sage further suggests that such citizens understand debate as a guard against elite conspiracy, thus contributing to a balance in power between the *dēmos* and elites.

Active negotiation between elites and citizen audience colors Plutarch's discussion of *ekklēsia* politics. Even as "the many" (οἱ πολλοί)[99] vigilantly assess various measures and speakers, the elites in this scenario are able to pass the motions that they find beneficial only by adopting the dynamics, and one suspects also the rhetoric, required by the citizen body. The elite politicians Plutarch counsels therefore are constrained by the *dēmos* to a certain extent, even as they seek to manipulate the assembly to their own ends within the accepted framework of persuasion and judgment.[100]

Dio's civic speeches complement Plutarch's political writing by demonstrating that intense assembly discussion was neither confined to Greece in the first century nor performed only as an elite fiction. In one speech geared toward achieving at least outward harmony for a Roman official visiting Prusa, he attempts to constrain dynamic argumentation in the assembly. Dio's forty-eighth oration is a speech given to the assembly in his native Prusa which, as previously mentioned, had only recently regained the right to assemble from the Roman authorities.[101] Dio addresses the *ekklēsia* in a way that suggests there were tensions between the people and elected officials of the city, perhaps over matters of money.[102] Whatever the cause for tension, Dio pleads that the assembly temporarily set aside the matters over which they have been "shouting" (περὶ μὲν τῶν ἄλλων ὧν ἐβοᾶτε ὑπερθέσθαι).[103] He argues that there is no advantage for involving outsiders in the citizens' internal struggles,[104] especially the Roman official Varenus who has the power

---

a decision has first been made. His opponent Diodotus argues in contrast that repeated deliberations are the only way of correcting mistakes and the only way that Athenians can best anticipate future events.

99. *Praec. ger. rei publ.* 813 B.

100. Ober offers an explanation of this democratic interaction between speaker and the power of the collective audience that takes place through "the medium of speech" in a number of works. For one example, see Ober, "Power and Oratory in Democratic Athens."

101. The reason for the suspension of the assembly is not completely clear here, though Swain hypothesizes that it has to do with tension between masses and elite. Whatever the cause, this speech does give some idea of the real vulnerability of assemblies to Roman power. Swain, *Hellenism and Empire*, 234–35.

102. Dio, *Or.* 48.3,9.

103. 48.2.

104. 48.10.

both to authorize and to suspend meetings of the Prusan assembly.[105] For Varenus' visit, Dio urges the assembly to exercise self-control and to demonstrate a semblance of unity. Once the visit is completed, if the citizens still cannot be persuaded to unite, it will be acceptable for them to speak out and even to shout as their fellow citizens act as judges and arbitrators.[106]

This speech shows certain significant similarities with Plutarch's discussion above. In both cases, there is a move by elites to limit intense argumentation in the assembly. However, both writers depict a *dēmos* anxious to embrace argumentative debate, debate interpreted by some as a sign of healthy democracy. "The many" in Plutarch's assembly look for intense debate, even as Dio's Prusan compatriots try to continue heated exchanges during civic proceedings. Both authors present this behavior as disorderly and even dangerous. However, in both cases, Dio and Plutarch intimate their awareness of counter-arguments that such interaction is part of a constructive process. While Plutarch acknowledges some in the assembly envision disagreement insuring responsible decision-making, Dio's Prusans understand themselves to be resolving the city's problems using the political tools of speech and audience deliberation. In these terms, Plutarch and Dio represent tension familiar from classical texts between the perspective that decision-making through assembly debate produced the wisest course for the *polis*, and the contradictory, elite position that such debate should be limited, or controlled by elites with greater wisdom and self-control. However, Dio's forty-eighth oration also brings to the topic of *ekklēsia* debate another theme in the work of both authors which is located very much in their own place and time—the consideration of Rome in civic politics.

Dio and Plutarch prioritize involvement in *polis* politics over interaction with the empire. Yet the empire looms large in their political writings. Indeed, these authors' commentary on the *ekklēsia* must be contextualized by their relationship with Rome as provincial elites. The very complexity of their status as Greek elites with many loyalties helps to illustrate the difficulties involved in establishing and describing continued *ekklēsia* discourse in the first century. For Dio and Plutarch, the *ekklēsia* exists as a node of tension around which they negotiate a degree of self-government for Greek cities under the empire. Upholding this institution appears essential to their larger goal of fostering independence, even as they portray the debate characterizing the democratic assembly as a significant threat to this project.

---

105. 48.1; 3.

106. 48.3. Καὶ δικασταῖς καὶ διαιτηταῖς ἀλλήλοις χρησάμενοι, τότε ἐξέσται καὶ λέγειν καὶ καταβοᾶν.

As *polis* citizens,[107] both Dio and Plutarch express the desire that their cities retain as much independence and self-rule as possible under the Roman Empire. Their writings depict the empire's threat to local independence as a kind of background noise, a persistent accompaniment to any discussion on civic politics. While Dio and Plutarch occasionally point out the advantages to Roman rule,[108] they also project a sense of the Empire as a menacing aggressor waiting to be unleashed. For both, the primary trigger for this Roman threat seems to be the actions of the people, both the masses and the elites, as they carry out tumultuous assembly debate. Dio and Plutarch seek to convince their audiences that harmony represents the best way to secure peace and relative freedom under the Romans.

Dio and Plutarch both describe Roman rule as a type of slavery that can be only partially avoided through achieving civic harmony.[109] For his part, Dio advises citizens of municipalities like Tarsus or Prusa to avoid completely bowing to Roman demands. However, he also counsels these same citizens against becoming overly visible in the eyes of the empire, thus risking entirely the important freedom of speech ($\pi\alpha\rho\rho\eta\sigma\iota\alpha$).[110] In these terms, Roman authority endangers the very freedoms most associated with the democratic *ekklēsia*. With such advice, Dio offers his audience a seemingly easy choice: save democratic freedoms by achieving harmony, or lose them through discord. However, those citizens that both Dio and Plutarch describe as dedicated to the democratic practice of the *ekklēsia* may well have viewed this as a false choice. Debate, and indeed dissention, remained

107. Mitchell suggests that in Greek cities of the Roman Empire, "[w]ith rare exceptions, the whole free adult male population was entitled to attend assemblies" and therefore might be considered citizens. In this, Greek cities of the first century CE resembled classical Athens. Mitchell argues that there was not a wealth requirement for natives of a city to claim citizenship, but such a requirement might be in place for outsiders hoping to gain citizenship. Dio provides one example: *Or.* 34.23. Mitchell, *Anatolia*, 1:203.

108. Swain suggests that those passages where Plutarch mentions the peace of his own time may well be a testimonial for benefits of Roman rule. See *Pyth. orac.* 408 B-C; *An seni* 784 F. Swain, *Hellenism and Empire*, 180. Dio himself may imply a support of Rome when he remarks on the benefits of kingship. *Or.* 3.46ff.

109. Swain notes that Dio's only mention of the relative peace that prevailed under the Romans speaks of it as a commodity that has been traded for freedom, resulting in slavery for many. Swain notes that this is particularly significant since this freedom is seen by "moderns" as the main benefit of Roman rule for the Greeks. *Hellenism and Empire*, 209. *Or.* 31.125.

110. *Or.* 34.38–39. Jones argues that complaints in this case mean successful prosecutions of certain Roman governors, leading to unpopularity at Rome. Jones, *The Roman World of Dio Chrysostom*, 76ff.

an elemental (though never uncontroversial) part of the democratic freedom practiced in the Greek *polis*.

Plutarch shares Dio's anxiety over Roman interference as well as his strategy of compromising democratic dynamics to maintain an acceptable level of freedom. Like Dio, Plutarch describes Roman rule as a type of slavery that can be mitigated but never entirely escaped. Plutarch also speaks of a delicate balance that the statesmen in Greek cities should achieve between urging obedience to Rome and preserving a certain level of freedom and self-government in civic affairs. Plutarch writes, "When the leg has been bound, it is necessary not to submit the neck, as some do who, by referring everything, great or small, to the leaders, bring the reproach of slavery upon their country, or rather wholly destroy its government, making it terror stricken, timid, and powerless in everything."[111] Avoiding this greater slavery means maintaining the authority of the most essential civic institutions of council, assembly, and courts.[112] To save these institutions, the statesman must foster harmony between citizens in several ways.

Plutarch urges politicians to avoid speeches inciting the wider population to any kind of unrest or rebellion. In particular, Plutarch advises that politicians steer clear of classical topics like the battles of Marathon, Eurymedon or Plataea that foster pride and false confidence among first-century audiences.[113] At the same time, these politicians must avert dissension among elites that could also endanger a city's freedom.[114] To answer all these concerns, Plutarch advises, "The statesman should soothe the ordinary citizens by granting them equality and the powerful by concessions in return, thus keeping them within the bounds of the local government and solving their difficulties as if they were diseases, making for them, as it were, a sort of secret political medicine."[115] Here, keeping tension within the bounds of the city involves turning disagreement into a matter of secrecy or sickness to

---

111. *Praec, ger. rei publ.* 814 F (Fowler, LCL). . . . μηδὲ τοῦ σκέλους δεδεμένου προσυποβάλλειν καὶ τὸν τράχηλον, ὥσπερ ἔνιοι, καὶ μικρὰ καὶ μείζω φέροντες ἐπὶ τοὺς ἡγεμόνας ἐξονειδίζουσι τὴν δουλείαν, μᾶλλον δ' ὅλως τὴν πολιτείαν ἀναιροῦσι, κατάπληγα καὶ περιδεᾶ καὶ πάντων ἄκυρον ποιοῦντες.

112. 815 A. Here the in-fighting between elites leads to calling in the Romans, thus destroying the authority of these institutions. ἐκ τούτου δὲ καὶ βουλὴ καὶ δῆμος καὶ δικαστήρια καὶ ἀρχὴ πᾶσα τὴν ἐξουσίαν ἀπόλλυσι.

113. 814 A.

114. Ibid.

115. Ibid. Δεῖ δὲ τοὺς μὲν ἰδιώτας ἰσότητι, τοὺς δὲ δυνατοὺς ἀνθυπείξει πραΰνοντα κατέχειν ἐν τῇ πολιτείᾳ καὶ διαλύειν τὰ πράγματα, πολιτικήν τινα ποιούμενον αὐτῶν ὥσπερ νοσημάτων ἀπόρρητον ἰατρείαν.

be quarantined. However, it also means fostering the political equality that characterized the classical democratic city.

The very apprehension these authors share over dissension in the *ekklēsia* exposes the continued association of assemblies with the kind of debate that they want to quell in favor of harmony. Indeed, Dio and Plutarch both convey to their readers their own participation in the competition, dissent and the tumult of the assembly in their time. Dio's and Plutarch's call for harmony and unity must not be taken as evidence that such harmony was the norm, or even the desired state, for the majority of citizens that they address. Instead, their unease with debate combined with hints they provide that many citizens preferred to retain contest and argument in the assembly setting may substantiate Salmeri's contention that provincial elites had much more to lose by Roman intervention than the general population.[116] While vociferous assembly debate could pose a serious threat to the position of a Dio or a Plutarch, those at a lower social strata might experience few consequences affecting livelihood or social position and, at the same time, receive benefits associated with self-determination. Such self-interest may help to contextualize Dio's and Plutarch's ambivalence toward the *ekklēsia*. This ambivalence reflects both the provincial experience under the empire as well as the traditional tension between elites and the larger population of the democratic city.

Their Roman context may have shaped Dio and Plutarch's interests and, to an extent, their rhetoric concerning civic government. Nevertheless, any explanation of these authors' engagement with the political practice of the civic sphere must place the empire's influence in conversation and struggle with ideals originating with classical democracy. Dio and Plutarch's mobilization of democratic, *ekklēsia* discourse witnesses negotiation and contestation over civic concerns, including leadership, that signals an authoritative *polis* assembly in the first century CE.

## Conclusion

This chapter began with a visit to the vibrant, raucous assembly that Dio imagines in the *Euboicus*. Together, the writings of Dio and Plutarch attest that the lively, democratic *ekklēsia* of the *Euboicus* was not merely an artifact of the classical past that Dio evokes for a later audience. Instead, these authors engage the *ekklēsia* as a key civic institution in the political discourse and practice of the first century. Plutarch and Dio describe the assembly both in Greece and Asia Minor as a powerful corporate actor determining

---

116. Salmeri, "Dio, Rome, and the Civic Life," 74–5.

its leadership and public policy. The assembly's survival as an institution may be partly explained by the importance of the Greek city itself as an administrative unit within the wider empire, expected to govern itself in most respects.[117] However, the first-century assembly perhaps owes a greater debt for its survival to a Greek heritage of democracy that included an emphasis on political citizen equality and persuasive assembly speech. Democratic discourse itself remained a key element of the Greek identity that characterized the eastern Roman Empire, an identity always in a complex relationship with the empire.

As in the classical period, Dio and Plutarch's *ekklēsia* remains an arena for the negotiation of various socio-political tensions. Josiah Ober has pointed out that the classical *ekklēsia* was a powerful location for the mediation of the elite and the masses in Athens.[118] The assembly of this later era remained one place where such tensions were played out and negotiated. As I have demonstrated, Plutarch and Dio discuss the relationship of poor to wealthy and high born to low in the context of the assembly. These authors both show that the assembly could provide the context for influencing the elite to contribute resources of wealth and public service to the *polis*, even as it remained a place where political equality was constantly renegotiated on the part of the city's lower social strata. Dio and Plutarch also witness the ongoing debate over democracy itself fostered by the *ekklēsia*. This debate included the nature of citizenship, leadership, and the limits of freedom on the part of both speakers and audiences. Finally, the *ekklēsia* was also a location in, and about which, the relationship between Greek cities and the Roman Empire might be explored. Because the *ekklēsia* retained close associations with concepts of Greek freedom and identity, the assembly provided a natural location to examine, and strain against, the limits of freedom and expression under Roman rule.

---

117. Mitchell, *Anatolia*, 1:210.
118. Ober, *Mass and Elite*.

# 3

# Moses in the *Ekklēsia*:
## *Josephus' Use of Democratic Discourse*

## Introduction

IN JOSEPHUS' ANTIQUITIES, MOSES, THE GREAT ORATOR, BRAVELY ADDRESSes an angry *ekklēsia* as it levels accusations of tyranny against him. His political acumen lies in his ability to speak frankly, yet persuasively, to the democratic assembly as he copes with the challenge of unrest and division. This unrest, this *stasis*, has been fomented by Korah, an opponent accusing Moses of using his influence and wealth to bypass the authority of the πλῆθος in making an important appointment. With masterful rhetoric, Moses' *ekklēsia* defense demonstrates that it is he, and not Korah, who truly champions political equality and freedom within the Israelite "*dēmos*."[1]

Except for the names, we might mistake this for a political scenario from the classical literature of democratic Athens. However, the first-century Jewish author Josephus here uses the civic *ekklēsia*, and its attendant democratic discourse, as the context for his re-writing in the *Antiquities* of Korah's dramatic rebellion from Numbers 16. Within the *Antiquities*' "translation project,"[2] the Korah episode is critical to establishing Moses

---

1. This presentation of Moses' leadership abilities, as well as the account of unrest instigated by Korah and Zambrias, are all found in book 4 of the *Antiquities*.

2. For a presentation of a range of views on the meaning Josephus ascribes to "translation" in the *Antiquities* (*Ant.* 1.5 as one instance), and its relation to his overall project, see Sterling, *Historiography and Self-Definition*, 252ff; Feldman, *Josephus's Interpretation of the Bible*, 44ff. Feldman contends that Josephus' understanding of translation in this instance included the meaning of interpreting the Scriptures, a practice that seems to include "paraphrasing or amplifying" (44). For his part, Sterling argues that he uses this term as a way of asserting the accuracy of his project as "*the* history of

as an ideal leader, and arguably, Josephus' greatest biblical hero. I will demonstrate that Flavius Josephus liberally employs the political language and dynamics of the Greek *ekklēsia* to develop Moses' excellence in leadership according to the ideals of ancient democratic discourse. In this representation, Moses is distinguished not only by his rhetorical abilities and strength of character but also by his commitment to the foundational democratic principles of individual political equality paired with respect for the authority of the πλῆθος.

Josephus' deployment of democratic discourse in his portrait of Moses[3] registers the pervasiveness and value of this discourse for Josephus' Greco-Roman audience. In these terms, his strategic use of democratic *ekklēsia* discourse also reveals democracy as part of the legacy—the negotiation—of Hellenism for first-century Jews. Josephus' own negotiation between this Greek discourse and the biblical narrative in the Korah episode not only throws into high relief his use of vocabulary and dynamics from the democratic *ekklēsia* but also engenders a creative tension that alters the landscape of both the Bible and the political assembly. As a product of this tension, Josephus revisions the Israelites as an *ekklēsia* whose interaction with the statesman and lawgiver Moses shows the freedom they have gained in the Exodus is a democratic freedom based in political equality for each "citizen." In the following chapters, I will show that Josephus' construction of Moses' leadership according to democratic discourse has resonance with the rhetorical construction of leadership in 1 Corinthians, a letter written by another first-century Jew. Likewise, I suggest that this construction of Israel as a democratic *ekklēsia*, a departure from the Septuagint usage for this term, provides an important parallel for the Corinthians' understanding of their identity as *ekklēsia*.

## Josephus' Use of the Title *"Ekklēsia"*

In the Korah episode examined in this chapter, Moses confronts several vibrant, noisy gatherings of the Israelites in the *ekklēsia*. Josephus' description of these gatherings—and his depiction of the period building up to the first assembly—feature the *topoi* and logic of democratic discourse. Within this re-writing of a key biblical story, Josephus' employment of the term

---

the Jews for Greeks." Sterling further asserts that this accuracy means that the *Antiquities* becomes a definitive translation of scripture that puts it on "equal footing with the LXX and actually displacing it" (*Historiography and Self-Definition*, 255).

3. Feldman calls this portrait a "veritable aretalogy." *Josephus's Interpretation of the Bible*, 377.

*ekklēsia* for a democratic assembly confounds any firm division between a "biblical" use of this word and its usage in a Greek political context. In this way, Josephus' deployment of the word *ekklēsia* problematizes scholarship which has insisted on this firm division in first-century parlance, a division in which the "religious" meaning of the term in the Septuagint contrasts with the secular, political use of the term in reference to the civic assembly. Both Josephus' departures and his convergences with the Septuagint use of this term witness a range of meaning for *ekklēsia* in the work of this first-century Jewish author, including the powerful resonance of the term with democratic, political practice.

The contribution that Josephus makes to understanding first-century use of the word *ekklēsia* must be contextualized by scholarship on the Septuagint deployment of the term. Scholarship addressing the Septuagint's use of this term has sought to distinguish its deployment from that of another term, "*synagōgē*." In the Septuagint, the words *ekklēsia* and *synagōgē* both often translate the same Hebrew word *qahal*, a term used in the Hebrew Bible for a wide range of gatherings.[4] Some scholars have assigned special meaning to *ekklēsia* as a word choice Septuagint translators made to emphasize the role of the Israelites as the people of God. These scholars starkly contrast the employment of the word *synagōgē* with this use of *ekklēsia* in the Septuagint. In their arguments, the term *synagōgē* functions as a more general word for meeting or assembly, while *ekklēsia* is invested with powerful specificity in its relation to the gathering of the chosen people, most notably in the giving of the law in Deuteronomy 23:1–8.[5] This line of reasoning would grant *ekklēsia* a more "religious" meaning in contrast to *synagōgē*.[6] In turn, this reasoning relates closely to the contention that the Septuagint determined the use of *ekklēsia* by the early Christians as a community title.[7]

Arguments against this perspective emphasize that it is by no means clear that translators of the Septuagint assigned special religious meaning to

4. Schmidt, "*Ekklēsia*." Also see Campbell, "The Origin and Meaning of the Christian Use of the Word *Ekklēsia*"; Schrage, "'*Ekklēsia*' und 'Synagoge.'"

5. Schrage provides a thorough overview of scholarship making this type of a claim. Schrage, "'*Ekklēsia*' und 'Synagoge,'" 180–81. For several examples, see Rost, *Die Vorstufen von Kirche und Synagoge im Alten Testament*; Holl, *Der Kirchenbegriff des Paulus in seinem Verhälnis zu dem der Urgemeinde*, 45.

6. McCready, "*Ekklēsia* and Voluntary Association," 61–62. While McCready suggests that "*ekklēsia*" in the Septuagint translates the word *qahal* when it designates a wide variety of meetings, including meetings to bear arms, he still suggests that the Hebrew *qahal*, and the Greek title *ekklēsia* as it is later used by Christian communities share a similar meaning: "It refers to people who have an ambition to form a new religious and social entity" (61).

7. Schmidt, "*Ekklēsia*," 514.

*ekklēsia* over and against *synagōgē* or associated this word more closely with the Israelites as the chosen people.[8] Both *synagōgē* and *ekklēsia* are associated with what might be termed religious gatherings, including the gathering of the Israelites to receive the law at Sinai. Schrage shows that both these words were used in translating passages touching on the law,[9] and both are also designated "of the Lord."[10] However, these two words also translate the word *qahal* when it is used for many different types of gatherings, including the "gathering of evildoers" in Psalm 26:5 (translated ἐκκλησία πονηρευομένων) and in Ezekiel 27:27 the population of Tyre (translated συναγωγή).[11] In fact, the main difference between the two appears to be that *synagōgē* is used to translate both *qahal* as well as another Hebrew term for gathering, *edah*, while *ekklēsia* translates only *qahal*.

Josephus parts ways with the Septuagint usage of both these terms in several ways that are significant for the wider topic of *ekklēsia* discourse.[12] The first obvious difference between the usage of the words *ekklēsia* and *synagōgē* in the Septuagint[13] and in Josephus is that *synagōgē* appears only rarely in Josephus. While the Septuagint applies the term *synagōgē* to a wide range of gatherings, Josephus employs the term less often and in a much more limited way. *Synagōgē* is used in the *Antiquities of the Jews* to refer to collections of books (*Ant.* 1.10), and of water, and food (15.346). This term

8. Writing of *ekklēsia* in the Septuagint, Georgi explains, "This word does not appear as a technical term in the Greek of the Jewish Bible or of the Jewish community; nor is it typically religious." Georgi, "The Interest in Life of Jesus Theology," 57. Campbell and Schrage both make extended arguments to support this point and to show the interchangeability of synagogue and *ekklēsia* in the Septuagint.

9. *Ekklēsia* thus appears in passages like Deut 4:10 and 9:10 associated with the law. However, synagogue is also used in key passages concerning the giving of the law such as 5:22. Schrage, "'Ekklēsia' und 'Synagoge,'" 182.

10. For example ἐκκλησία κυρίου appears in Deut 23:2, but συναγωγὴ κυρίου is used to translate *qahal* in Num 16:3 and *edah* in Num 27:17. Ibid., 183.

11. The Septuagint edition used is *Septuaginta* (ed. Alfred Rahlfs; Stuttgart: Deutsche Bibelgesellschaft, 1979).

12. This chapter will not address in detail the difficult question of Josephus' sources for the *Antiquities*. For an analysis of the state of the question as to Josephus' use of Septuagint, Hebrew text, or paraphrases of the Bible, see Feldman, *Josephus's Interpretation of the Bible*, 30–36. Concerning sources for the Pentateuch, Feldman suggests here, "There is, however, a greater degree of agreement between the Hebrew and Greek texts of the Pentateuch than with other books of the Bible, and Josephus himself is freer in his paraphrase of the Pentateuch than he is with the later books of the Bible, making it difficult to be sure whether he is using a Hebrew or a Greek text at any given point" (30).

13. The Septuagint utilizes *ekklēsia* approximately seventy times, against over 200 uses of *synagōgē*. Ibid., 179–180.

also appears both in the *Antiquities* and in the *Jewish War*, seemingly in reference to actual buildings where Jews gathered for religious purposes in Antioch (*War* 7.44), the Phoenician city Dora (*Ant.* 19.300–305), and the Hellenized city of Caesarea Maritima (*War* 2.285; 2.289).

In contrast to the term *synagōgē*, Josephus draws on the word *ekklēsia* far more frequently. Josephus primarily applies *ekklēsia* to large meetings of people in various times and places. In a number of passages, Josephus draws on *ekklēsia* in the traditional political sense when he depicts assemblies in Greek cities. Notably, he describes decrees passed by assemblies like those in Athens[14] and Pergamon,[15] as well as civic assemblies that had implications for the Jewish people in Antioch[16] and Alexandria.[17] Outside of these examples of the civic assembly in Greek cities, Josephus also utilizes *ekklēsia* when describing assemblies that met in Palestine during the second temple period up to, and including, the Jewish War against Rome.[18] Moreover, he also applies this word to a number of gatherings in his reinterpretation of the Bible in the *Antiquities*.[19] As in the Korah episode, these last two usages of *ekklēsia* in Josephus often include not only vocabulary but also dynamics that place these passages in close conversation with *ekklēsia* discourse in its Greek political context. While Josephus' use of *ekklēsia* retains some of the Septuagint's range in naming a variety of gatherings with this title, Josephus also demonstrates the possibility of exploiting the Greek, democratic valences of the word to describe Jewish political practice in his own time and in his re-visioning of biblical scenes. In the analysis that follows, I address one episode from the *Antiquities* that vividly realizes this potential.

---

14. *Ant.* 14.150.
15. Ibid., 14.252.
16. *War* 7.47.
17. Ibid., 2.490.

18. Two interesting examples for this study include the speech given by Ananus to the *ekklēsia* convened during the Jewish War (ibid., 4.162ff), and also the use of the *ekklēsia* in the speech of Jesus, another priest (ibid., 4.255). In both these examples, Josephus utilizes Greek political language associated with the *ekklēsia* to reinforce these priests as positive figures in the narrative.

19 In several cases, including *Ant.* 6.222 (1 Sam 19.19) and 9.250 (2 Chron 28.14), Josephus uses the word *ekklēsia* when interpreting biblical passages where the Septuagint also uses this term. However, much more often, Josephus uses the word *ekklēsia* regarding passages where the Septuagint has chosen synagogue.

## Stasis, Politics, and *Ekklēsia* in Josephus

From the beginning of his re-telling, the alterations that Josephus makes to the Korah episode from Numbers 16 highlight his engagement with Greek political discourse. As it stands in Numbers, this story provides a justification for the preeminence of the Aaronide priesthood over and against the Levites, despite Aaron and Moses' shared bloodlines with some Levites.[20] By contrast, Josephus' expansion of this story frames it as an occasion of strife, of *stasis*, which has no parallel among "either Greeks or barbarians."[21] In this rendition, Moses' ability to confront and resolve this *stasis* showcases his leadership skills. Indeed, much of this episode can be read as a meditation on correct leadership. In this definition of leadership, and in his appeal to the *topos* of *stasis*, Josephus exploits Greek democratic discourse in his portrayal of Moses as an ideal leader and statesman.

While Josephus represents the unrest created by Korah as particularly grave, *stasis* itself is not an unusual topic in his writings. Instead, *stasis* represents a common motif of both the *Antiquities* and the *Jewish War*.[22] Scholars like Louis Feldman and Tessa Rajak identify the theme of *stasis* as part of Josephus' wider concern with politics,[23] a concern that displays what Rajak terms Josephus' "Jewish-Greek political thought."[24] These scholars recognize Josephus' focus on *stasis* in particular, and politics in general, as an appeal to an audience steeped in these subjects within Greek literature.[25]

20. Levine, *Numbers*, 428–430.

21. *Ant.* 4.12.

22. Feldman, *Josephus's Interpretation of the Bible*, 140. Feldman notes that this the theme of *stasis* not only runs through much of Josephus' interpretation of the Hebrew Bible but in Josephus' analysis "it was civil strife that cost the Jews most dearly in the war against the Romans."

23. In the introduction to the *Antiquities*, Josephus signals the place politics will have in this work, declaring he will provide an overview not only of Jewish history but a consideration of the Jews' political constitution as well. *Ant.* 1.5. The extent of Josephus' interest in politics within the *Antiquities* generates some debate in the secondary scholarship. Feldman and Rajak identify politics as only one theme among others that determine the work. By contrast, Steve Mason contends that Josephus frames the whole of the *Antiquities* to demonstrate that Judaism can be recognized in Greco-Roman terms as both a *politeia* and a philosophic system in which Greeks could find much to admire. Rajak, "The *Against Apion* and the Continuities in Josephus' Political Thought," 195–196; Feldman, *Josephus's Interpretation of the Bible*, 140ff.; Mason, "Should Any Wish to Enquire Further," 82.

24. Rajak, "The *Against Apion* and the Continuities in Josephus' Political Thought," 199.

25. Feldman argues that Hellenistic audiences might identify with this theme through knowledge of a writer like Thucydides (2.53.1). Feldman, *Josephus's*

Josephus' engagement with such tradition evidences the complicated relationship of subject people in the Greek East with the forces of Hellenism. As Rajak points out, for Palestinian Jews like Josephus, the pervasive Greek culture they experienced was associated with three empires—Ptolemaic, Seleucid, and Roman. In the case of this last empire, "Roman rule in the east drew on the Greek language, incorporated Greek political ideas and fostered Greek literature."[26] Perhaps in part because of the close ties of Hellenism with Roman political power, the scholarship on Josephus has, in the main, not acknowledged democratic discourse as part of his conversation with Greek culture—nor the way his appropriation of the *stasis topos* reflects that discourse.

Certainly audiences familiar with classical Greek literature would recognize the theme of factionalism and its ramifications for democratic *ekklēsia* politics and civic stability.[27] According to Demosthenes, Lysias, and Thucydides, *stasis* hinders, or even makes impossible,[28] the func-

---

*Interpretation of the Bible*, 140. The nature of the audience Josephus addresses in the *Antiquities* and elsewhere has been a point of contention in the recent scholarship on Josephus. Mason includes a survey of the various answers given to the question of audience in the scholarship. His own argument insists that Josephus writes for a sympathetic, Gentile audience primarily located in Rome, an audience that would have been interested in Judaism as a *politeia*. By contrast, Rajak suggests an audience composed of Hellenistic Jews for all of Josephus' works, Jews located in cities throughout the empire who were in need of encouragement following the destruction of the Temple. Feldman describes the audience in part as non-Jews, and partly "secularly educated Jews." Likewise, Sterling posits a mixed audience for the *Antiquities*. He suggests that Josephus writes this work as an apologetic history directed to Greek cities of the Diaspora, Roman authorities, and Judeans, attempting to convince all that his version of Hellenized Judaism "would reconcile the antagonistic elements of his world and establish a place for the Jewish nation in the new world after the revolt." Mason, "Should Any Wish to Enquire Further," 65–72, 95–97; Rajak, "The *Against Apion* and the Continuities in Josephus's Political Thought," 197; Feldman, *Josephus's Interpretation of the Bible*, 140; Sterling, *Historiography and Self-Definition*, 309.

26. Rajak, "Judaism and Hellenism Revisited," 3.

27. *Stasis* was described as a critical danger to civic government. Speaking through the democratic Syracusan leader Hermocrates, Thucydides informs the reader that *stasis* is the "chief cause of ruin to cities." νομίσαι τε στάσιν μάλιστα φθείρειν τὰς πόλεις. Thuc. 4.61 (Smith, LCL). For another example, see Dem. 18.61. For a detailed discussion of *stasis* in the classical period, see Ober, "Political Conflicts, Political Debates, and Political Thought."

28. Thucydides records that his hero Pericles refuses to call an assembly at one point because the city is in such a state of disorder as people gather in groups to dispute the present state of affairs that they cannot be counted on to make a good decision. 2.21. The vocabulary for the groups into which people are divided in this passage is ἔριδι.

tioning of assembly politics that benefit the common good. Such authors suggest that *stasis* in the *ekklēsia* context is driven by private interests and selfishness, whether it be the desire to best others in the assembly[29] or the pursuit of monetary gain.[30] Economic and social disparity takes a starring role within these discussions over the origins of *stasis*. In fact, the tension between those of high birth and wealth and the many without these attributes haunts much of the writing over classical democracy. When it comes to *stasis* within such democracies, Aristotle argues that responsibility lies with "the notables" (οἱ γνώριμοι). This group, he contends, are discontented with the terms of the democratic system since "they have an equal share though they are not equal."[31] In Josephus' narration, it is this dissatisfaction that drives Korah to act against Moses.

In the original biblical story from Numbers 16, Korah and his confederates protest that Aaron and Moses have set themselves up above the rest of the Israelites by awarding the priesthood to Aaron. Two other prominent Israelites, Datham and Abiram, join Korah in criticizing Moses for abusing his authority. The situation is largely resolved and Moses' authority confirmed when the people gather the next day at Moses' command, and divine action makes a swift end of Korah, Datham, Abiram, and all their allies. By contrast, Josephus' considerable expansion of this biblical narrative[32] not only plays out Korah's challenge and Moses' defense in persuasive speech before an active audience but also gives a rationale for Korah's rebellion that coheres with classical Greek discussions of *stasis*.

In the *Antiquities*, Korah's resentment stems from his own fine lineage and wealth. According to Josephus, Korah feels that he should have received the honors of leadership in place of Moses, since Korah is of equal birth but richer than Moses. Entirely absent from the biblical narrative, the issue of wealth inequality motivates Korah's agitation even as it runs throughout discussions of political equality in this episode. In the case of Korah, Josephus' rationale for this character's motivations closely matches Aristotle's description of *stasis*' origins in a democracy. Like Aristotle's "notables," Korah chafes against his "equality" out of a conviction of his own superiority. However, Josephus adds yet another reason for Korah's indignation that is highly revealing for the construction of leadership in this episode. Korah's

---

29. Dem. 31.1–2.

30. Lys. 18.6–17.

31. Aristotle, *Pol.* 1303b5 (Rackham, LCL). . . . ὅτι μετέχουσι τῶν ἴσων οὐκ ἴσοι ὄντες.

32. Feldman points out that together the stories concerning Korah and Zambrias make up more than half of the narrative material in book 4 in the *Antiquities*. Feldman, *Josephus's Interpretation of the Bible*, 390.

resentment is located not only in his wealth and birth but also in his abilities as a persuasive speaker to assemblies (δήμοις).³³ This ability, used in the correct manner, becomes essential for Josephus' definition of the ideal leader—a definition that Korah can never meet because he does foment *stasis* out of his own selfish ambition.

Korah's attempt to assail Moses' and Aaron's position, and to gain the priesthood for himself, begins with Korah addressing his own kinsmen, the Levites. Korah argues to this group that Moses has not relied on a decree of the people to decide who should hold the office of priest. Instead, Moses has tyrannically cast his vote alone in giving the office to Aaron.³⁴ Josephus' choice of vocabulary is significant in this opening section. Not only does Korah claim that Moses is exercising power in a tyrannical mode (τυράννων) but he also speaks negatively of Moses casting his vote alone (αὐτοῦ ψηφισαμένου).³⁵ The Greek term ψηφίζομαι had a technical usage primarily related to civic voting.³⁶ Notably, this word had a close connection to the procedure of the assembly. Not only did this term designate voting in the *ekklēsia* but decisions of the assembly were also known as ψήφισμα.³⁷ Josephus' use of the word evokes an *ekklēsia* context by contrasting Moses' solitary voting with an action taken by the people as a whole. As ψηφίζομαι has a connection to the ancient assembly, so the word δόγμα, which Josephus uses for a decree of the people, was also a word relating to popular decision in a democracy.³⁸ Couched in the vocabulary of civic democracy, Korah's rhetoric thus relies on an assumption of communal decision-making as a superior political process—while a leader acting unilaterally is understood as a threat to the people's welfare.

Korah also accuses Moses of scheming to gain power. He argues that Moses' underhanded actions are actually more damaging than open violence since the people are unaware of the way that they are being fooled. Korah's arguments contrasting correct leadership to this corrupt practice are presented in this way:

33. *Ant.* 4.14.

34. Ibid., 4.15–16 (Thackeray, LCL). "In defiance of the laws he had given the priesthood to his brother Aaron, not by the common decree of the people but by his own vote, and in a tyrannical fashion was bestowing the honors upon whom he wished." ... παρὰ τοὺς νόμους μὲν τἀδελφῷ τὴν ἱερωσύνην Ἀαρῶνι δόντα, μὴ τῷ κοινῷ δόγματι τοῦ πλήθους ἀλλ' αὐτοῦ ψηφισαμένου, τυράννων δὲ τρόπῳ καταχαριζομένου τὰς τιμὰς οἷς ἂν ἐθελήσῃ.

35. Ibid., 4.16.

36. For examples, see Lys. 12.43–45; Thuc. 7.48.

37. For more about voting at Athens, see Hansen, *The Athenian Democracy*, 147.

38. Dem. 18.154; 5.19.

> For one who is conscious of being worthy to gain promotion seeks to obtain it by persuasion, without boldly using violence; but those who are incapable of obtaining honors by just means, while they do not apply violence because they wish to be taken for good people, with cunning carry out evil to gain power.³⁹

This passage illustrates significant claims about the exercise of power that are determined by democratic discourse. Korah's arguments rest on the supposition that someone gaining authority through force is exercising an illegitimate form of power that marks them as a substandard leader. Such a description of leadership resonates with the negative model of tyrant that is often the foil for descriptions of democracy in the ancient world.⁴⁰ That Josephus is in conversation with this model is evident both in his description of leadership in the passage and in the explicit accusations of tyranny that Korah and the people level against Moses in this episode.

The ideal of the persuasive speaker provides a counterpoint to the tyranny Josephus implies in this passage. This description suggests a leader should speak persuasively in order to have power conferred upon them by the people. Such a description of leadership prefigures the *ekklēsia* context in the next part of the story. Moreover, the honest and persuasive statesman evokes the Greek ideal of democratic power dynamics. However, this ideal is often contrasted, as Josephus does here, with dishonest assembly speakers seeking to mold the people to their own goals.⁴¹ In this passage, Josephus' illustration of leadership with the figures of tyrant, honest and dishonest persuasive speakers shows that his construction of leadership, like that of Dio Chrysostom and Plutarch, is heavily influenced by democratic discourse.

Josephus' introduction thus frames the Korah episode in the discursive terms of the democratic political context. At the same time, Korah's persuasive speech to his kinsmen also provides roles for the story's major characters within this environment. Korah defines his own villainy in the narrative as the one dishonestly seeking to persuade the assembly for his own benefit. However, this passage also lays the groundwork for the heroic and persuasive statesman in the image of a Pericles, a position that Moses

---

39. *Ant.* 4.17 (Thackeray, LCL). ὅστις γὰρ αὐτῷ σύνοιδεν ὄντι λαβεῖν ἀξίῳ πείθει τυγχάνειν αὐτὸν καὶ ταῦτα βιάσασθαι μὴ θρασυνόμενος, οἷς δὲ ἄπορον ἐκ τοῦ δικαίου τιμᾶσθαι βίαν μὲν ἀγαθοὶ βουλόμενοι δοκεῖν οὐ προσφέρουσι, τέχνῃ δ' εἶναι κακουργοῦσι δυνατοί.

40. Dio Chrysostom offers a nice description of tyranny that touches on its use of force in comparison with other forms of government. See Dio, *Or.* 3.44–48.

41. For a passage that alludes both to tyranny and dishonest assembly speakers, see Eur. *Supp.* 410–35.

will soon personify. Finally, this opening section introduces the reader to the corporate presence of the people and their role in forming decisions for the group. This foreshadows the active role of the πλῆρος when the people come together in the assembly.

## The Assembly Convenes: Enter Moses the Orator

In Josephus' account, Korah succeeds in whipping up a frenzy against Moses and Aaron, first among his tribe, and then throughout the multitude (τὸ πλῆθος). A spontaneous assembly results which Josephus designates "*ekklēsia*."[42] All the Israelites rush to this assembly, loudly proclaiming Moses a tyrant in imposing his authority to name Aaron the high priest.[43] This noisy assembly of τὸ πλῆθος replaces the much less dramatic confrontation of Korah and his 250 compatriots against Moses and Aaron in Numbers 16. Likewise, Moses' brief command to Korah and his associates from Numbers is replaced in the *Antiquities* with a significant speech by Moses, the gifted rhetor.

Josephus' description of a spontaneous and tumultuous assembly originating in the concerns of the "many" finds significant parallels within Greek literature from the classical period as well as in the first-century writings of Dio and Plutarch.[44] These descriptions convey the power and agency of the *ekklēsia* as a corporate entity that acts in the interest of the people. In Josephus' narrative, the threat of tyranny brings together this *ekklēsia* as

42. Josephus specifically uses the word *ekklēsia* to describe this meeting as the Greek above shows. However, the Septuagint consistently uses synagogue in this scene, applying it both to the whole Israelite people in Num 16:3 (notably this verse uses τὴν συναγωγὴν κυρίου), as well as to those who belong to Korah's faction alone in Num 16:5–6. The Hebrew Bible uses *edah* for the 250 leaders from the "assembly" (16:2), but uses *qahal* elsewhere in the passage both for all the Israelites as an entirety, as well as for the portion associated with Korah.

43. *Ant.* 4.22 (Thackeray, LCL). The first part of the passage concerning the people gathering and leveling accusations against Moses reads: ἀνηρέθιστο δὲ καὶ τὸ πλῆθος καὶ βάλλειν τὸν Μωυσῆν ὡρμήκεσαν, εἴς τε ἐκκλησίαν ἀκόσμως μετὰ θορύβου καὶ ταραχῆς συνελέγοντο, καὶ πρὸ τῆς σκηνῆς τοῦ θεοῦ στάντες ἐβόων διώκειν τὸν τύραννον καὶ τῆς ἀπ' αὐτοῦ δουλείας ἀπηλλάχθαι τὸ πλῆθος, τῇ τοῦ θεοῦ προφάσει βίαια προστάγματα κελεύοντος. "But the crowd was equally excited and eager to stone Moses; and, coming together in the assembly chaotically with tumult and uproar, they stood before the tabernacle of God and were shouting to banish the tyrant and let the people be rid of their bondage to one who, in the pretended name of God, imposes his despotic commands."

44. For examples of tumultuous assemblies and their interactions with speakers, see Aeschin. 2.4; Aristotle, *Rhet.* 1355a2–3; Dio, *Or.* 48.2; 7.23ff. For two examples of "spontaneous" assemblies, see Acts 19:29ff; Chariton, *Chaereas and Callirhoe* 8.7.1.

corporate actor. As in classical literature, this accusation of tyranny suggests that a leader is exercising undue influence to the detriment of the people's authority and well-being.[45] In Greek democratic tradition, such an abuse of power damages the ability of the *dēmos* to carry out self-determination both in the speech and the decision-making of the assembly. In this passage, the Israelites' protest against tyranny resists such a threat to the authority of the *ekklēsia*. In this way, Josephus makes an intriguing cultural translation of the claim by Korah and his companions in Numbers 16:3 that Moses and Aaron have set themselves above the rest of the Israelites.

If Josephus departs from the biblical script with this portrayal of the Israelites as a powerful *ekklēsia*, he also retains God's overarching authority from Numbers. Throughout the story, these two types of authority exist in uneasy tension. Here, at the beginning of the first assembly, the Israelites claim that Moses has not received God's command, implying that they would have accepted God's direct order if it were given to them. However, the people also contend that if God *had* decided to put Aaron in this position, he would not have chosen Moses to confer the honor but would have let the people appoint Aaron priest.[46] This last argument illuminates the Israelites' expectations in this story. While they recognize God's authority, they also assume that as a corporate body they have the opportunity to take part in the process of appointing leaders who will serve them. As the people recognize God's authority in this scenario, they also expect God's acknowledgment of their rightful role in deciding leadership for their own community.

The noisy gathering of the people εἴς τε ἐκκλησίαν and their shouted accusations bring Moses himself to the assembly in *Ant.* 4.24. Josephus has transformed the Israelites into an *ekklēsia* in his revision of Numbers 16. Now he passes Moses through the prism of democratic discourse as well. Moses' curt instructions from Numbers for offering incense the next day has, in Josephus' telling, become an eloquent oration defending his leadership, and God's action. As Moses turns to shout across the assembly at Korah, thereby beginning his speech, Josephus transforms the tongue-tied Moses of Numbers into a gifted orator. He makes this transformation explicit as he explains that Moses, in addition to his many other positive attributes, is also

---

45. For several references to tyranny and its detrimental effects for the people, see Dem. 6.25; Lys. 2.17–19.

46. *Ant.* 4.23 (Thackeray, LCL). τὸν γὰρ θεόν, εἴπερ αὐτὸς ἦν ὁ τὸν ἱερασόμενον ἐκλεγόμενος, τὸν ἄξιον ἂν εἰς τὴν τιμὴν παραγαγεῖν, οὐχὶ τοῖς πολλῶν ὑποδεεστέροις ταύτην φέροντα προσνεῖμαι, κρίνοντά τε παρασχεῖν Ἀαρῶνι ταύτην ἐπὶ τῷ πλήθει ποιήσασθαι τὴν δόσιν, ἀλλ' οὐκ ἐπὶ τἀδελφῷ καταλιπεῖν.

"naturally suited to converse with the people."[47] This description of Moses' verbal talents coheres with similar characterizations of this leader elsewhere in the *Antiquities*. For instance, Josephus reports that at Elim, Moses and not Aaron spoke before the angry Israelites, demonstrating he was "most persuasive in conversing with the people."[48] Moses' successful interaction with the crowd justifies Josephus' final description of Moses as someone who "in speech and in conversing with the people was found agreeable in every way."[49]

In these passages, Josephus alters Moses' persona so as to resemble the successful statesman of the democratic *ekklēsia*. With this alteration, Moses' deficiencies of speech as reported in Exodus 4:10 and 6:12 have vanished. As at Elim, Moses no longer requires Aaron as a spokesman before Pharaoh since Moses is more than capable of speaking for himself in all situations.[50] Josephus renders his hero as a skilled orator exercising power through persuasive speech. Louis Feldman argues that such a transformation owes much to Josephus' defense of Moses as leader and lawgiver in light of Greek culture.[51] To be truly great as a wise lawmaker, Moses must demonstrate his wisdom through speech.[52] I would go a step further to suggest that in order to demonstrate Moses' excellent leadership in Greek terms, Josephus has not only changed Moses into a fine speaker but also an orator of the *ekklēsia*. According to Greek democratic discourse, statesmen prove their worth not simply in giving a speech but by speaking persuasively with the people.[53] Likewise, Moses' excellence as a speaker is described specifically in his ability to address, and to persuade, the πλῆθος.

If Josephus transforms Moses to a statesman of the *ekklēsia*, this identity remains in conversation with the other more traditional roles of prophet and lawgiver. In fact, these three roles are tightly connected. Josephus writes

---

47. Ibid., 4.25 (Thackeray, LCL). δεξιὸς ὢν καὶ κατὰ τἆλλα καὶ πλήθεσιν ὁμιλεῖν εὐφυής.

48. Ibid., 3.13 (Thackeray, LCL). ὢν καὶ πλήθεσιν ὁμιλεῖν πιθανώτατος. Josephus shifts the biblical narrative of Exodus 16 in which the grumbling of the hungry Israelites prompts God to tell Moses that food will come to the people in the wilderness. In that narrative, God speaks to Moses who then relays the message to Aaron so that he might make an announcement to the people. By contrast, Moses faces the angry people alone in Josephus' account.

49. Ibid., 4.328 (Thackeray, LCL). Εἰπεῖν τε καὶ πλήθεσιν ὁμιλῆσαι κεχαρισμένος τά τε ἄλλα.

50. Compare Exodus 5:1 with *Ant.* 2.281.

51. Feldman, *Josephus's Interpretation of the Bible*, 397–401.

52. Ibid., 400.

53. Feldman himself points to Pericles' example as a statesman in Thuc. 2.60. Ibid.

that Moses' ability to inspire faith in his words remains alive in Josephus' own day through the laws that still speak to people.[54] Josephus argues that Moses was only able to accomplish what he did as a speaker, calming the Israelites and delivering the laws, because "God was with him, preparing the people to submit to his words."[55] In his final enumeration of Moses' virtues, Josephus speaks of his role as a prophet in very similar terms. No other prophet was Moses' equal since "in whatever he would say one seemed to hear God himself speaking."[56] While Josephus might describe Moses with the virtues and practical ability of a democratic leader, this leadership is only made possible by Moses' relationship to God as prophet and as lawgiver. It is this figure—prophet, statesman and lawgiver—that confronts Korah across an angry assembly.

## Moses' First Speech: Equality and Competition

Moses commences his speech before the assembly dramatically, shouting with all his might at Korah (πρὸς δὲ τὸν Κορῆ βοῶν ἐφ' ὅσον ἐδύνατο).[57] This confrontational performance grants Moses the appearance of strength and certainty as he speaks before an assembly predisposed against him. While Moses ostensibly directs his speech to Korah, it is clear that Moses, "so gifted in moving a crowd,"[58] aims not just to challenge Korah but to persuade the wider assembly audience. With this speech, Josephus replaces Moses' basic command and condemnation of Levite ambition in Numbers with an impassioned self-defense that incorporates suggestions for ending the community's strife. Moses' speech asserts not only his commitment to God but also his preference for equality and competition in the *ekklēsia* context.

Even as Moses declares it was God's command and not his own choice that resulted in Aaron's appointment, he also assures his audience that he personally thinks all are worthy of this honor even if they lack the wealth and other distinctions that someone like Korah possesses.[59] The preference

---

54. *Ant.* 3.317.

55. 3.316 (Thackeray, LCL). ὁ γὰρ θεὸς αὐτῷ συμπαρὼν ἡττᾶσθαι τοῖς λόγοις αὐτοῦ τὸ πλῆθος παρεσκεύαζε.

56. 4.329–30 (Thackeray, LCL). προφήτης δὲ οἷος οὐκ ἄλλος, ὥσθ' ὅ τι ἂν φθέγξαιτο δοκεῖν αὐτοῦ λέγοντος ἀκροᾶσθαι τοῦ θεοῦ.

57. 4.25 (Thackeray, LCL).

58. 4.25. This description of Moses immediately precedes his address.

59. 4.25–26 (Thackeray, LCL). Speaking to Korah: "ἐμοί," φησίν, "ὦ Κορῆ, καὶ σὺ καὶ τούτων ἕκαστος," ἀπεδήλου δὲ τοὺς πεντήκοντα καὶ διακοσίους ἄνδρας, "τιμῆς ἄξιοι δοκεῖτε, καὶ τὸν ὅμιλον δὲ πάντα τῆς ὁμοίας οὐκ ἀποστερῶ τιμῆς, κἂν ὑστερῶσιν ὧν ὑμῖν ἐκ πλούτου καὶ τῆς ἄλλης ἀξιώσεως ὑπάρχει. "'To me Korah,' he said, 'you and each of

Moses evinces for equal opportunity in leadership starkly contrasts Korah's motivations as Josephus has described them. While Moses expresses his inclination toward equal opportunity regardless of wealth or position, Korah seeks the priesthood out of a feeling of entitlement based both on birth and wealth.

Moses further argues in his own defense that he would not have betrayed either the laws or God in appointing Aaron priest. In a fascinating move, Moses actually claims that Aaron is in this position partly through the people's decision. With somewhat convoluted logic, Moses argues that what God has granted, it might be supposed the people also supported with their decision.[60] Moses thus suggests that the decision of the people matters, though it stands in complicated relationship with God's authority.

Moses' initial defense supports equal opportunity, the peoples' right to decision, as well as his own obedience to the laws. The inclusion of such loyalties within a passionate *ekklēsia* speech burnishes Moses' image as a democratic orator. The contention that honors and leadership should not depend on wealth or birth is a familiar theme from Greek democratic discourse. Moses' position also correlates with the reverence in classical literature for the rule of law, seen as guarantor of equality in the *polis* and the foundation for the people's continuing authority.[61] In this light, Moses' backing of law and equality within the *ekklēsia* also locate him in the Greek political landscape.

By declaring the priesthood open for competition, Moses proves that the egalitarian values he espouses are more than lip service. In contrast to the biblical account, Moses of the *Antiquities* announces that Aaron will at least temporarily give up the priesthood so that it may be openly sought by the "citizens" at large.[62] What was voiced as a command in Numbers 16:6–7 that Korah and his associates present themselves the following day, now takes on the guise of opportunity for all those who want to contend for the priesthood (ὅσοι τῆς ἱερωσύνης ἀντιποιεῖσθε).[63] Moses tells the assembly

---

these men'—indicating the two hundred and fifty—'seems worthy of honor; indeed, I would not rob this whole assembly of similar honor even though they lack what you possess from wealth and other distinctions.'"

60. 4.30–31 (Thackeray, LCL). ὃ γὰρ ἔδωκεν ὁ θεὸς οὐχ ἡμάρτομεν τοῦτο καὶ βουλομένων ὑμῶν λαβεῖν νομίζοντες.

61. Feldman suggest that Moses' concept of law within a community is at least in part influenced by Thucydides' emphasis on following traditional law, and the disaster that results when they are disregarded. Feldman, *Josephus's Interpretation of the Bible*, 114.

62. *Ant.* 4.29.

63. 4.32.

that this contest, centered on offering incense, will take place before "all the people."⁶⁴

In his version of the Numbers story, Josephus has shifted what was essentially an activity of divine confirmation into a contest to be decided in the assembly by a vote (ψηφοφορίαν) resulting in an "elected" official.⁶⁵ This shift reflects the close relationship between competition and equality within *ekklēsia* discourse.⁶⁶ In this discourse, the *topos* of democratic equality relates less to natural parity between citizens than to equal opportunity for political participation and competition.⁶⁷ To be sure, the biblical foundation of the story makes for interesting alterations in what one might expect from "competition" in an *ekklēsia* setting. Most notably, this is an election to be decided by God's vote rather than that of the πλῆθος.

If, in Moses' plan, God will cast the deciding vote for high priest, the *ekklēsia* audience still retains voice and authority in this narrative. This particular assembly ends with the people ratifying Moses' proposals.⁶⁸ Josephus describes the people's approval of Moses' counsel by writing, "The people assented to his words, which indeed were, it seemed excellent for the people" (ἐπένευσαν δὲ τοῖς εἰρημένοις· καὶ γὰρ ἦν καὶ ἐδόκει χρηστὰ τῷ λαῷ).⁶⁹ Josephus' wording in this case evokes the standard enactment formula of the democratic assembly, "It appeared right to the *dēmos*" (ἔδοξε τῷ δήμῳ).⁷⁰ However, Josephus also includes in this formulation the common benefit of Moses' plan for the people. In this scene, Moses has acted as the democratic leader before the assembly, arguing for a particular course of action to be taken by the people. Moses only sways the people, and they only enact his plan, because he convinces them his proposal is indeed beneficial to their interests.

---

64. 4.34 (Thackeray, LCL). ἐν φανερῷ παντὶ τῷ λαῷ.

65. 4.34. Josephus explains that whoever is picked by God, will be elected priest. Οὗτος ὑμῖν ἱερεὺς κεχειροτονήσεται. The verb χειροτονέω is significant here since its meaning of raising one's hand was very much associated with the process of voting in the assembly. For examples relating to elected officials, see Lys. 28.14; Dem. 4.26.

66. For examples discussed in previous chapters, see Dem. 18.109, 320; Plutarch, *Praec. ger. rei publ.* 804 C. Thucydides gives a very nice description of the interaction between equality and competition in Pericles' funeral speech: Thuc. 2.37.

67. Hansen provides a helpful discussion of this distinction in terms of classical democracy. Hansen, *The Athenian Democracy*, 83–84.

68 *Ant.* 4.35.

69. 4.35 (Thackeray, LCL); my translation.

70. For discussion of this formula and its use, see Hansen, *The Athenian Democracy*, 139.

In Greek literature about the *ekklēsia*, the interests of the people, or the "common good," serve as a measuring stick by which to judge the performance of both leaders and the assembled *dēmos*. Ideally, this greater good should govern the speeches of leaders and the decisions taken by civic assemblies.[71] In the *Antiquities*, the people recognize that Moses speaks to their benefit, and they use their corporate authority to endorse his proposal. Meanwhile, Moses' ability to direct the energies of the people away from *stasis* and toward that common good confirms his excellence as a leader. In this way, his actions and abilities strongly contrast Korah's selfish motivations and his duplicitous claims to foster the common good.[72]

## Day Two: Divine Action in the *Ekklēsia*

Josephus resumes his account on the second day of the Korah episode by describing the *ekklēsia* meeting gathered to choose the high priest. This assembly meeting serves as the frame for the dramatic events of this day and the next, which end not with democratic participation but rather with the divine action and wrath of God in Numbers. The inclusion of both *ekklēsia* and dramatic divine action highlights the tensions inherent in the "translation" project that Josephus has undertaken. In this particular episode, God's action—His vote—twice confirms Aaron's position as priest. However, that divine action plays out against the continued participation of the Israelites as *ekklēsia* and the leadership of Moses as combined prophet and democratic rhetor. Moses' own success in bringing the *stasis* plaguing the Israelites to an end depends not only on God's action but also on bringing the people together in one place as an *ekklēsia*.

On the second day of Korah's *stasis*, the people remain a vivid presence within the *ekklēsia*. As the assembly opens, Josephus' description of the audience reinforces the involvement of the people in the choice of priest, even as the process is further framed in terms of a competition, with those participating labeled "τῶν περὶ τῆς ἱερωσύνης ἀγωνιζομένων."[73] In this case, the assembly again proves to be noisy and turbulent.[74] While the people in

---

71. For examples, see Dem. 18.273;278; 321.

72. *Ant*. 4.20 (Thackeray, LCL). ἐβούλετο μὲν οὖν ταῦτα λέγων ὁ Κορῆς τοῦ κοινοῦ προνοεῖσθαι δοκεῖν, ἔργῳ δὲ εἰς ἑαυτὸν ἐπραγματεύετο τὴν παρὰ τοῦ πλήθους τιμὴν μεταστῆσαι. "Now by saying these words Korah wished it to appear that he was concerned for the common good; in reality, he was attempting to have the place of honor granted to him by the people."

73. 4.35–36.

74. The word that Josephus uses to describe the tumult of the assembly, θορυβώδης, in its verbal, adjectival, and substantive forms is used often in conjunction with the

the first day's assembly of this episode were unified by anger against Moses, Josephus now presents an assembly divided by disparate desires and emotions. Josephus notes three divergent perspectives within the assembly. The first, represented by those "making trouble," would be pleased if Moses was actually convicted of a crime.[75] The second group consists of wiser members of the assembly who are hoping events of the *ekklēsia* will save the people from further disorder. This group recognizes continuing *stasis* or division as a threat for the stability of their system of government.[76] This second group forms a positive foil, both for the troublemakers seeking Moses' downfall as well as for the third group, "ὁ δὲ πᾶς ὅμιλος." Josephus describes the third group, the crowd, as tempestuous by nature and easily swayed by speakers. This crowd relishes the opportunity to challenge those in authority.[77]

This description of the *ekklēsia* attests to the continuing role of the assembled Israelites in the story, even as it draws on the negative and positive potential of assembly participation. Here Josephus contrasts wisdom and respect for government with division and inconstancy. The assembly that possesses these positive virtues is frequently presented in Greek literature as both an ideal and a requirement for successful democratic government.[78] Wisdom and respect for government translates into responsible behavior and concern for the common good. In contrast, the irresponsible *ekklēsia* audience seeks entertainment and is easily swayed by speakers who mix that entertainment with unhealthy doses of flattery.[79] Meanwhile, the

---

*ekklēsia*, describing the noise of the audience in both praise and displeasure. See Dio, *Or.* 32.11; Thuc. 8.92.

75. *Ant.* 4.36 (Thackeray, LCL). The first division of the crowd: . . . καὶ τῶν μὲν εἰς ἡδονὴν λαμβανόντων εἰ Μωυςῆς ἐλεγχθείη κακουργῶν. "Some would have taken pleasure in seeing" Moses convicted of a crime.

76. Ibid. The second division: τῶν δὲ φρονίμων εἰ πραγμάτων ἀπαλλαγείησαν καὶ ταραχῆς· ἐδεδίεσαν γὰρ μὴ τῆς στάσεως προιούσης ἀφανισθῇ μᾶλλον αὐτοῖς ὁ κόσμος τῆς καταστάσεως. "Other wiser ones (would take pleasure in Moses) escaping from troubles and tumult, for they feared, if sedition gained ground, a further effacement of the order of their constitution."

77. Ibid. ὁ δὲ πᾶς ὅμιλος φύσει χαίρων τῷ καταβοᾶν τῶν ἐν τέλει καὶ πρὸς ὅ τις εἴποι πρὸς τοῦτο τὴν γνώμην τρέπων ἐθορύβει. "But the rest of the assembled crowd, by nature rejoicing in decrying those in authority and altering its opinion according to what anyone said, was in an uproar."

78. Demosthenes gives one view of ideal *ekklēsia* behavior over and against division in the *Second Olynthiac* (2.29–31). Dio Chrysostom suggests democracy requires both virtue and the soundness of mind, or wisdom (σωφροσύνη), on the part of the people that Josephus mentions for the "best" of the three groups above: Dio, *Or.* 3.47.

79. Dem. 18.138; Dio, *Or.* 32.26–27.

tumultuous *dēmos*, torn by divisions, is portrayed as the very threat to good government that Josephus' "good" assembly members believe it to be.[80]

While Josephus begins his account of the second day of the "rebellion" by describing the people in the assembly, the focus soon shifts to the main actors in the biblical account. Josephus converts the Numbers (16:12) refusal of Datham and Abiram to come at Moses' command to a refusal to attend the assembly. In reply, Moses takes chief councilors and confronts these leaders. Josephus again transforms a relatively brief speech given by Moses in the biblical account into an impressive oration. Moses' ultimatum remains from Numbers 16:28–30—that God should prove his worthiness by having the earth swallow the rebels and their families. However, this short communication expands into another full defensive speech, this time summarizing Moses' service to the Israelites over time.

While Moses' second major speech in the Korah episode is not strictly an *ekklēsia* speech, it reinforces the image of Moses as democratic leader. While Moses supposedly addresses God in this impassioned communication, Josephus reveals that he speaks loudly enough to be heard by all the crowd.[81] Before this audience, Moses gives a ringing defense of his leadership from the time he left a life of comfort in order to lead the Israelites out of Egypt. The overall theme of this defense is Moses' devotion to the Hebrews, proved over time by his work "first for their freedom, and now for their salvation."[82] Moses states this devotion explicitly in terms of the common good, arguing that he would never govern (πολιτευσάμενος) against the common good (ἐπὶ βλάβῃ τοῦ κοινοῦ) by acting in his own selfish interests rather than at God's command.[83] Moses also here reiterates his commitment to equality, explaining that he has never acted in the interest of the wealthy to condemn "poverty that deserved to win."[84]

Through this second speech, Josephus reaffirms Moses as the paragon of leadership according to Greek *ekklēsia* discourse. Moses remains the great orator, leading through persuasion and dedicated to equality and self-sacrifice in the interest of the common good. As Moses speaks before the people in the mode of a Demosthenes or Pericles, the reintroduction of the biblical narrative jars the reader. Paralleling Numbers 16:28–30, Moses

---

80. Dem. 2.29–31.

81. *Ant.* 4.40 (Thackeray, LCL). γεγωνότερον ἐκβοήσας, ὡς ἀκουστὸν πάσῃ τῇ πληθύι γενέσθαι. "... calling out in ringing tones, so as to be heard by all the crowd..."

82. 4.42 (Thackeray, LCL). καὶ πρότερον μὲν ὑπὲρ τῆς ἐλευθερίας αὐτῶν, νῦν δ' ὑπὲρ τῆς σωτηρίας μεγάλους ὑπέστην πόνους...

83. 4.46 (Thackeray, LCL).

84. Ibid. οὔτε πλούτῳ κατέκρινα πενίαν νικᾶν δυναμένην.

finishes his speech by suggesting his worth as a leader will be proved by God ordering the ground to swallow Datham, Abiram, and their families.[85] At the completion of Moses' speech, this catastrophic event occurs, complete with an earthquake and booming crash as the ground duly swallows Datham, Abiram, and their relatives.

The Korah episode ends in Josephus' account with a return to the *ekklēsia* setting. In this case, such an environment forms an uneasy pairing with events carried over from the biblical narrative. The active crowd belonging to the first *ekklēsia* and the beginning of the second now becomes a mute witness to the demise of Korah and his associates. When Moses brings forward the claimants for the priesthood in order to see who will be "elected" (ἢ κεχειροτονημένος),[86] fire consumes those competing for the honor, leaving only Aaron unscathed. As in Numbers, even these divine acts do not completely convince the people, and they proceed to blame Moses for the deaths of the rebels. The influence of the people does not entirely disappear in Josephus' narrative. Instead, their dissatisfaction leads Moses to bring them together once again in the *ekklēsia*, not to convince them verbally, but to demonstrate God's actions in making Aaron's staff alone bloom among those offered by other Israelite leaders. With this final divine act, peace is achieved at last, and Aaron's priesthood is accepted.

The conclusion of the Korah episode highlights the tension in Josephus' writing between democratic dynamics and views that are distinctly undemocratic. Several times within this account Josephus clearly questions the people's actions and ability as a governing body. Yet he also recognizes their authority as an *ekklēsia* audience and the potential for their positive democratic participation. Moses' own virtues as a leader are made manifest in democratic interaction with the Israelite *ekklēsia*. His persuasive speeches in this episode demonstrate his oratorical skill and ability to "converse with the crowd." These same speeches showcase Moses' preference for equality in the *ekklēsia* setting and his respect for the people's decision. In Josephus' account of the Korah episode, Moses and the Israelites participate in a democratic system that determines the basis for understanding leadership and community interaction. Nevertheless, Josephus ends the account not with the people's decision or with persuasive speech but with God's demonstrations of divine favor. Here we certainly see what Tessa Rajak has labeled "the creative fusion of a non-Greek literary culture with Greek ideas."[87] In this

---

85. Moses requests that this takes place but also asks that God spare those who do follow his commandments, granting them peace and harmony. *Ant.* 4.50.

86. 4.54.

87. Rajak, "The *Against Apion* and the Continuities in Josephus's Political

case, Josephus' deployment of *ekklēsia* discourse interacts with the sovereign God so prevalent in biblical accounts, including that of Numbers 16.[88]

Josephus' choice to illuminate the virtues of Moses within the context and dynamics of the democratic *ekklēsia* in this episode speaks to the pervasiveness and power of democratic discourse in the first century. Like his contemporaries Plutarch and Dio, Josephus must make his arguments about leadership and community formation intelligible to an audience steeped in the Greek democratic model. This participation in democratic discourse does not mean that Josephus, like Dio and Plutarch, refrains from expressing reservations about the democratic system. With these authors, Josephus shares not only concerns about the abilities of *ekklēsia* participants and leaders to serve the common good but also a political scenario in which democratic *ekklēsia* politics must negotiate with the ultimate authority of a sovereign beyond the control of the πλῆθος. In these terms, Josephus' depiction of the Israelite assembly might well strike a chord with audiences familiar both with democratic discourse and with the political realities of life under the Roman Empire.

## Conclusion

This chapter has explored Josephus' re-reading of a key biblical episode with the lens of *ekklēsia* discourse. In the fourth book of the *Antiquities*, Josephus re-imagines a tumultuous period between Moses and the Israelites with the vocabulary and logics of ancient democracy. Josephus describes the Korah episode from Numbers 16 as a moment of *stasis*, arising from the tensions of wealth inequality. Much of the following action of the story in the *Antiquities* takes place within the context of the gathered *ekklēsia*. Moses' worth is proven in this context by his ability to persuade the people toward the common good and away from destructive *stasis*. Moses' great speaking ability, his integrity, and commitment to equality allow him to end this grave *stasis* and to take on the persona of a Periclean democratic leader.[89] In this narrative, Moses' role as democratic rhetor is matched by the Israelites' identity as an *ekklēsia*—as a *dēmos*. Moses proves his leadership skills, in part, by negotiating with this powerful, mercurial corporate body.

---

Thought," 199.

88. Elsewhere in the *Antiquities*, Josephus suggests this ideal can be realized in aristocratic government where the people live in accordance with the laws under God as their true ruler. *Ant.* 4.223.

89. For Feldman's description of Moses in the model of Pericles, see Feldman, *Josephus's Interpretation of the Bible*, 377, 441.

Josephus' version of the Korah episode demonstrates that his engagement with the Hellenism of his day includes Greek democratic discourse associated with the civic *ekklēsia*. In contrast to the Septuagint, Josephus' use of the word *ekklēsia* in this episode includes the full democratic valence of the term. Josephus' choice to re-imagine this episode, and Moses' part in it, as a moment of civic *stasis* resolved in an *ekklēsia* setting speaks to the pervasive influence of this discourse in the first century. As shown in earlier chapters, *ekklēsia* discourse continued to shape ideals of leadership and community interaction in the first century. Josephus exploits this discourse to burnish his own hero Moses as a democratic orator, gifted in "conversing with the crowd." Indeed, in this episode, Moses becomes a hero by confronting problems of economic inequality, *stasis*, duplicitous leadership, and fickle crowds—issues that would be strikingly familiar to those acquainted with debates inherent to ancient democracy.

The complexity and challenge of Josephus' translation project in the *Antiquities* is shown not just by his transformation of Moses into a statesman and the Israelites into an *ekklēsia*, but by the interaction of biblical material with this Greek democratic content. In this narrative, Josephus offers the ideal of human equality at the core of free democratic participation. This ideal accompanies the active presence of a corporate *ekklēsia* and leadership exercised through persuasive speech. However, Josephus also retains a divine authority that overshadows human politics, both aristocratic and democratic. In the Korah episode, neither democracy nor divine sovereignty replaces one another. Instead, they exist in tension throughout the narrative. As I have suggested, this tension between sovereignty and democracy also would likely have been familiar to Josephus' Greek speaking audience within the Roman Empire—and to the audience that Paul addresses in his first letter to the Corinthians.

# 4

# Speech and Wisdom of the Corinthian *Ekklēsia*

## Introduction

PAUL OPENS THE LETTER 1 CORINTHIANS BY WARMLY PRAISING THE WISdom and speech of his correspondents. He tells the Corinthians that their relationship with Jesus means that, "in every way you have been enriched by him, in speech and knowledge of every kind."[1] Yet Paul soon characterizes the Corinthians as immature, worldly and contentious in both their speech and wisdom. This worldliness, this immaturity, starkly contrasts with Paul's portrayal of his own speech and wisdom which, while lacking eloquence, is filled with the maturity of "spirit and power" (1 Cor 2:4). Scholars have read the early chapters of Paul's letter as revealing the Corinthians' divisiveness,[2] their lack of self-control or their compromising "Greekness."[3] I argue instead that the focus on speech in these early chapters of 1 Corinthians is a sign of the democratic discourse I have explored in previous chapters.

Earlier chapters have substantiated the continuing vitality of democratic discourse in the first century and its contributions to political practice and debates over citizenship and leadership in the Greek *polis*. Analyzing this discourse in 1 Cor 1–4 highlights speech as a site of struggle between

---

1. 1 Cor 1:5: ἐν παντὶ ἐπλουτίσθητε ἐν αὐτῷ, ἐν παντὶ λόγῳ καὶ πάσῃ γνώσει. The Greek edition of the New Testament used in this chapter is Nestle-Aland 1993. I follow the New Revised Standard Version unless otherwise noted.

2. Mitchell (*Paul and the Rhetoric of Reconciliation*) and Martin (*The Corinthian Body*) have made particularly important contributions to this interpretation of 1 Corinthians.

3. For instance, Betz argues that in 1 Corinthians Paul confronts this community's "Hellenistic religiosity," that makes possible both "libertinism" and "radical asceticism." Betz, "The Problem of Rhetoric," 24–25.

Paul and his Corinthian audience—and as a key to understanding the contestation over power that marks the letter as a whole. In particular, my analysis seeks to illuminate the social context of the letter and the way this context both shapes and constrains Paul's argumentation. I argue that Paul's rhetoric is designed to address a community that understood itself in terms of ancient Greek democracy and its principal institution, the *ekklēsia*.

In this chapter, I first challenge New Testament scholarship which has dismissed the democratic *ekklēsia* as a viable institution in the first century CE by showing that the *ekklēsia* remained a source of practice, identity, and discourse in the early empire. Secondly, I will discuss speech, and specifically wise speech, as a critical *topos* of first-century democratic rhetoric, which, like its classical predecessor, structured the nature of citizen participation and leadership in the context of the *ekklēsia*. Ultimately, I contend that reading 1 Cor 1–4 in light of *ekklēsia* discourse provides new insights into Paul's rhetoric, which seeks to establish his authority through negotiation with a powerful democratic assembly composed of individuals with equal voice.

## The First-Century *Ekklēsia*: Institution and Discourse

Biblical scholars have been inattentive to democratic discourse in 1 Corinthians because they have assumed that the political institutions of democracy, including the *ekklēsia*, were moribund, if not entirely absent, in the first century CE.[4] Richard Horsley represents this wider consensus when he asserts:

> Under imperial Roman rule, then, the last vestiges of democracy were undermined as the oligarchies gained control of or simply abolished the city assemblies, gradually destroyed the law courts (*dikasteria*), and by attaching liturgies to magistracies, established a property requirement for holding public office ... With the weakening or abolition of the assemblies and law courts, two of the traditional functions of rhetoric disappeared.[5]

As I have shown, this portrait of the Greek city reflects over a century of influential research in classics. Indeed, Horsley echoes the claim of G.E.M. de Ste Croix and I. Lévy[6] that the Greek civic assembly during the Ro-

---

4. Recent New Testament scholarship addressing the influence of politics on early Christian communities and texts has, for the most part, emphasized the relationship of Christians to the Roman Empire. For two recent examples, see Elliott, *The Arrogance of Nations*; and Kahl, *Galatians Re-Imagined*.

5. Horsley, "Rhetoric and Empire," 79.

6. Lévy describes an assembly isolated from any serious decision-making,

man period was increasingly ornamental, manipulated by elite councilmen and magistrates serving as Rome's chosen representatives in each district.[7] By questioning the viability of the *ekklēsia*, the principal institution of the democratic polis, this assessment leads to the inevitable conclusion that democracy itself had become obsolete in the early Empire.[8]

In New Testament scholarship, the democratic, civic roots of the *ekklēsia* tend to be invoked only to then be dismissed as the source of the name and practice of early Christian assemblies. By accepting classicists' contention that the democratic *ekklēsia* had become irrelevant in the first century CE, New Testament scholarship largely disregards democratic discourse as operative when analyzing the term *ekklēsia* itself, and in assessing the community dynamics and rhetoric that are consistent with *ekklēsia* practice. The scholarly consensus locates the origin for *ekklēsia* as a Christian community title in the Septuagint,[9] which, as I have explained, uses *ekklēsia* to translate the Hebrew *qahal* for gatherings.[10] This scholarship often highlights the Septuagint's use of the term for the gathered Israelites as the chosen people, especially at the time the law is given in Deuteronomy

---

writing, "Mais, si l'*ekklēsia* est associée, au moins nominalement, au vote des decisions générales, la boulè statue seule sur tout ce qui a pratiquement une importance réelle" ("Études sur la vie municipale de l'Aie Mineure sous les Antonins. I," 215). Further, Lévy describes this weakening of the assembly in terms of the city government: "L'affaiblissement de l'*ekklēsia*, ou plutôt son annihilation, tel est, à l'époque Antonine, le phénomène capital de la vie constitutionnelle de la cite grecque" (218). For other influential studies following Lévy's lead, see Ste Croix, *The Class Struggle in the Ancient Greek World*; Jones, *The Greek City from Alexander to Justinian*; Millar, "The Greek City in the Roman Period"; Magie, *Roman Rule in Asia Minor*.

7. Ste Croix suggests that the assembly fell into complete political insignificance by the beginning of the Principate in Greece and by the mid-second century CE in Asia Minor. Ste Croix, *Class Struggle*, 527, 532–33.

8. Here, Horsley is again in good company with scholars like Jones, who contend that democracy had ceased to function for Greek cities as a political system of any significance even by the beginning of the second century BCE. Jones, *The Greek City*, 170.

9. A few New Testament scholars are an exception to this trend in their arguments that the *ekklēsia* title has a political valence connected with the civic assembly. However, these scholars have not explored the continuing strength of democratic discourse in the first centuries CE, nor connected that discourse with the civic assemblies that still met during the early empire. See Peterson, *Ekklesia: Studien zum Altkirchlichen Kirchenbegriff*, 15–26; Berger, "Volksversammlung und Gemeinde Gottes"; Van Kooten, "Ἐκκλησία τοῦ θεοῦ"; Zamfir, "Is the *ekklēsia* a Household (of God)?"

10. Schmidt writes on this matter: "Constitutive for the Christian ἐκκλησία within Greek usage is the line from the Septuagint to the NT. Only on this line does the word take on its particular significance." Schmidt, "*Ekklēsia*," 514. See also Meeks, *The First Urban Christians*, 108; McCready, "*Ekklēsia* and Voluntary Associations," 60–61. More recently, see Trebilco, "Why Did the Early Christians Call Themselves ἡ ἐκκλησία?"

(23:1–8).[11] Following this reasoning, the Christian phrase "*ekklēsia* of God" (1 Cor 1:2; 10:32) finds its roots in the Septuagint's "*ekklēsia* of the Lord" (ἐκκλησία κυρίου)[12]—both phrases demonstrating that the Christians chose the title for its "particular religious significance."[13] As I have shown, the Septuagint's application of this term to a wide range of gatherings lacking religious significance undermines this explanation for the Christian appropriation of the word.[14] This explanation of the Christian title *ekklēsia* with select aspects of its Septuagint usage also neglects the most common employment of the word from the classical period into the first century—the designation of the civic, political assembly of citizens.

Although New Testament scholars routinely claim the Septuagint as the source of the *ekklēsia* title, they often explain the form and interaction of early Christian communities by drawing parallels with other social groups active in the first century CE. In this pursuit, Wayne Meeks' identification of four ancient "models" to compare and contrast with the Christian *ekklēsia* has often guided the scholarly conversation in recent decades.[15] In the case of each model—household, synagogue (συναγωγή), voluntary association, and philosophical school—Meeks indicates similarities with the Christian *ekklēsia*, but he explains that each model ultimately falls short of explaining the form of early Christian communities. Among the most serious discrepancies between his models and these Christian communities, Meeks

11. Schrage provides a thorough overview of scholarship making this claim. Schrage, "'*Ekklēsia*' und 'Synagoge,'" 180–81.

12. Meeks notes the presence of this phrase, especially in Deut 23:2, 3, 4 and Judg 20:2. Meeks, The *The First Urban Christians*, 230. Likewise, Schmidt, "*Ekklēsia*," 527–29.

13. McCready, "*Ekklēsia* and Voluntary Associations," 47.

14. Georgi, "The Interest in Life of Jesus Theology," 57. For extended arguments on this point that also show the interchangeability of *synagogē* and *ekklēsia* in the Septuagint, see Schrage, "'*Ekklēsia*' und 'Synagoge'"; Campbell, "The Origin and Meaning of the Christian Use of the Word *Ekklēsia*."

15. Originally published in 1983, Meeks' *The First Urban Christians* has influenced a large number of studies investigating the similarities of the early Church to these particular models. Adams provides a helpful survey of this scholarship over the last decades. Adams, "First-Century Models for Paul's Churches." Some of the most extensive recent work on ancient institutions as a model for early Christians centers on what Meeks designates "the voluntary association." For a sample of this work, see Kloppenborg, "Greco-Roman *Thiasoi*"; Kloppenborg and Wilson, *Voluntary Associations in the Graeco-Roman World*; Ascough, *Paul's Macedonian Associations*; Harland, *Associations, Synagogues, and Congregations*. Stowers focuses on the philosophical school model ("Does Pauline Christianity Resemble a Hellenistic Philosophy"). For a critique of Meeks' failure to include sanctuary space among these models, see Økland, *Women in Their Place*.

recognizes the contrast between the Christians' more democratic gathering and the hierarchy of the Greco-Roman household, even as he points out that the social diversity in the Christian *ekklēsia* was uncommon in voluntary associations. However, the influence of democratic *ekklēsia* discourse on early Christianity would account for these very discrepancies. The civic *ekklēsia* embodied the democratic interaction lacking in the hierarchical organization of the ancient household. Meanwhile, a socially diverse range of citizens participated in civic assemblies, a contrast to Meeks' description of voluntary organizations as homogeneous.[16] Meeks himself attributes any democratic currents present in Pauline communities to the influence of voluntary associations set up "according to the model of the classical *polis*," a model he does not specifically associate with the *ekklēsia*.[17] Meeks thus ascribes any democratic practice or ideology in the Christian *ekklēsia* to voluntary associations or synagogues which are themselves appealing to the classical past. In this way, Meeks does not acknowledge *ekklēsia* democracy as an active, first-century discourse shared alike by Christian communities, voluntary associations, and synagogues.[18]

My previous chapters have demonstrated that portrayals of the *ekklēsia*'s waning, or even non-existent, role in first-century Greek cities do not account for the growing evidence scholars have amassed to the contrary. Textual and inscriptional sources exhibit the continuing legislative authority of the *ekklēsia* in cities of the Greek East.[19] Meanwhile, first-century states-

16. Meeks, *The First Urban Christians*, 76ff; McCready, "*Ekklēsia* and Voluntary Associations." Harland and Kloppenborg contend that voluntary associations were much less homogeneous than Meeks suggests (Harland, *Associations, Synagogues, and Congregations*; Kloppenborg, "Greco-Roman *Thiasoi*").

17. Meeks, *The First Urban Christians*, 78.

18. With regard to synagogues, voluntary associations, professional clubs, religious cults and funeral societies, Schüssler Fiorenza explains: "These 'private' organizations did not adopt the structures of the patriarchal household, however, but utilized rules and offices of the democratic assembly, i.e., the *ekklēsia* of the *polis*." While she has not disproved the common assumption that the civic *ekklēsia* was moribund in the first century CE, Schüssler Fiorenza provides a marked contrast to Meeks in that she has consistently understood this title in democratic terms. Schüssler Fiorenza, *The Power of the Word*, 108. For an earlier example, see Schüssler Fiorenza, *Bread Not Stone*, xiv.

19. For some overview of this evidence in the early Empire, see Salmeri, "Dio, Rome, and the Civic Life of Asia Minor." Likewise, Ma shows that inscriptional and textual evidence registers democratic thought and practice associated with the assembly throughout the Hellenistic period and into the first century CE (2000a, 2000b). Ma, "The Epigraphy of Hellenistic Asia Minor" and "Public Speech and Community in the Euboicus." See also Gruen, "The Polis in the Hellenistic World," 354; Quass, *Die Honoratiorenschicht in den Städten des griechischen Ostens*, 361–62; Rogers, "The

men like Dio Chysostom and Plutarch acknowledge the continuing necessity of crafting their rhetoric toward a powerful assembly. The unfettered democratic practice and decision-making characterizing classical Athens may have been impossible under the Romans. Nevertheless, the developing portrait in classics scholarship of active, democratic *ekklēsiai* in Greek cities of the empire seriously undermines earlier historical models in which the *ekklēsia* was seen as only the rubber stamp for a powerful *boule* or council, itself dominated by omnipresent Roman power.[20]

That citizens continued to meet and to exercise political power in civic assemblies significantly questions the disappearance of the democratic *ekklēsia* under the Romans. However, I have shown that evidence for the vitality of democratic thought is not limited to the physical theater or Pnyx, but is witnessed in *ekklēsia* discourse, the logic and *topoi* that marked constructions of democracy in the first-century Roman Empire. The civic assembly sustained and replicated *ekklēsia* discourse. However, this democratic discourse also constituted a prevalent type of social knowledge and cultural logics maintained by a variety of institutions[21] that were part of the Greek cultural context. My own work has examined one such institution, education, and shown it to be critical in the replication of this discourse. Certainly, the process of Greek *paideia* helped to socialize students into the Greek democratic city and formed those students as speaking, discerning, democratic citizens.

## The Speech Topos in *Ekklēsia* Rhetoric

In previous chapters, I have shown that during Paul's lifetime the emphasis on free citizen speech was the critical rhetorical *topos* connecting democratic

---

Assembly of Imperial Ephesos"; Mitchell, *Anatolia*, 201–4. Likewise, Philippe Gauthier shows many similarities between the Hellenistic city assembly in form and function with the classical democratic assembly, directly contradicting Jones' picture of a decisive break with democratic tradition already in the Hellenistic period. Gauthier, "Les cités hellénistiques," 219–21. By contrast, see Jones, *The Greek City*, 177.

20. Here the work of Mitchell has been influential in showing that there are only a small number of specific instances that can be demonstrated for direct Roman involvement in Greek *polis* government, as the Romans were generally content to let cities determine their own government. Mitchell, *Anatolia*, 210. Likewise, Mitchell (ibid., 201–4) and Guy MacLean Rogers ("The Assembly of Imperial Ephesos") have seriously questioned the assertion that the civic councils usurped all real political power from the civic assemblies.

21. Foucault understands discourse as sustained through, but not limited to, particular institutions. Foucault, *The Archaeology of Knowledge*, 45.

discourse in the early empire with its powerful classical antecedent. As in classical Athens, this freedom of speech appears not only as the foundation of the democratic system but also as the act defining the citizen subject. In the literature I have examined, first-century authors continue to portray the right of addressing the citizen assembly as a realization of the freedom and equality defining democratic citizenship and participation. Likewise, these authors share with classical literature a portrayal of the democratic *ekklēsia* in which leadership plays out in this free speech before a critically engaged audience, itself composed of citizens with the right to speak in agreement or opposition.

Paul's own emphasis on speech in 1 Corinthians is closely linked with wisdom in the early chapters of the letter, thus reflecting another facet of democratic discourse. In democratic discourse from the classical period into the first century, the role of speech as the currency of democratic citizenship was paired with its ideal complement, wisdom on the part of both speakers and audiences.[22] Thucydides succinctly explains the dynamics of this partnership in a speech by Athenagoras of Syracuse, "While the wealthy are the best guardians of property, the wise (ξυνετούς) would be the best counselors, and the many, after hearing matters discussed would be the best judges; and that these classes . . . enjoy a like equality in democracy" (Thuc. 6.39.1–2).[23] While other classical authors share Thucydides' insistence that democracy depended on wise counselors or speakers,[24] these authors also betray a common assumption that the wisdom of the *dēmos* exceeds the wisdom of the individual.[25] For his part, Aristotle approves of limited democracy because the many exhibit significant "virtue and wisdom" (ἀρετῆς καὶ φρονήσεως) when they gather in assembly or court—a collective virtue and wisdom that surpasses even that of the few possessing the greatest virtue in the city (Aristotle, *Pol.* 1281b5). Likewise, Demosthenes courts his audience by claiming, "You the many are not expected to speak as well as the

---

22. While Betz notes the connection between wisdom and speech in ancient discussions over rhetoric, he does not locate this pairing in the conversation over democracy in the ancient world. In this way, Betz misses the contribution that this pairing makes to the struggles and debates in regard to democracy and the relationship of masses and elites within this political system. Betz, "The Problem of Rhetoric and Theology," 26–36. By contrast, see Ober, *Mass and Elite*, 163–166.

23. Smith, LCL.

24. For instance, Dem. 1.1; 8.71. Ober argues that the ability of educated elites to offer valuable, well-crafted advice delineates the usefulness of these elites to the city, and provides context for the constant negotiation of power between mass and elites. Ober, *Mass and Elite*, 317–20.

25. Ibid., 163–66.

orators, but you, especially the older ones of you, are expected to have intelligence equal or better than that of the speakers" (45.2).[26] In both examples, the ability—one might term it the special talent—of the *dēmos* to arrive collectively at wisdom enables citizens to practice the self-rule characterizing democracy.

As I have demonstrated, Plutarch and his near-contemporary Dio Chrysostom give particularly valuable witness to the continuing emphasis on *polis* citizenship and *ekklēsia* speech in the first and early second century CE. While these authors specify persuasive speech as the medium of civic participation and leadership, they also echo classical authors in suggesting that this speech must be paired with wisdom. Plutarch calls for the persuasive speech of the statesman (πολιτευομένου) or counselor (συμβουλεύοντος) to be full of true practical wisdom (φρονήματος ἀληθινοῦ)[27] and foresight (Plutarch, *Praec. ger. rei publ.* 802 F). Likewise, he quotes Euripides from *Antiope*, "For one wise counsel over many hands is victor" (σοφὸν γὰρ ἓν βούλευμα τὰς πολλὰς χέρας νικᾷ), in order to argue that "one sensible and persuasive expression of opinion accomplishes the greatest and most excellent public measures" (μία γνώμη λόγον ἔχουσα καὶ πειθὼ τὰ κάλλιστα καὶ μέγιστα διαπράττεται τῶν κοινῶν) (Plutarch, *An seni* 790 A).[28] Dio also repeatedly stresses wisdom in his own speech. Though Dio downplays his knowledge and speaking ability, he indicates that his service to the people resides in his wise words.[29] In addition, he shares with classical authors the expectation for wisdom on the part of the *ekklēsia* audience. For instance, speaking to the *ekklēsia* of his native Prusa, Dio acknowledges that the audience is capable of understanding and claims that above all he hopes they should "have the character which is Greek and be neither ungrateful nor unintelligent (ἀξυνέτους)" (*Or.* 43.3).[30]

Dio and Plutarch actively engage in the democratic thought and practice that continued to permeate the Greek East of the first century CE, the cradle for the growing Christian movement. Likewise, I suggest that Paul and his correspondents in first-century Roman Corinth also knew and mobilized *ekklēsia* discourse. At first glance, Corinth's history seems to make such a claim counterintuitive. In 146 BCE, the Romans defeated and largely

---

26. Ibid., 164.

27. My translation.

28. Fowler, LCL.

29. See, for instance, Dio's comparison of himself to the wise (σοφὴ) owl in *Or.* 12.7. Likewise, the question of wisdom in his speech arises, among others, in *Or.* 42.1; 47.1.

30. Crosby, LCL.

destroyed the powerful ancient Greek city of Corinth. Corinth owed its decline but also its resurrection as a vibrant city, to the Romans that resettled the city as a colony in 44 BCE. James Walters details two recent trends in scholarship on Roman Corinth from the time of this refounding to the first and second centuries CE. On the one hand, scholars increasingly recognize that "refounded Corinth was a more typical Roman colony with a stronger Roman character than has been assumed."[31] However, another group of scholars argues that "The civic identity of Roman Corinth began to change during the Augustan period and accelerated through the second century as the city became increasingly integrated into the surrounding Greek world, a transition already evident by the time of Claudius."[32] This second group of scholars explores the complex negotiation between Greek and Roman identity as witnessed in Corinth's archaeological record. This record attests that, even as a Greek population was reestablished in Corinth soon after its defeat in 146 BCE[33] and became more visible in the first century CE,[34] Roman colonizers highlighted Corinth's Greek past in order to validate Roman rule. Christine Thomas explains that this focus on Corinth's traditional Greek identity[35] speaks to a hybrid discourse that was exploited by Romans and Greeks alike. Romans might use this discourse toward justifying their rule, but Greeks also "enthusiastically adopted this emphasis on Greek heritage . . . to depict a world in which most traces of Roman influence have faded from view."[36]

---

31. Walters, "Civic Identity in Roman Corinth," 397. Cf. Walbank, "The Foundation and Planning of Early Roman Corinth"; Romano, "Urban and Rural Planning."

32. Walters, "Civic Identity in Roman Corinth," 397. For examples of this scholarship, see Spawforth, "Roman Corinth," 169–75; Bookidis, "Religion in Corinth."

33. Bookidis, "Religion in Corinth," 149. Gebhard and Dickie recognize this Greek resettlement. Gebhard and Dickie, "The View From the Isthmus," 261–78. Millis describes the population of the early colony as dominated by Greek freedmen, who maintained their Greek identity even as they were able to manoeuver in the Roman culture that was also part of Corinthian culture and identity. Millis, "Social and Ethnic Origins."

34. Walters agrees with Spawforth ("Roman Corinth," 173–75) that under Claudius and Nero "the city itself was becoming more integrated into its Greek context," an integration witnessed by Greek notables appearing for the first time as magistrates of Roman Corinth. Walters, "Civic Identity in Roman Corinth," 408.

35. This was visible, for instance, in the renewal of Greek sanctuaries now marked by Roman architecture and religious practice. For an exploration of this Roman renewal of traditional Greek sanctuaries, see Bookidis, "Religion in Corinth"; Thomas, "Greek Heritage in Roman Corinth and Ephesos."

36. Thomas, "Greek Heritage," 141.

The Roman orator Favorinus, speaking to Corinthians in the early second century CE, suggests that this trajectory of Corinthian Hellenization included Greek *paideia*[37] and an awareness of the democratic discourse which had its own place within Greek identity under Rome. In his Corinthian oration, Favorinus rhetorically courts the Corinthians, both by asserting that they have been thoroughly Hellenized like him (*Or.* 37.26) and by naming them as Greek heirs to classical Corinth (*Or.* 37.1; 7; 16).[38] Further, he contends that these classical ancestors, and thus his audience, are distinguished by their support of democracy and the freedom from tyranny.[39] Hence one can argue that Greek-speaking inhabitants of first-century Roman Corinth were participants in the increasing Hellenization of their city and would have known democratic discourse centered on *ekklēsia* speech—a discourse itself thoroughly implicated in Greek culture and *paideia*.[40]

## The Corinthian *Ekklēsia*: Speech and Wisdom in the Christian Assembly

When Paul wrote to Corinth in the middle of the first century, I argue both he and his audience were immersed in this *ekklēsia* discourse. In 1 Corinthians, the extensive use of the word *ekklēsia* itself signals this discourse insofar as this letter claims an exceptional place in the New Testament, with the largest concentration of the term *ekklēsia* outside of the Book of Acts.[41] However, the significance of this expression for indicating the pres-

37. Given Favorinus' urging for the attainment of Greek culture (*Or.* 37.27), Dutch concludes that Greek *paideia* was indeed available to Corinthian youths (Dutch, *The Educated Elite*, 145). Certainly Favorinus compares himself to the Corinthians in this speech, suggesting that both have become thoroughly Greek through interaction with Greek culture (*Or.* 37.26).

38. For further discussion of Favorinus and the appeals he makes to the Corinthians based on their "Greek" identity, see König, "Favorinus' *Corinthian Oration*."

39. Favorinus suggests that the Corinthians were foremost among the Greeks for cultivating justice: "For I ask you, was it not they who put an end to the tyrannies in the cities and established the democracies and freed Athens from her tyrants . . ." (*Or.* 37.16; Crosby, LCL). See also *Or.* 37.17–20. This appeal to the Corinthians as supporters of democracy is interesting given the history of classical Corinth, which maintained a democratic regime for only a short time in the fourth century BCE. For a treatment of this period, see Hamilton, "The Politics of Revolution in Corinth."

40. For a survey of the rich body of literature devoted to analyzing this early Christian community at Corinth, see Horrell and Adams, "Introduction," 1–43.

41. The word *ekklēsia* does not appear in the Gospels, with the exception of Matt 16:18; 18:17. Nor does it appear in 2 Timothy, Titus, 1 and 2 Peter, or 1 and 2 John. The majority of instances appear in Paul's letters or in those letters that were written using

ence of democratic discourse lies not only in its frequency but also the way in which the word is defined and the *topoi* that accompany it. Here, as in civic parlance, Paul applies this term to a corporate body defined not as a location but instead as the group coming together in a gathering (1 Cor 11:18). Moreover, the prominence of the word "*ekklēsia*" pairs with the focus on speech and wisdom in 1 Corinthians. Beginning with the opening thanksgiving, speech and wisdom emerge as central concerns in this letter. While Paul's other letters combined only use the words σοφία and σοφός six times, 1 Corinthians employs this vocabulary twenty-eight times. Likewise, the word λόγος[42] features more prominently in the Corinthian correspondence than in Paul's other letters, appearing twenty-six times in 1 and 2 Corinthians compared to thirty-eight occurrences in the five other undisputed Pauline epistles together with Colossians and Ephesians.[43]

Scholars have recognized the centrality of speech and wisdom[44] in 1 Corinthians and have located that emphasis in the Hellenistic cultural and political context of the letter. For instance, Dale Martin and Lawrence Welborn hypothesize that Paul's arguments over speech and wisdom reflect the role of Greco-Roman rhetoric in Corinthian strife, a strife that each author relates to class conflict within the community.[45] Martin, in particular, suggests that Paul problematizes rhetoric because rhetorical ability and education are such critical status indicators in the ancient world, linked to elite possession of wealth, beauty, and noble birth.[46] Martin argues that for Paul

---

his name and authority (46 out of 114 usages are in the Pauline literature). Revelation is also distinguished by the high incidence of the word *ekklēsia*. See further Coenen, "Church, Synagogue," 298.

42. As Betz points out, λόγος has a range of meanings in the Greco-Roman world. Betz argues for its translation as speech in this case over "reason as a faculty of thought" (34) based on context, not least the pairing of λόγος and σοφία as in other ancient discussions of rhetoric. Betz, "The Problem of Rhetoric and Theology," 34–35.

43. Beyond 1 Corinthians, σοφία and σοφός only appear in Romans and 2 Corinthians within the Pauline correspondence, with five occurrences in Romans and one in 2 Corinthians. Finally, the word γνῶσις appears sixteen times in 1 and 2 Corinthians but only seven times in the rest of the undisputed Pauline, Deutero-Pauline, and Pastoral Epistles. For a survey of scholarship considering the relationship between γνῶσις and λόγος in 1 Cor 1:5, see Fee, *The First Epistle to the Corinthians*, 39.

44. For agreement with this translation, and, even more specifically, that this speech can be identified as rhetoric, see Wire, *Corinthian Women Prophets*, 49–54; Castelli, "Interpretations of Power," 208; Pogoloff, *Logos and Sophia*, 105; Litfin, *St. Paul's Theology*, 2–10; Martin, *The Corinthian Body*, 49–50; Welborn, *Politics and Rhetoric*, 29–30.

45. Martin, *The Corinthian Body*, 49–54; Welborn, *Politics and Rhetoric*, 29–32.

46. Martin, *The Corinthian Body*, 49–54.

to persuade those within the community who claim such status to lower themselves voluntarily, Paul must first stake his own claim to high status and leadership. At the same time, Paul ultimately rejects the status upholding elite power as damaging to community and valueless in comparison with divine speech and wisdom. To support this argument, Martin exploits assumptions regarding ancient democracy that I have already examined. Along with Stephen Pogoloff, on whom he relies in this discussion, Martin portrays first-century rhetoric as divorced from a democratic context. In an echo of the quotation I gave from Horsley at the beginning of this chapter, Pogoloff claims that, "under the Empire the practical public value of rhetoric declined as opportunities for free political speech were curtailed."[47] Since Martin and Pogoloff envision rhetoric permeating the Greco-Roman city, they assert that civic elites were trained in rhetoric primarily for the purpose of the classroom, the rigors of declamation and the cachet of status, but not for the civic *ekklēsia*.[48] For these scholars, rhetoric no longer figures into the complex negotiation between speakers and powerful citizen audiences in the democratic *ekklēsia*[49] but represents the one-sided exercise of power by the educated upper classes. In turn, this understanding of rhetoric and politics means that the function of rhetoric is largely equated in the Greek and Roman political contexts, and these scholars draw examples freely from each in order to tease out Paul's arguments. Continuing vitality of democratic discourse and practice in the first-century Greek East problematizes this view of rhetoric and power and, in the process, raises a new set of questions regarding the debates over speech between Paul and the Corinthians. Not least, we must consider the possibility that a community engaged with democratic discourse might view rhetorical speech and wisdom not primarily as a marker of elite status and class conflict, but rather as the act that defines collective authority—together with individual freedom and equality.

47. Pogoloff, *Logos and Sophia*, 175.

48. Martin, *The Corinthian Body*, 49–51; Pogoloff, *Logos and Sophia*, 175–77.

49. Martin does give several examples of democratic rhetoric that challenge the benevolent patriarchalism that he suggests is the rule in the ancient world. He notes that the classical authors Isocrates and Demosthenes both give speeches in which they reject the hierarchy headed by the strong, wealthy, and educated elements of society, and instead question whether it is "just" for the strong to rule over the weak, or if indeed the *dēmos* should be in the true position of power. Martin reasons that each addresses Athenians "during a time when the constitution was democratic and the air filled with populist rhetoric"—circumstances that allowed benevolent patriarchalism to be set aside "at least momentarily." However, Martin does not seriously investigate this democratic ideology—or audiences—in the context of the Roman Empire. Martin, *The Corinthian Body*, 44.

Paul opens 1 Corinthians (1:1–9) by applauding the *ekklēsia*, singling out their speech and wisdom for notice. Paul explains that the Corinthians have the grace of God through Christ Jesus and states in 1:5: "in every way you have been enriched in him, in speech and knowledge of every kind" (ὅτι ἐν παντὶ ἐπλουτίσθητε ἐν αὐτῷ, ἐν παντὶ λόγῳ καὶ πάσῃ γνώσει). Here, Paul might have specified any number of gifts that the Corinthians possess, and in letters to other communities Paul does praise his audience for specific spiritual gifts highly valued throughout his writings, including faith (1 Thess 1:3) and love (Phil 1:9). However, beyond the grace of God in Christ, this thanksgiving only mentions Corinthian enrichment in speech and knowledge (1 Cor 1:5).[50] Unique among Paul's epistles, this praise of Corinthian speech and wisdom is even more striking because Paul goes on to challenge systematically the group's use of these gifts. Scholars have explained this dissonance between Paul's initial approbation and later critique as part of Paul's rhetorical appeal to the Corinthians' own vision of themselves in order to make them more receptive to later criticism. For instance, Margaret Mitchell and Ben Witherington argue that Paul's opening compliments to the community serve the rhetorical work of an *exordium* or προοίμιον designed to "make the hearers attentive, receptive, and well-disposed, and orient them to the argument to follow."[51] In fact, such an *exordium* was a common strategy in ancient *ekklēsia* speeches.[52] Paul's use of this strategy shows that he shapes his rhetoric toward a group valuing speech and wisdom as part of their collective identity.[53] This thanksgiving intimates not division

50. For some analysis of the scholarship on Paul's attribution of λόγος καὶ γνῶσις to the Corinthians, along with an argument for the former as referring to rhetoric, see Betz, "The Problem of Rhetoric and Theology," 26–36.

51. Mitchell, *Paul and the Rhetoric of Reconciliation*, 194–97. Witherington III adds that the προοίμιον also fulfills the task of "encapsulating the main themes of the speech or letter." Witherington III, *Conflict and Community*, 87. See also Aune, *Prophecy in Early Christianity*, 186.

52. Mitchell provides numerous examples from the classical period onwards. *Paul and the Rhetoric of Reconciliation*, 194–97.

53. Betz shares Mitchell's and Witherington's perception that this initial praise appeals to Corinthians self-understanding. Of this portion of the thanksgiving, Betz writes, "[I]t provides the basic assumptions for his arguments in the letter. In this case the formula not only states the Corinthians' self-praise but must also contain Paul's critique and the clue to the following arguments" ("The Problem of Rhetoric and Theology," 33). Likewise, Stowers recognizes that Paul uses foreshadowing in the thanksgiving: "In 1 Corinthians (1:4–9), he gives thanks for the speech, knowledge and spiritual gifts of the Corinthians. In chapters 1–4, 8, and 12–14 the reader learns that the improper use of wisdom, knowledge, charismatic speech, and spiritual gifts are, according to Paul, central problems for the Corinthian church." Stowers, *Letter Writing in Greco-Roman Antiquity*, 22.

based on an unequal distribution of speech and wisdom, but rather that the community understood its members as all possessing powerful speech and wisdom by virtue of their relationship with Christ.

Beginning with 1 Cor 1:17, a critique of worldly wisdom and eloquent, persuasive speech governs Paul's rhetoric, indicating the presence of *ekklēsia* discourse. With this verse, Paul initiates his challenge of the value of speech and wisdom practiced by the community. Indeed, Elizabeth Castelli views the relationship between power, speech, and knowledge as the most contested terrain between Paul and the Corinthians within this letter.[54] Paul constructs his own authority based on this relationship, even as he questions Corinthian power as exercised through speech and wisdom. Paul claims in 1 Cor 1:17 that his own ministry to the Corinthians lacked "eloquent wisdom" (οὐκ ἐν σοφίᾳ λόγου) which endangers the power of the cross. 1 Cor 1:17 bridges a discussion of Corinthian factionalism associated with different leaders to a later discussion contrasting God's wisdom with that of the world.[55] In this verse, Paul introduces the word σοφία[56] into the debate, indicating that the following argument about wisdom has some relationship to leadership—specifically his own. This disavowal of eloquent wisdom reappears in 1 Cor 2:1, where he again insists that his initial proclamation did not feature "lofty words or wisdom."[57] Likewise, in 1 Cor 2:4–5, Paul states that he did not use "persuasive words of wisdom" (ἐν πειθοῖς σοφίας λόγοις)[58] so that the Corinthians' faith did not rest on "human wisdom" (ἐν σοφίᾳ ἀνθρώπων). With these statements, Paul rhetorically constructs his image as a leader who neither values nor employs eloquent, persuasive speech, itself linked with worldly wisdom. With Pogoloff, one might conclude that Paul uses this claim to make a surprising break with the dominant culture in which persuasive, eloquent speech is so integral to "the Hellenistic role of the ideal public figure."[59] However, within *ekklēsia*

---

54. Castelli, "Interpretations of Power," 208.

55. For discussions over the "parties" and "slogans" represented in 1 Cor 12, see Conzelmann, *1 Corinthians*, 33–34; Mitchell, *Paul and the Rhetoric of Reconciliation*, 84–86.

56. Conzelmann notes the substitution of γνῶσις from 1:5 with σοφία in 1:17, but suggests that, as they are both linked with λόγος, their very interchange "shows that the two expressions cannot be strictly distinguished from each other." Conzelmann, *1 Corinthians*, 54.

57. ἦλθον οὐ καθ'ὑπεροχὴν λόγου ἢ σοφίας.

58. I follow the translation of Barrett and Conzelmann. For the challenging nature of manuscript variants for this verse, see Barrett, *First Epistle to the Corinthians*, 62; Conzelmann, *1 Corinthians*, 55.

59. Pogoloff, *Logos and Sophia*, 134.

discourse, such a claim can be construed not as a radical rejection of personal status and authority by the speaker—or yet again as a rather empty rhetorical strategy employed to gain audience favor[60]—but instead as an essential element in the elite speakers' negotiation of the power and authority of "the many."

From the classical period into the first century CE, Greek texts concerned with democracy reveal a tension centered on the role of elite orators. The democratic assembly required educated elite speakers who could provide the *dēmos* with wise advice and thoughtful options for future action. However, this recognition of elite rhetors' worth to the common people, the *idiōtai*,[61] was balanced by a fear that elite rhetors[62] would not serve the common good with wise advice.[63] Instead, Athenians harbored a strong anxiety that these orators would use their skills to deceive or mislead their audience, thus threatening the democratic process itself. As Ober explains, "The orator who put great store by his speaking ability was not merely unseemingly vain but threatened the whole state. He set himself above the decrees of the Assembly (e.g., Dem. 51.22) and believed that his ability to speak well gave him immunity from prosecution (Aristot. *Rhet.* 1372a11–17)."[64] In this atmosphere, elite speakers employed a variety of rhetorical strategies designed to preclude accusations that their own polished speech threatened the *dēmos*. In one such strategy, applied both to the assembly and court, the orator claimed that it was his opponents who were "sophists," well-trained, clever speakers that used rhetoric toward selfish or even evil ends.[65] An equally prevalent, and not unrelated, rhetorical *topos* found the speaker characterizing himself as unskilled and inexperienced at crafting rhetoric. This last strategy, the "unskilled speaker" *topos*,[66] became an especially useful element in the rhetor's tool kit.[67]

---

60. Martin, *The Corinthian Body*, 52.

61. In the classical period, this word came to denote a common citizen who was not a political expert. For this use, see Aeschines 3.233. However, Lycurgus (1.79) uses the word in a stricter sense, suggesting that all citizens not serving in magistracies or on juries were *idiōtai*. For further discussion, see Ober, *Mass and Elite*, 111.

62. Although classical authors often contrast the expert political speaker, the rhetor, with the *idiōtēs*, Ober explains that expert politicians were not a legally defined group. Ibid., 108.

63. Ibid., 165–68.

64. Ibid., 169.

65. For examples, see Dem. 35:40–43 and 19.246–50; Aeschin. 1.173.

66. This is Ober's description of the strategy. *Mass and Elite*, 177.

67. Cf. Lys.17.1; 31.2,4; Dem. 55.2; 1.19–20.

Ober explains that self-presentation as an inexpert or inexperienced speaker was one of the "fictions" in the democratic assembly that allowed elite leaders to make common cause with their audiences by signaling that they supported equality in the political realm.[68] At the same time, this rhetorical strategy could accomplish further benefits for a civic leader. The unskilled speaker *topos* also allowed an orator to make a significant truth claim. Speakers thereby asserted that they were using words supposedly so lacking in sophistication that they could only represent the truth—a truth entirely to the benefit of the audience.[69] By taking on the guise of the amateur citizen speaker, elite rhetors could also use this *topos* to persuade—and even critique—their audience, hinting that resistance to the speaker's proposals exposed the *dēmos'* preference for eloquence or entertainment over substance.[70] In most cases, the well-crafted orations of those employing this strategy revealed it to be an obvious fabrication.[71] As one of the finest orators of his age, Dio Chrysostom provides an excellent example of the elite rhetor who repeatedly, and with great eloquence, denies his ability to speak with any skill whatsoever.[72]

In 1 Corinthians, Paul's own finely chosen words for an *ekklēsia* audience undermine his claims of limited rhetorical ability.[73] As in the civic *ekklēsia*, I would suggest that Paul employs this *topos* toward reinforcing his leadership within the community, even as he also uses it to challenge the authority of his audience. Paul may present himself as an inadequate speaker in part to establish his credentials with a group primarily composed of non-elites. Scholars have commonly derived a description of the Corinthians' stratified class and status out of Paul's statement in 1:26 that few at the group's founding could be labelled well-born (εὐγενεῖς), powerful (δυνατοί), or wise "according to the flesh" (σοφοὶ κατὰ σάρκα) (1 Cor 1:26).[74] L. L. Welborn recognizes that these words, along with their paired

---

68. *Mass and Elite*, 191.

69. For classical instances of this rhetorical strategy, see Lys. 19.2; Dem. 21.141–42. This strategy also found its way into first-century oratory; see Dio, *Or.* 35.1.

70. Aeschin. 1.30–31; Dem. 18.138.

71. Ober, *Mass and Elite*, 175.

72. Dio provides particularly excellent examples of this strategy in *Or.* 12.15–16; 42.1–3; 47.1. This last speech was given to the civic assembly in Dio's native Prusa.

73. Martin, *The Corinthian Body*, 47–54. Schüssler Fiorenza has characterized Paul's rhetoric as deliberative discourse, in which the speaker appeals to the audience to make the correct decision for the future. Moreover, she notes that this is the type of rhetoric associated with the civic assembly. *Rhetoric and Ethic*, 121.

74. Meeks, *The First Urban Christians*, 67–69, 157–58; Theissen, *Social Setting*, 72; Welborn, *Politics and Rhetoric*, 23–24.

opposites used by Paul in the next verses, were associated not only with status but also with political allegiances in the ancient world. While "powerful," "wise," and "well-born" were often terms applied to wealthy supporters of oligarchy, the words "foolish" (μωροί), "weak" (ἀσθενεῖς), and "lowly born" (ἀγενεῖς) often appeared as descriptors for the economically disadvantaged supporters of democracy.[75] Rather than envisioning the "few" wealthy and powerful members of the community as his target audience in these early chapters of 1 Corinthians,[76] I suggest that Paul crafts his rhetoric toward the wider community dominated by non-elites. Indeed, Paul's exercise of the unskilled speaker *topos* is most easily explained as a strategy directed toward such a group. However, we must also explain Paul's transition from this initial sketch of the Corinthians in 1 Cor 1:26–28 to a description of the wider group with other status indicators such as powerful, rich, and royal (1 Cor 4:8–10). Paul's division of worldly and human wisdom is the key to this explanation. Together with the unskilled speaker *topos*, this conversation facilitates Paul's unique truth claims in the letter. At the same time, he appears to use both the inexpert speaker strategy and his characterization of wisdom to secure the role of the common man, the *idiōtēs*,[77] for himself—a role he sets against his construction of the Corinthians as "elites."

In 1 Cor 1:18, Paul commences a lengthy argument distinguishing two types of wisdom: the wisdom of God, and the wisdom of the world (1 Cor 1:20–21). This division of wisdom effectively divides human beings into two groups as well. Paul places himself among those who speak and possess divine wisdom. By contrast, Paul aligns the Corinthians with the inferior wisdom of the world.[78] Defining the two types of wisdom through association with other entities and concepts, Paul attributes to God's wisdom the message of the cross (1:18, 23; 2:2) and divine power (1:24; 2:4–5). This divine wisdom has an eternal quality manifested through the foolish and weak in the eyes of the world (1:27–28; 2:7). Moreover, only those who are

75. For Welborn's discussion, and classical examples, see Welborn, *Politics and Rhetoric*, 21–22.

76. Welborn, *Politics and Rhetoric*, 23–24: Martin, *The The Corinthian Body*, 67.

77. Significantly, in his ongoing conversation with the Corinthians, Paul uses this very terminology in 2 Corinthians 11:6 to describe himself, arguing that he is an "*idiōtēs* in speech" (ἰδιώτης τῷ λόγῳ) if not in knowledge.

78. Wire argues that in this discussion over speech and wisdom, Paul sets aside the "persona of the peacemaker" that he has assumed in order to deal with conflict in Corinth. In the wisdom discussion, by contrast, Wire contends that Paul "defends himself and shows he has been charged with not speaking wisdom in Corinth." Wire, *Corinthian Women Prophets*, 49–54. While I do not necessarily follow Wire in reading Paul as defending himself against a particular charge of not speaking wisdom, I agree with her that Paul uses arguments over speech and wisdom to defend his leadership.

mature and spiritual can recognize this wisdom (2:6, 13–15). Paul claims that it is this very wisdom which characterizes his own leadership. Paul's proclamation to the Corinthians embodied this wisdom, since it did not contain persuasive words, but "a demonstration of spirit and power" (ἐν ἀποδείξει πνεύματος καὶ δυνάμεως) linked with the very power of God (1 Cor 2:4). In fact, the very weakness and fear that Paul demonstrates in his proclamation (1 Cor 2:3) become assets since they illustrate his own separation from fleshly matters.

In stark contrast to divine wisdom, Paul establishes the inferiority of worldly wisdom by linking it with the human (2:5), the fleshly (3:1–4), and, by extension, with immaturity (2:6; 3:1–4). As the wisdom of God is by implication eternal, this other wisdom must be transitory. In fact, Paul ties this wisdom to the rulers of this age (ἀρχόντων τοῦ αἰῶνος τούτου) who are "doomed to perish" (2:6). Likewise, Paul ascribes this lesser wisdom to other groups, notably the scribe or debater (1:20),[79] and the "Greeks" who seek wisdom (1:22). Finally, Paul couples worldly wisdom with persuasive, eloquent speech, which becomes the antithesis of his own message of divine wisdom (1:17; 2:1; 2:4).

The connection of eloquent wisdom to certain groups significantly shapes the portrait that Paul develops of his Corinthian audience. Scholars have long sought to explain the connection between these groups that enables Paul to use them as a foil to divine wisdom. Recognition of the political valence of these words in the Hellenistic world reveals some of their rhetorical power in the early chapters of 1 Corinthians. With regard to the wise man, scribe, and debater of 1 Cor 1:20, scholars have often understood one or more of these figures as belonging to a Jewish context and associated the remaining terms with the Hellenistic world.[80] Arguably, a place also may be found for all three within the Greek democratic environment strongly associated with paired wisdom and speech—a pairing that also

---

79. This noun (συζητητής) is rarely used, found only here and in Ignatius' quotation of the verse in *Eph* 18:1. However, the verb (συζητεῖν) is more common. Mitchell notes that it is found elsewhere in the New Testament, both in the sense of "to discuss" (Mark 1:27; Luke 24:15) and "to dispute" (Mark 8:11; Luke 22:23). For a fuller discussion of the term, see Mitchell, *Paul and the Rhetoric of Reconciliation*, 87–88. See also Schneider, "συζητέω, κτλ," *TDNT* 7:747–48.

80. For instance, Mitchell reckons the wise man to be a Hellenistic moral-philosophical sage, the scribe is his Jewish counterpart, and the disputer is a combination of both. Mitchell, *Paul and the Rhetoric of Reconciliation*, 88. Martin takes a similar tack, explaining the scribe as Jewish, and the other two as Greco-Roman characters. The wise man is the "Hellenistic moral-philosophical sage" and the debater, "a rhetorically trained person who might join in actual or staged debates on any number of topics in a law court, a lecture hall, or a private home." Martin, *The Corinthian Body*, 47.

frames this passage in 1 Corinthians. Indeed, the focus on speech and wisdom that forms the context of this discussion means that the "wise person" (σοφός) may well designate the wise leader who applies his wisdom to political speech.[81] Meanwhile, although "scribe" (γραμματεύς) was certainly used in a Jewish context, it was also a common title for certain magistrates in the Greek democratic *polis*.[82] A first-century author like Plutarch attests this use (*An seni* 796E5), even as Acts 19:35 uses the term to describe an official associated with the Ephesian civic *ekklēsia*. Likewise, the extremely unusual συζητητής may be used in 1 Cor 1:20 to evoke not only, as Martin suggests, someone rhetorically trained for debate, but also someone who carried out such debate within a Greek political context. Finally, Paul uses ἀρχῶν in 1 Cor 2:6 and again in 2:8 as a key word to define the temporary and immature nature of wisdom "of this age." Dio Chrysostom and Plutarch show that, during the first century CE, this term could be employed as a general word for political leaders.[83] However, these authors also utilize the word ἀρχῶν according to its most common meaning in classical Athens: to signify an elected office-holder. Thus it was often used as a foil for "private citizens"—the *idiōtēs*.[84] Paul's description of those who crucified the Lord with the aid of this word (2:8) suggests that its meaning in 1 Corinthians may not be exhausted by its democratic connotations. Nevertheless, Paul clearly draws upon the term's association with political leadership. His rhetoric brings together the resonance of ἀρχῶν with that of "scribe," "wise man," "debater" and the "Greeks who seek wisdom" in order to craft a vision of those that Paul contends are "worldly" in their speech and wisdom. In this vision, Paul's construct is an influential figure who acts in a public,

81. In addition to the examples already provided, see Dio, *Or.* 47.3 and 52:11–12. The first of these passages uses the word σοφός to discuss the place of the philosopher—Mitchell's "Hellenistic moral-philosophical sage"—in the politics of his native Greek city.

82. Such an opposition between Jewish and Greek contexts can be misleading since scholars have shown that Jews and Greeks in the first century CE shared a common thought world that included shared political discourse. See further Rajak, "The Against Apion"; Feldman, *Josephus's Interpretation of the Bible*, 140–45.

83. Cf. Dio, *Or.* 3.127; 13.33; 56.2. Plutarch, *Sept. sap. conv.* 149 A; 151 A.

84. Lycurgus (1.79) suggests that the *politeia* is composed of three types of people: the ἀρχῶν, the juryman, and the *idiōtēs*. Dio (*Or.* 49.11) attests the usage of ἀρχῶν as an office in several places, notably in a speech in which he discusses his own candidacy for this office (see also *Or.* 47.19). Plutarch uses this terminology numerous times in his political treatises, *An seni respublica gerenda sit* and *Praecepta gerendae rei publicae*. I offer two particularly helpful examples: in *Praec. ger. rei publ.* 816 F, Plutarch discusses the limited amount of time that office-holders rule in a democracy; likewise, in the same treatise (813 C) Plutarch speaks of such offices as elected (χειροτονοῦσιν).

political context with "human" wisdom and speech as the hallmarks of leadership and authority.

By the beginning of chapter three, Paul has laid the necessary groundwork to establish that the Corinthians themselves possess inferior worldly, or human, wisdom. In 1 Cor 3:1, he describes the Corinthians as possessing the characteristics of this worldly wisdom, naming them "fleshly" (σαρκίνοις) and "infants in Christ" (νηπίοις ἐν Χριστῷ). Paul asserts continued jealousy and quarrelling in the community—including claims of allegiance to Paul and Apollos (3:4)—to support his contention that the Corinthians are not yet spiritual people (3:1). Because they are immature, fleshly, and contentious, the Corinthians can only be aligned with worldly wisdom and its accompaniment in Paul's rhetoric: eloquent and persuasive speech. Likewise, through association, they can be understood—like the ἀρχῶν, like the συζητητής—to be politically powerful by human standards. Nevertheless, Paul indicates that they are separated from true power and true wisdom. After praising their speech and knowledge in 1:5 as a fulfillment of their life in Christ, Paul now defines the Corinthians by wisdom and speech that lack divine power, and thus, has no place in the Christian *ekklēsia*.

Castelli reads "echoes of the competing discourse of Corinthian power" in Paul's arguments.[85] While Paul's arguments legitimize his own authority over and against his audience, even affording him a unique authority as builder and "father," Castelli hypothesizes that the "Corinthians as knowers and speakers seem to understand power as a fluid, surging quality, occupying different bodies at different moments and with varying intensities." This description of the community's exercise of power closely parallels ancient *ekklēsia* discourse and practice in which every citizen had the right to speech and thus to power that shifted with each new discussion and speaker. However, a recognition that Paul and the Corinthians do indeed participate in *ekklēsia* discourse allows us to be more specific about the exercise of authority, not only by individuals (Paul among them) but also by the community as an *ekklēsia*.

Paul attributes to his Corinthian audience paired "worldly" wisdom and persuasive speech, thus recalling the pairing of speech and wisdom in the *ekklēsia* by ancient authors from the classical period into the first century CE. These ancient authors largely judged democracy's success by the wisdom of speech on the part of citizen leaders and wise discernment of that speech by the *ekklēsia* itself. In the case of the Corinthian community, Paul's arguments not only suggest that the Corinthians looked for this type of wisdom among their leaders but also that, as a group, they also claimed

---

85. Castelli, "Interpretations of Power," 208–9.

excellence in speech and wisdom. Indeed, Paul's first appeal to the Corinthians as ones gifted in speech and wisdom indicates that, as a group, they saw themselves as possessing those very skills that defined both citizenship and superior leadership in the democratic city.[86] Within *ekklēsia* discourse, the right of each citizen to speech also rendered each member of the assembly as an active, discerning participant in the powerful whole of the *dēmos* itself. Each speaker coming before the assembly had to negotiate with this powerful *dēmos*, navigating possible critique and debate over their leadership. In 1 Corinthians, Paul intimates that debate within the community centers on his own leadership. Moreover, the signs of Corinthian debate over leadership accompany Paul's efforts to destabilize Corinthian confidence in the very speech and wisdom grounding their authority as an *ekklēsia*.

If one recognizes the prevalence of democratic discourse in Paul's rhetoric, one can see how he uses it to negotiate with an audience steeped in this discourse. Paul's rhetoric indicates that the Corinthians expected leadership through persuasive speech and that they understood themselves to be empowered to judge those who acted as leaders. At the same time, Paul's discussion of speech and wisdom works to privilege his voice as a leader in the community. The very act of persuasion that Paul uses in this effort shows that he is negotiating with the authority of the Corinthians in the model of an *ekklēsia* audience endowed with the power to make decisions. However, Paul also seeks to erode the community's authority relative to his own.

Paul may draw on the unskilled speaker *topos* in part to appeal to an audience that understood itself as a democratic *ekklēsia* because his strategy allows him to distance himself from negative understandings of elite orators in a democratic context. However, the use of this strategy in accompaniment to the division of human and divine wisdom also enables Paul to gain a significant rhetorical advantage over his audience. By denying his ability to use the persuasive speech that he associates with human leadership, Paul emphasizes his access to the divine truth not yet possessed by the Corinthians. Likewise, as Paul's rhetoric distances him from expert, wealthy politicians, this rhetoric also comes to equate the Corinthians with the very powerful elites that Paul aligns with human wisdom and eloquent speech. This contrast comes to a climax in 1 Cor 4:8–13 where the Corinthians are characterized as rich and fulfilled kings,[87] while Paul and his fellow apostles

---

86. Wire concurs that such an expectation shapes Paul's rhetoric. She notes that Paul focuses on oral expression in his exposition on wisdom—and suggests that he takes such a tack with the Corinthians because "they demand such speech of their leaders and are themselves speakers." Wire, *Corinthian Women Prophets*, 54.

87. ἤδη κεκορεσμένοι ἐστέ, ἤδη ἐπλουτήσατε, χωρὶς ἡμῶν ἐβασιλεύσατε (1 Cor 4:8). Wire (*Corinthian Women Prophets*, 168) describes this as a "complaint" against

are hungry, thirsty, weak, poorly clothed, and beaten. I would argue that Paul, with the aid of these comparisons, seeks to present the Corinthians themselves as suspect according to the standards of democratic discourse. Perhaps even more damaging within this discourse, Paul uses the distinction between worldly and divine wisdom to question the Corinthians' ability to arrive at truth through the very type of debate and judgment that characterizes the civic assembly—debate that is here directed toward Paul's own leadership.

Paul's challenge to Corinthian speech and collective judgment echoes ancient critics of democracy who question the capability of the gathered *dēmos* to govern effectively in the *ekklēsia*.[88] Such critique calls into question the legitimacy of the Corinthians as a governing body. Here, his portrayal of wisdom and speech as being of two types—divine and worldly—defines *ekklēsia* authority and participation heavily in Paul's favor. According to this redefinition, the wisdom and speech that Paul associates with the Corinthians can no longer be considered an effective basis for conducting the community's affairs or for arriving at truth. As in elite critiques of democratic government in the ancient world, Paul labels the Corinthians as immature because their wisdom is shown to be lacking in critical ways. Their worldly speech and wisdom fall short of that essential truth related to God and to Christ and, by Paul's account, can only lead further away from such truth. Meanwhile, Paul asserts possession of the infinitely better, yet mysterious, divine wisdom and speech, thus placing himself among the ones who judge all things yet are subject to no one else's judgment (1 Cor 2.15).

---

Corinthian claims of power based in the resurrection, while Martin (*The Corinthian Body*, 65–66) considers this to be an ironic contrast meant to critique the few among the Corinthians who were exalting themselves over others. However, it is worth noting that this characterization of the *ekklēsia* as "king" also finds a place in first-century discussions of democracy, as we can see in Dio's suggestion (*Or.* 32.27–28) that the power of the gathered assembly can be manifested in resemblance to a reasonable and righteous king, or perversely, in approximating a cruel tyrant.

88. One can hear echoes of a range of democracy's critics in 1 Corinthians. Certainly Paul shares the concerns voiced by an author like Thucydides, namely that *ekklēsia* audiences appreciated eloquence over true wisdom. This comes through clearly in the famous speeches recorded by Thucydides for Cleon and Diodotus (Thuc. 3.37.1–48.2). A concern for the wisdom of the governing *dēmos* also comes through in discussions of "excessive" freedom which means that "even women and slaves" have a freedom that matches that of citizens. For this critique, see Plato, *Resp.* 8.557 B. Likewise, concern about democracy centers on the idea that this political system is a tyranny of the poor and the disadvantaged, and that a *dēmos* dominated by the poor will only seek their own interests rather than the best and wisest course for the city as a whole. See Plato, *Resp.* 8. 557 A; Aristotle, *Pol.* 1279 B–1280 A; 1290 A–B; Ps.-Xen. [*Ath.*] i.4–9. See also Isoc., *De Pace* 8.128.

When Paul associates himself with superior, divine wisdom, he appropriates an authority that he denies to the Corinthian *ekklēsia*. Indeed, Paul appeals to this divine authority in arguing that he is impervious to the Corinthians' judgment (1 Cor 2:14; 4:3–4). An awareness of *ekklēsia* discourse allows the reader of 1 Corinthians to discern the ways in which Paul's rhetoric works not to affirm his "authority as an apostle among apostles," but rather to negotiate with the Corinthians' own power in a bid to establish Paul's unique claims to authority as the community's "sole founder and father."[89] I would argue that Paul rhetorically sustains his claims to unique authority by introducing the issue of division into the community's discussion. In these terms, Paul may be understood to reinterpret Corinthian debates over leadership and shared governance—debates which are themselves located in democratic discourse—as divisive party strife illustrating Corinthian immaturity.[90] However, the most serious division that Paul introduces into these early chapters regards the nature of wisdom and speech. Paul's rhetoric indicates that the Corinthians envision themselves as transformed in Christ.[91] Indeed, Schüssler Fiorenza describes the contents of 1 Corinthians as follows: "The whole letter documents this baptismal self-understanding of the many who were nothing in the eyes of the world before their call, but who now have freedom, knowledge, wisdom, riches, and power over their own bodies and life in their new kinship-community."[92] According to this description, the Corinthians would most likely consider their democratic power of speech and decision to be based in their new relationship with the risen Christ. However, Paul undercuts this very claim to be unified in superior speech and wisdom, contending instead that only a limited number of Christians speak "true," divine wisdom. With the intimation that the Corinthians do not speak this wisdom, Paul questions the very basis for Corinthian power as a discerning assembly. In the context of such *ekklēsia* discourse, Paul carefully fashions his arguments toward an assembly with the authority to make communal decisions. At the same time, Paul rhetorically undermines the authority of this body to debate and to critique his own leadership.

---

89. Schüssler Fiorenza, *Rhetoric and Ethic*, 119. Schüssler Fiorenza notes that Paul's claim that he has begotten the community as father, and that he has the power to command and punish, demonstrates that he intends more than simply asserting that "he shared access to divine power for building up the community and the Corinthians and other apostles" and thus has status as an apostle among other apostles. Similarly Castelli, "Interpretations of Power," 213–14.

90. Ibid., 118

91. Wire, *Corinthian Women Prophets*, 31, 187.

92. Schüssler Fiorenza, *Rhetoric and Ethic*, 122.

## Conclusion

My interpretation of the early chapters of 1 Corinthians in terms of *ekklēsia* discourse indicates that Paul constructs his authority and directs his message to a community deeply informed by the logic of Greek democracy. I have shown that into the first century CE, a vital democratic discourse constructed citizenship, civic participation, and leadership in terms of public speech of the *ekklēsia*. Moreover, authors belonging to the early empire retained the classical connection of that speech to wisdom on the part of speakers and audiences alike. Scholars such as Betz, Martin, and Welborn have contextualized the pairing of speech and wisdom in 1 Corinthians within ancient rhetoric.[93] However, they have not considered the place of this rhetoric in democratic discourse centered on the *ekklēsia*, thus overlooking Paul's subtle power negotiation with his Corinthian audience. With an awareness of democratic discourse, Paul's division of speech and wisdom into worldly and divine types becomes not just a theological claim but also a fundamentally political one. Recognizing Paul's rhetorical exercise of power through the deployment of *ekklēsia* discourse reveals the Corinthians' understanding of their own authority as a discerning assembly made up of participants with equal voice. In turn, such a reading of the argument precludes acceptance of Paul as a univocal source of authority and theology and instead foregrounds his debates and negotiation with a diverse audience. Viewing the Corinthian church as a democratic assembly—where all participants share a right to leadership through deliberative speech, and all listeners share a claim to judgment—reconfigures our understanding of Paul's own leadership, as well as our expectations for the way the community might respond to a letter like 1 Corinthians.

A recognition of *ekklēsia* discourse in the first century CE not only illuminates Paul's initial rhetorical strategies in 1 Corinthians but it also brings into high relief later passages of this letter that display the *topos* of speech. As I have demonstrated, speech holds special significance within democratic discourse as that action by which citizenship is realized—an action that further defines freedom and equality as they exist within democracy. In the next chapters, I extend this analysis of democratic discourse to later parts of the letter that also center on *ekklēsia* speech. In these chapters, I interrogate Paul's rhetoric for further insights into the construction of citizenship in the Corinthian assembly. Specifically, I will question the ways in which we may revise our understanding of women's citizenship and

---

93. Betz, "The Problem of Rhetoric and Theology"; Martin, *The Corinthian Body*; Welborn, *Politics and Rhetoric*.

participation in this community in light of ancient democratic discourse. I will show that Paul's own rhetoric genders speech in order to solidify the boundaries he seeks to create regarding Corinthian citizenship. In the current chapter, I have demonstrated that the presence of *ekklēsia* discourse in 1 Corinthians reconfigures our understanding of the exercise of communal and individual exercise of power in this group. Moving forward, I suggest that we must not only question how such discourse circumscribed Paul's rhetoric and authority but also how it may have empowered the full range of individuals claiming citizenship in the Christian *ekklēsia*.

# 5

# The Gendering of Democratic Participation

## Introduction

IN THE EARLY CHAPTERS OF 1 CORINTHIANS, PAUL ENHANCES HIS OWN AUthority while undermining that of the Corinthians by asserting difference with regard to speech and wisdom. Paul defines his own wisdom and speech as superior to that of the Corinthians, even as he asserts divisions regarding wisdom within the community. In yet another respect, Paul asserts difference in speech among the Corinthians. He also deeply genders speech in 1 Cor 11:2–16, deploying cosmology, the Genesis creation narratives, and the *topoi* of hair and veiling toward a construction of women's speech as disordered and lacking in reason and intellect. As I have shown in previous chapters, speech and its discernment in the *ekklēsia* context marked citizenship in the discourse and practice of the Greek democratic *polis*. Meanwhile, those deploying this democratic discourse regularly identify wisdom associated with reason and self-control as the necessary ingredient if such speech and discernment is to benefit the *polis*. Within *ekklēsia* discourse, a gendering of speech that asserts essential difference between men and women's speech in wisdom and self-control has profound implications regarding citizenship and leadership. Indeed, Paul's rhetoric in this passage can also be located in democratic discourse in which speech is gendered as part of the policing of the boundary between the free, male, native-born citizen, and the non-citizens of the Greek *polis*, children, foreigners, and the women and slaves Charles Hedrick calls "utter anticitizens."[1] At the same time, the indication in 1 Corinthians that women were speaking and

---

1. Hedrick, "The Zero Degree of Society," 302. Hedrick makes the point that in contrast to children or metics, women and slaves do not have the potential to gain full citizenship.

discerning in the community assembly also registers the ongoing tensions and contest in this discourse around women's speech and citizenship represented in ancient texts from the classical period forward.

In this chapter, I will first consider gendering of speech within ancient democratic discourse and attend to the way that assertions of gender difference constructed the speech of women as unsuited for the *ekklēsia* context. However, I will also explore the tensions in the discourse regarding women's public, political speech that show the negotiations, the debates, and potential inherent in this same democratic discourse toward women's inclusion as citizens.

I will finish with an examination of 1 Cor 11:2–16. In these verses, Paul genders speech and speakers in the Corinthian community, grounding women's essential difference and inferiority in a divinely given hierarchy. As in the wider *ekklēsia* discourse of the Greco-Roman world, such a reification of gender boundaries regarding the type of speech and wisdom at home in the *ekklēsia* context serves the contention that women are unsuited to performance of citizenship and instead contribute dangerous disorder to the public, political context. As I will show, this construction of gender has implications not only for the free women of the Corinthian community but also for the slaves as well. Certainly, I will show that women and slaves were often addressed together in ancient democratic discourse and found wanting as citizens according to a similar logic.

If this chapter traces Paul's argumentation toward the foreclosure of women's full citizenship in the Corinthian *ekklēsia*, it will also demonstrate that Paul's rhetorical arguments in 1 Cor 11 suggest an audience that does engage the radical potential of democratic discourse to extend citizenship to the full range of *polis* inhabitants—including slaves and women. For the Corinthians, such radical potential seems to be strengthened by the spiritual and social transformation of baptism set forth in a formula like Gal 3:28, a formula which promises that in Christ, "There is no longer Jew or Greek, there is no longer slave or free, there is no longer male and female." Though Paul's argumentation in 1 Cor 11:2–16 has been powerfully deployed so as to enforce hierarchy within the church context and beyond, I contend that the activity of the Corinthians and the counter-argument suggested by Paul's own rhetoric reveals the radical potential for equality and freedom for *all* members of the Christian *ekklēsia*—a radical potential facilitated by both democratic discourse and the theological claims of the earliest followers of Jesus as Christ.

# I. Gendering of Speech/Wisdom within Democratic Discourse

## *The Logic of Exclusion and Citizen Identity*

The last chapter shows that a construction of democratic citizenship informs Paul's rhetoric in 1 Corinthians. In classical Athens, where it originated, this construction of citizenship applied to a broad range of the population. By the fifth century, all free, native-born males over eighteen years old, rich and poor, urban and rural dweller, met together in the civic *ekklēsia*. As Philip Manville points out, this citizenship had little of the passive, abstract legal status we assign to the term in the modern world. Instead, citizenship in the classical, democratic *polis* was defined by the active, public participation of the individual in the day-to-day politics of the city.[2] By the fourth century, citizens received pay for serving in the *ekklēsia* or court, thus making such civic involvement more realistic and practical for the full range of citizens. Even as this large, politically active citizen body came into being, Athenian law and practice intensified the boundary between the citizen and the non-citizen within the *polis*.

By the time of Kleisthenes, free-born Athenians could no longer become debt slaves. The "sanctity of their persons," their claim to freedom as citizens, was guaranteed.[3] Likewise, by the time of Kleisthenes, Athenian law restricted citizenship only to those who had an Athenian father—a law later emended to require that both parents of a citizen were free-born Athenians.[4] For foreigners, the path to citizenship also became more difficult during the time of Kleisthenes. All these reforms solidified the citizen boundary, with free, native-born, adult males on one side, and non-citizens—women, slaves, foreigners, and children—on the other. In turn, the meaning and value of citizenship in the democratic *polis* came to be defined against non-citizenship. With no groups is this process more clear than with the "utter anticitizens" of the classical *polis*: women and slaves.[5]

2. Manville, *The Origins of Citizenship*, 5.

3. Ibid.

4. Under Pericles, the Athenians passed a law in 451 BCE requiring "Athenian parentage on both sides" for citizenship. Moreover, as time went on, "mixed marriages" of citizens and non-citizens came to be highly penalized in Athens. Hansen, *The Athenian Democracy*, 53.

5. The case of women is particularly complex when it comes to the question of citizenship. As I will show, free born women were effectively excluded from political participation. However, their status as citizens "counted" when it came to producing the children who would be future citizens of the *polis*.

Sheldon Wolin describes democracy as essentially different from other political systems in that, "It was and is the only political ideal that condemns its own denial of equality and inclusion."[6] In these terms, the exclusions of classical democracy may have formed the "constitutive outside"[7] of the citizen subject, but these exclusions were also sources of tension and struggle in a discourse characterized by the promise of equality to "the many." In democratic discourse, the exclusions of women and slaves in particular were justified with assertions of essential difference and inferiority from the socially perfect citizen. The constant reiteration of those differences served to foreclose the possibility of women and slaves acting as full citizens, even as the very necessity of that reiteration attests the possibilities of disrupting the citizen boundary.

In the *Politics*, Aristotle gives one notable performance of the logic of exclusion and citizen identity. While Aristotle has been described as an antidemocratic writer, his own participation in democratic discourse registers with his definition of the ἄνθρωπος. Aristotle argues that the *polis* is the natural *telos* of various human partnerships, even as the human is by nature a political animal (ὁ ἄνθρωπος φύσει πολιτικὸν ζῷον).[8] Moreover, Aristotle contends that this political identity results because humans alone of the other animals possess speech as well as the ability to exercise wisdom (φρόνησις) and virtue (ἀρετή).[9] Here, Aristotle naturalizes the broad enfranchisement of Athenian citizenship with his contention that speech, wisdom, and virtue are inherent possessions of the human being. Those very qualities and abilities that come to characterize successful democratic participation are constructed as the natural and, arguably, most essential qualities of the fully realized human being, the person Aristotle identifies elsewhere as the free, male citizen. When Aristotle describes the nature of women and slaves, these same qualities and abilities are marked by their lack or defect.

Holt Parker suggests that Aristotle's arguments regarding women and slaves are part of his larger reasoning strategy of "resolving" contradictions regarding appearance or phenomenon. In the case of women and slaves, "There is a phenomenon: slaves and women appear to be fully human and rational. There is a contradiction: if so, it would be wrong to rule over them

---

6. Wolin, "Transgression, Equality, and Voice," 80.

7. With this language, I am indebted to Butler's consideration of citizenship as constructed by discourse of sex and gender. Butler, *Bodies that Matter*, 3, 49.

8. Aristotle, *Pol.* 1253a1–5.

9. Ibid., 65–66. Aristotle, *Pol.* 1253a10–35.

absolutely."[10] Indeed, Aristotle here confronts the essential dilemma for anyone who might want to justify exclusions of certain groups from democratic citizenship. If these groups are indeed fully human with the ability to rationally speak and deliberate, then their exclusion is no longer morally or logically justified within the discourse of democracy. Aristotle himself appeals to nature in order to claim that appearances in this case are misleading since women and slaves are morally and intellectually different from the male citizen.

Aristotle's arguments about the nature of women and slaves are intertwined through the early part of the *Politics*. As a first step to establishing a social hierarchy, Aristotle investigates the relationship of those "unable to exist without one another." Here, Aristotle begins with the union between female and male for the continuation of the species. He uses this pairing as the basis for his next argument from nature: that there is likewise a union of those naturally suited to rule and with those inherently inclined to being ruled. In this pairing, the ruler is distinguished from the natural slave by the ability to "foresee with his mind."[11] With this train of logic, Aristotle introduces several themes that become essential to his insistence that neither slaves nor women can be placed on a level plane with citizens. On the one hand, he argues that slaves and women are each part of a natural whole. Moreover, he establishes the idea of hierarchy within such pairings that he will further develop with respect to both women and slaves going forward. Parker contends that these two initial pairings are foundational to the arguments about difference and subordination that Aristotle makes in the *Politics*. The male/female division furnishes Aristotle with an example of natural difference, while by definition the master/slave division demonstrates hierarchy. "Aristotle's primary move here is to blur the two categories as much as possible. He will establish a vocabulary and use analogies that are valid for one case and then subtly apply them to the other."[12]

Aristotle naturalizes the social hierarchy in which women and slaves play a part by extrapolating yet another pairing—that of soul and body. The relationship of soul and body illustrates Aristotle's outright contention that "in every composite thing, where a plurality of parts, whether continuous or discreet, is combined to make a single whole, there is always found a ruling

---

10. Parker, "Aristotle's Unanswered Questions," 75. For Aristotles's formulation of this question, see *Pol.* 1259b35–40.

11. Τὸ μὲν γὰρ δυνάμενον τῇ διανοίᾳ προορᾶν ἄρχον φύσει. *Pol.* 1252a32 (Rackham, LCL).

12. Ibid., 77.

and a subject factor."[13] With regard to the soul and body that together compose every animal, the soul is the obvious master of the body, controlling the "appetites" and emotions. Aristotle contends that for the individual "animal" this relationship of ruler soul to ruled body is highly advantageous, and its reversal can only be harmful. Likewise, Aristotle presents as advantageous other "natural" hierarchies. Man is superior to animals, even as "the male is by nature superior and the female inferior, the male ruler and the female subject."[14] The slave also benefits as the subordinate to a master since he "participates in reason so far as to apprehend it but not to possess it."[15]

Aristotle clinches his argument that women and slaves exist as subordinates that are naturally ruled, and never the reverse, by insisting that their soul—and by extension their virtue—is essentially distinct from that of *polis* citizens. He first divides the soul itself into dual virtues, the rational (λόγος) virtue which rules, and the irrational (ἀλόγος) which is ruled. In the case of women, slaves, and children, Aristotle claims that they possess the soul differently than the free adult male. He writes, "And all possess the various parts of the soul, but possess them in different ways; for the slave has not got the deliberative part at all, and the female has it, but without full authority, while the child has it, but in an undeveloped form."[16] This description precludes all three from rule since, "the ruler must possess intellectual virtue in completeness."[17] Moreover, Aristotle uses this vision of the soul's possession as the basis for his contention that all possess the moral virtues, "but not in the same way, but in such measure as is proper to each in relation to his own function." In the case of courage, for instance, the man has the "courage of command, and the other that of subordination."[18] Aristotle further illustrates this difference in virtue by citing Sophocles, "Silence gives grace to a woman"[19]—a clear contrast to male virtue based in rational speech.

13. Aristotle, *Pol.* 1254a29-31. ὅσα γὰρ ἐκ πλειόνων συνέστηκε καὶ γίνεται ἕν τι κοινόν, εἴτε ἐκ συνεχῶν εἴτ' ἐκ διῃρημένων, ἐν ἅπασιν ἐμφαίνεται τὸ ἄρχον καὶ τὸ ἀρχόμενον.

14. Ibid., 1254b13-15. ἔτι δὲ τὸ ἄρρεν πρὸς τὸ θῆλυ φύσει τὸ μὲν κρεῖττον τὸ δὲ χεῖρον, τὸ μὲν ἄρχον τὸ δ' ἀρχόμενον.

15. Ibid., 1254b22-25.

16. Ibid., 1260a12-15. Καὶ πᾶσιν ἐνυπάρχει μὲν τὰ μόρια τῆς ψυχῆς, ἀλλ' ἐνυπάρχει διαφερόντως· ὁ μὲν γὰρ δοῦλος ὅλως οὐκ ἔχει τὸ βουλευτικόν, τὸ δὲ θῆλυ ἔχει μέν, ἀλλ' ἄκυρον, ὁ δὲ παῖς ἔχει μέν, ἀλλ' ἀτελές.

17. Ibid., 1260a15. Διὸ τὸν μὲν ἄρχοντα τελέαν ἔχειν δεῖ τὴν διανοητικὴν ἀρετήν.

18. Ibid., 1260a23.

19. Ibid., 1260a31. Γυναικὶ κόσμον ἡ σιγὴ φέρει. Here, he quotes Sophocles, *Ajax* 293.

Ultimately, Aristotle justifies the exclusion of women and slaves from citizenship not only by arguing that they are naturally subordinate to the free, adult male but also by locating that subordination in their lack of rationality, their very inability to deliberate. Women and slaves may appear to be fully human like male citizens, and they may even understand reason, but their natures preclude them from exercising such reason in the way a citizen, a natural ruler, would. Women's lack of reason, and by implication their inability to control their appetites and emotions, means that the virtue befitting this group is silence—the absence of the very deliberative speech that characterizes citizenship.

With this discussion, Aristotle participates in the wider construction of women (and slaves) within democratic discourse as incapable of citizenship. Though his argumentation on this topic may be more sustained than other classical authors, his key suppositions are echoed by other writers. Like Aristotle, these authors present women as essentially different than men, distinguished by their lack of rationality and judgment. In turn, this lack of rationality means a lack of self-control—an inability for women to govern their appetites or desires. Such a construction appears in Xenophon's *Symposium* where Socrates remarks, "Woman's nature is really not at all inferior to man's, except in its lack of judgment and physical strength."[20] Euripides, too, attests to this common explanation of women's inherent abilities, writing in *Hippolytus*, "But will you say that folly (τὸ μῶρον) is not to be found in men but is native to women?"[21] In his prosecution of Timarchus, Aeschines draws on these perceived differences between men and women to suggest, "a woman does wrong according to her nature."[22] Aeschines insists that it is wrong to condemn a woman for acting according to her nature while allowing the man who has done wrong against his to serve as a speaker, an adviser in the assembly.[23] Meanwhile, Aeschines' contemporary, the orator Demosthenes, submits that a man may be found incompetent when compromised by old age, drugs, disease, madness—and "the influence of a women."[24]

The portrayal of women as essentially "other" than the male citizen with regard to reason and self-control facilitates the assertions by Aristotle

---

20. Xenophon, *Symp.* 2.9–12 (Todd, LCL). ἡ γυναικεία φύσις οὐδὲν χείρων τῆς τοῦ ἀνδρὸς οὖσα τυγχάνει, γνώμης δὲ καὶ ἰσχύος δεῖται.

21. Euripides, *Hipp.* 966–70 (Kovacs, LCL). ἀλλ᾽ ὡς τὸ μῶρον ἀνδράσιν μὲν οὐκ ἔνι, γυναιξὶ δ᾽ ἐμπέφυκεν;

22. Aeschines, *Tim.* 185 (Adams, LCL).

23. Ibid.

24. Dem. 46.16 (Vince, LCL). γυναικὶ πειθόμενον

and others that women had no place in the public sphere. Rather, women found virtue both in the home and in their very lack of voice. As I have shown, Aristotle himself quotes one such witness to women's silence as virtue in Sophocles' *Ajax*. Sophocles' fellow playwrights offer further examples. Euripides' Macaria asks pardon for coming into the public sphere, since, "For a woman silence and discretion are the most honorable, along with staying in the home."[25] In *Seven Against Thebes*, Aeschylus also genders virtue and action along the same lines. Here, the character Eteocles addresses women of Thebes to say that matters of the city are a man's affair,[26] while "your business is to keep quiet and stay in the house."[27]

In the classical period, a construction of women as intellectually compromised and lacking in self-control served the foreclosure of their vocal participation in the public politics of the democratic *polis*. Nevertheless, classical authors convey considerable anxiety that women would not necessarily stay in the subservient position mapped out for them. Indeed, some of this anxiety involves democracy itself and its radical potential for empowering even those "utter anticitizens," women and slaves.

Two notable critics of democracy, the Old Oligarch and Aristotle certainly find great cause for concern in the very blurring of the citizenship boundary possible under the democratic system. In his fifth-century critique, the Old Oligarch airs such concerns directly following a conversation in which he decries the democratic system that "allows even the worst people to speak."[28] The Old Oligarch complains that in Athens you also find great licentiousness among the slaves and resident foreigners (metics), and that this licentiousness results from a system in which even slaves are not visibly different in appearance or dress from the individuals making up the "*dēmos*." In fact, the Old Oligarch points out the danger of hitting a slave in Athens where one might accidentally hit a citizen.[29] According to this author, the *dēmos* depends on the labor and money of slaves and metics, especially with regard to the fleet, to the point that Athenians have established "equality" between these groups and the citizens.[30] The choice

---

25. Euripides, *Heracl.* 475 (Kovacs, LCL); my translation. Γυναικὶ γὰρ σιγή τε καὶ τὸ σωφρονεῖν κάλλιστον εἴσω θ' ἥσυχον μένειν δόμων.

26. Aeschylus, *Sept.* 200–204 (Smyth, LCL). He adds, "Let no woman advise (βουλευέτω) on such matters"; my translation.

27. Ibid. 230–232. Σὸν δ' αὖ τὸ σιγᾶν καὶ μένειν εἴσω δόμων.

28. Pseudo-Xenophon, [Ath.] 1.6 (Bowersock, LCL). ἐῶντες καὶ τοὺς πονηροὺς λέγειν.

29. Ibid., 1.10.

30. Ibid., 1.11.

of vocabulary in this passage is significant. The Old Oligarch uses the word ἰσηγορία to denote equality given to these non-citizen groups. As I have discussed, this word defined freedom of speech within classical democracy and, by extension, the equality of all citizens. The Old Oligarch's critique here runs deeper than a complaint that slaves and metics look, and even act, too much like citizens. Instead, the use of this particular vocabulary suggests that the citizen boundary has been fully breached. Slaves and metics have appropriated the very right that makes them fully indistinguishable from their citizen neighbors. In turn, the Old Oligarch has given further weight to his earlier protest that democracy makes it possible for "the worst people to speak."[31]

Aristotle also expresses the concern that democracy may lead to the iniquity of non-citizens as well as the transgression of citizen boundaries. Aristotle' reservations with democratic government register in his exposition over the best and worst of the types of democracy. For Aristotle, the best democratic government is that in which the citizens are primarily agricultural workers, small land holders, whose work on the land and distance from the city limits their active involvement in politics. As a result, they can attend only a limited number of assemblies per year.[32] In this type of democracy, the best and highest offices would be held by those owning significant property or by those chosen on the grounds of capacity. Aristotle suggests that this will lead to a balance between the common people and the notables since the "best" will not be ruled by their inferiors, and the *dēmos* will be able to hold these magistrates to account through audits. Thus, Aristotle's superior democracy manifests with an agricultural *dēmos* possessing little time to carry out politics, dominated in its highest offices by the wealthiest citizens.

For Aristotle, the quality of democracy is lessened with each additional category of people registered as citizens. Thus, the worst form of democracy is that one in which "all" share rule. Indeed, this form of the *dēmos* comes into being by blurring the citizen boundaries Aristotle upholds, as the illegitimate and men with only one citizen parent are recognized as citizens. Not only does this type of democracy antagonize the notables and create disorder but Aristotle argues that this democracy also facilitates elements of tyranny. He names these elements as the license (ἀναρχία) of women, slaves, and children combined with the indulgence to "live as one likes."[33]

---

31. Ibid., 1.6.
32. Aristotle, *Pol.* 1318b10–15 (Rackham, LCL).
33. Aristotle, *Pol.* 1319b27–31. Τὸ ζῆν ὅπως τις βούλεται.

Together, Aristotle and the Old Oligarch's critiques register not only the inclusiveness of a wide range of the male population as citizens in democracies of their time period but also the possibility inherent in democratic discourse of extending citizenship to an even wider group. For these authors, the empowerment and active involvement of such a range of citizens engenders disorder and the transgression of boundaries that keep women, metics, slaves, and children as voiceless, non-political members of the *polis*. These authors thus witness the possibility of disruption, the "constitutive instabilities," in the construction of citizenship in the classical *polis*. Certainly the "gaps and fissures" of democratic discourse and citizenship are visible in other classical texts.

## *Women and Speech in Ekklesiazusae*

Before turning to the gendering of democratic discourse in the first-century, I want to visit one last classical text that proves especially valuable in demonstrating the instability of a citizen boundary maintained according to gender difference. Aristophanes' *Ekklesiazusae* offers a comedic scenario in which women become political actors in the assembly itself, using the legal conventions of that context to assume citizenship, and ultimately rule of the *polis*. The play opens with a gathering of women who reveal their preparations to infiltrate the assembly in order to gain a vote that will allow them to take over civic government from their male counterparts. To bring about this outcome, the women have taken on the appearance of men. Not only do they put on their husbands' clothing but they also have darkened their skin with tanning and have become "hairy." The women have abandoned shaving so that their hairy bodies will resemble those of men, and they bring false beards to don for the assembly.

The women match these physical preparations with practicing the type of speech fit for the assembly. During this practice session, the women, especially their leader Praxagora, show their apprehension and exercise of the conventions of assembly speech. Despite occasional mishaps (for instance, invoking the "two goddesses" and Aphrodite for their oaths),[34] Praxagora and her fellow speakers utilize phrases and rhetorical strategies strongly tied to the *ekklēsia*—including the claim not to be the best or most well trained speaker.[35] Praxagora, in particular, practices well-crafted rhetoric that earns the admiration of her companions for its quality and "wisdom"

---

34. Aristophanes, *Eccl.* 155, 189 (Henderson, LCL).

35. Such a claim to modest speaking talents can be seen at: Aristophanes, *Eccl.* 151.

(σοφή).³⁶ When asked where she learned to speak so skillfully, Praxagora says that she learned assembly speech when she lived near the Pnyx³⁷ and listened to the speeches given there. Indeed, Praxagora and her companions mobilize democratic discourse not only in their conventions of speech and argumentation but also in the claim that they speak in order to serve the common good of the city and its citizens.³⁸

Josiah Ober observes that the use of *ekklēsia* conventions in the first scene of *Ekklesiazusae* alerts the audience that this "play will mix together two seemingly incompatible categories: women—who were denied a political role in the *polis* as a function of their gender—and the political business of the assembly."³⁹ Certainly this is a "comic extension of the democratic-egalitarian ethos" beyond the usual male citizen boundary. However, Ober argues that this comedy does not represent a true overturning of Athenian practice and ideology. Praxagora and her companions exploit the "institutional machinery of the democratic state and its associated ideologies" to bring about comprehensive social change.⁴⁰ Aristophanes writes for an audience well aware of both democracy's track record and the potential for enacting social change that upset traditional hierarchies of power. The more challenging proposition for the playwright, and the one that Ober suggests determines the critical "bite" of the play, is to convince his audience that women had the capacity to exercise public, political power effectively—or even at all.⁴¹

In several respects, Aristophanes undermines "natural" gender differences used to justify and reinforce the idea that only biological males could exercise democratic citizenship. In the initial scene, the women's preparation to attend the assembly highlights a number of common gender indicators in ancient society. In fact, their preparations suggest a certain mutability of physical characteristics associated with gender. To "become men" in appearance they have only to put on men's clothes, false beards, and to change their bodies by allowing hair to grow in areas where they usually shaved it. Likewise, the telling whiteness of their skin connected to their life in the "private" realm of the home can be altered through exposure to the sun. Authors like Caroline Vander Stichele, Todd Penner, and Maud Gleason have shown that in antiquity hair was effective as a rhetorical tool

36. Ibid., 245.
37. The location for the Athenian assembly.
38. Aristophanes, *Eccl.* 105–10; 208–10.
39. Ober, *Political Dissent*, 129.
40. Ibid., 127.
41. Ibid., 130.

for asserting ontological gender difference and for crafting arguments about behavior and practice for individuals within the "body politic."[42] In his play, Aristophanes suggests that far from being a "natural" gender indicator, difference in hair between women and men is "an artifact of voluntary human action."[43] In these terms, difference in hair between the genders actually diverges from the natural tendency of women and men to have a similar amount and type of hair.

Questioning the construction of gender according to physical indicators certainly undermines a vision of essential and immutable gender difference. In turn, this has significant implications for a political system and discourse that bases its exclusions of women on an essentialist understanding of gender. However, Aristophanes offers an even more serious challenge to the exclusion of women from democracy in his portrayal of their capacity for rational thought and speech. The initial scene of the play finds these women fulfilling a carefully constructed plan, developed through an earlier process of democratic deliberation. Indeed, the phrase Praxagora uses to describe their earlier agreement, "it seemed right to my friends" (ἔδοξε ταῖς ἐμαῖς φίλαις), echoes the enactment formula of the assembly, "it seemed right to the *dēmos*" (ἔδοξε τῷ δήμῳ).[44] This phrasing indicates that the women have already acted out *ekklēsia* speech and deliberation, foreshadowing their success at the *Pnyx*.

The women further exhibit their ability to be members of the *ekklēsia* both in their initial practice session and in a later persuasive speech that Praxagora gives to a group of men that includes her own husband. In this practice session, Aristophanes does not entirely dispense with standard gender constructions, and in this first scene women express a fondness for alcohol and sex that squares with a vision of women strongly influenced by their appetites. However, their planning, their ability to keep secrets, and their gradual mastery of "male" *ekklēsia* speech all show that the women do possess self-control and rationality. Praxagora's speech, in particular, showcases a woman's ability to exercise wisdom and forethought in a political speech designed to benefit the city in which she claims an equal stake. Her explanation for her speaking skill implies that lack of exposure limits a woman's ability to perform political speech—not any inborn deficiency. In her persuasive speech later in the play, Praxagora further asserts that women possess good judgment in addition to their thrifty ability to manage

---

42. Penner and Vander Stichele, "Paul and the Rhetoric of Gender," 306; Gleason, *Making Men*, 113.

43. Gleason, *Making Men*, 136.

44. Aristophanes, *Eccl.* 18. Ober, *Political Dissent*, 129.

money.⁴⁵ This speech defending women's right to rule and laying out their plans for the *polis* again substantiates women's ability to practice the persuasive speech and wisdom required of democratic citizens.

Aristophanes' *Ekklesiazusae* confronts a similar question to the one that Aristotle poses at the beginning of the *Politics*. Do women have the same intellectual and speaking capabilities as male citizens? If so, how can their perpetual subjugation be justified? Aristotle answers his own question by arguing that the virtue, and thus the abilities, of women are distinct from those of free men. Thus, women are "naturally" suited to being ruled by those with superior deliberative and rational capabilities. By contrast, Aristophanes reveals tensions in a discourse that renders women as essentially "other" from male citizens. Aristophanes undermines fixed gender difference in several ways during the course of the play, most notably by highlighting the ability of women to deliberate with rational speech and judgment. Although this play does not reveal Aristophanes' own commitments with regard to women's political practice, his work certainly opens up the very possibilities for women as full democratic citizens that Aristotle seeks to foreclose.

## *"Keeping Silence": Plutarch's Gendering of Women's Speech*

Plutarch attests that democratic discourse of the first century continued to gender citizenship in such a way that women were constructed as unsuited to take part in public politics. At the same time, Plutarch's writings reveal tensions in the discourse that some scholars suggest reflect changing roles for women during the early Empire. In particular, two of Plutarch's works, his *Advice to the Bride and Groom* and *A Consolation to His Wife*, employ gendered discourse regarding the public behavior and speech of women. These two texts address both the ideal wife and marriage. In a *Consolation to His Wife*, Plutarch comforts his wife of many years after the death of a beloved child, all the while outlining the "correct" behavior for wives regardless of their circumstances. As the name suggests, Plutarch addresses his *Advice to the Bride and Groom* to a couple that are only embarking on their married life, with much of the text outlining conduct for a long and happy union.

While both these treatises speak of marriage as a partnership, Plutarch actually envisions a deeply unequal relationship between men and women,⁴⁶ arguing women should follow their husbands in a variety of ways.

---

45. Ibid., 598.
46. Foxhall makes this same point, including the observation that Plutarch even

Women should act as the "mirror" for their husbands' emotions, reflecting his feelings while possessing none of their own.[47] Men must also provide intellectual leadership within the home. Plutarch compares the development of a woman's intellect to the conception of a child. While the male and female union produces a healthy child, a woman on her own can only develop misshapen uterine growths "originating in infection."[48] To avoid comparable disfigurations of intellect, a woman must receive her husband's guidance as he brings to her superior ideas and doctrines.

In his *Advice*, Plutarch naturalizes the hierarchy between men and women with a further comparison reminiscent of Aristotle. Plutarch argues that a woman should be controlled by her husband, even as the body is ruled by the soul. Plutarch writes, "As, therefore, it is possible to exercise care over the body without being a slave to its pleasures and desires, so it is possible to govern a wife, and at the same time to delight and gratify her."[49] In common with earlier classical examples, Plutarch's formulation connects women with bodily appetites and desires, while urging men to provide the rational control these women lack.

For the virtuous wife, Plutarch outlines a limited public role. Plutarch does not consign women entirely to the home, but instead recognizes their presence at banquets, religious ceremonies, and the theater.[50] Nevertheless, even within those public contexts, Plutarch's virtuous woman should draw little attention. Plutarch expresses this sentiment in the letter to his beloved, grieving wife. He praises his wife for showing self-control in her emotions and in her simplicity of dress for the theater or procession.[51] Plutarch locates this simplicity of behavior and dress in the civic, political context by writing, "Neither is there any citizen (τῶν πολιτῶν) of ours to whom at religious ceremonies, sacrifices, and the theatre you do not offer another spectacle—your own simplicity."[52] While *Consolation* praises a woman's simple appearance for the public context, Plutarch's *Advice* insists that a woman's presence in that context must be governed by her husband's movements. For Plutarch, "a virtuous woman ought to be most visible in

---

talks of men and women possessing the same virtue—certainly a contrast to Aristotle's arguments in the *Politics*. Foxhall, "Foreign Powers," 145.

47. Plutarch, *Conj. Praec.* 140 A.
48. Ibid., 145 D.
49. Ibid., 142 E.
50. For a discussion of Plutarch's recognition of women's public roles, see Foxhall, "Foreign Powers," 145–47.
51. Plutarch, *Cons. Ux.* 609 A (Fowler, LCL).
52. Ibid., 609 D.

her husband's company, and to stay in the house and hide herself when he is away."[53] Upholding a firm distinction between public and private realms, he argues here that a woman can only enter the public without shame if she is attached to her husband.

Putting a final, significant restraint on women's public action in the *Advice to Bride and Groom*, Plutarch first relates the story of Pythagoras' wife who, when her exposed arm was complimented, exclaims, "But not for the public."[54] Plutarch contends, "Not only the arm of the virtuous woman, but her speech as well, ought not to be for the public."[55] He invokes a feminine ideal consisting of "womankind keeping at home and keeping silence."[56] A woman's speech is thus confined to the private setting where she is to speak to or "through" her husband. The only public outlet for a woman's voice is her husband speaking on her behalf, an eventuality a woman should accept since "like the flute-player, she makes a more impressive sound through a tongue not her own."[57]

Plutarch's construction of the ideal woman shares key elements with his classical forbearers. Like Aristotle, Plutarch draws on the body/soul dichotomy as the basis for his ontology of hierarchical difference between men and women. In Plutarch's presentation, women's difference is manifested in an inferior intellect and in a corresponding subservient nature that achieves its best form when ruled by the man. In common with classical authors, Plutarch's virtuous woman belongs primarily to the private context, and she is distinguished by her silence.

As I have shown, Plutarch elsewhere attests to a continuing construction of democratic citizenship based in the public speech and wisdom of the individual. With his description of ideal "womanhood," Plutarch, like Aristotle, renders women incapable of that citizenship. With their defective intellect and subservient nature, women have only a limited place in the public—and certainly no speaking role in that context. They are to "be seen but not heard," even as their appearance must demonstrate both simplicity and their faithfulness to their husband's leadership.

Despite strong similarities between Plutarch and classical authors regarding the construction of women's "nature," classics scholars Lin Foxhall and Jo Ann McNamara insist that Plutarch be read with an awareness of the historical changes that separate him from fourth- and fifth-century Athens.

---

53. Plutarch, *Conj. Praec.* 139 C (Fowler, LCL).
54. Ibid., 142 C. "ἀλλ' οὐ δημόσιος"
55. Ibid., 142 C–D. δεῖ δὲ μὴ μόνον τὸν πῆχυν ἀλλὰ μηδὲ τὸν λόγον δημόσιον εἶναι.
56. Ibid., 142 D. οἰκουρίας σύμβολον ταῖς γυναιξὶ καὶ σιωπῆς.
57. Ibid.

Plutarch is living in a different time than Xenophon did when he described the marriage ideal in *Oeconomicus*. Notably, Plutarch lives in a period in which the gendered division between public and private for elite women seems less solid.[58] Unlike Xenophon, Plutarch's writing does not assume the isolation of the young, elite wife to the home. Instead, Plutarch's very attempt to limit and control the public behavior of women reveals their presence in theater, procession, and temple, where they move amongst the male citizens. McNamara and Foxhall suggest that Plutarch's attempt to check the autonomy of women,[59] to assert an essential difference that renders women best suited for the home, comes in response to changing norms that meant women "were aggressively present at every public function and dangerously active in the formation of public policy."[60] In these terms, his rhetoric is not just a continuation of gendered democratic discourse from the classical period, but a renewal, or insistence on gender difference in light of changes that made women an increasing presence within the public sphere.

With women moving more freely in public during the first century,[61] their exclusion from full membership in the democratic *polis* might well have been further questioned or undermined. Plutarch's mobilization of gendered difference regarding women's ability to act, and most importantly, to speak in the public, political sphere makes sense as a strategy to limit this potential, seeking to address these existing tensions in the discourse. It is in this world—in this era—that Paul writes to Corinthian women and men in one early Christian community.

## II. Gendering of Speech, Gendering of Citizenship: 1 Corinthians 11:2–16

While Paul devotes considerable attention to speech and wisdom at various points in 1 Corinthians, he specifically addresses women as speakers

---

58. Foxhall, "Foreign Powers," 147.
59. Ibid., 150.
60. McNamara, "Gendering Virtue," 151.

61. Ibid., 156–57. Foxhall suggests that the Empire introduced Greek citizens of the East to the Roman legal status for women that granted them "a more formally constituted legal and political persona," than that available in traditional Greek society. While the Greek *poleis* did not institute this practice, it may have presented a threat to elites like Plutarch who wished to maintain those gender boundaries—even as men's "lives were less separated from women's lives." Foxhall, "Foreign Powers," 147. For more thorough conversation over changes for women in the first century BCE and CE, see Winter, *Roman Wives, Roman Widows*, 1–74; Fanthan, *Women in the Classical World*, 280–93.

in 1 Corinthians 11:2-16 and 14:33b-36. These two biblical passages have been among the most frustrating and challenging for biblical scholars and the focus of considerable debate. Much of this debate swirls around how these passages relate to each other, if they do at all. Scholars have generally read the first passage, 1 Cor 11: 2-16, as an argument about women's hair or head-covering during prayer and prophecy. They have interpreted this prayer and prophecy as occurring in a worship context, and correspondingly, often insist that Paul's comments on women's appearance are related to the "public" context of their speech.[62] By contrast, in 1 Corinthians 14:33b-36, Paul prohibits women's speech entirely in the *ekklēsia*, demanding their silence and submission in that context. Scholars have noted the seeming contradiction between these passages, with Paul forbidding the very speech in chapter 14 that he implicitly approves in 1 Corinthians 11. In the range of hypotheses for this contradiction, some, like Jerome Murphy-O'Connor, Gordon Fee, and Gerhard Dautzenberg, argue for parts or the entirety of 1 Cor 14:33b-36 as a later interpolation.[63] Conversely, others have argued a different type of speech is at issue in each passage[64]—or a different group of speakers, with 1 Cor 14:33b-36 addressed specifically to wives while 1 Cor 11:2-16 concerns unmarried women.[65]

I read these difficult verses as the product of Paul's participation in the democratic discourse of the Corinthian assembly. In 1 Cor 11:2-16, Paul constructs an essential gender difference regarding speech and speakers that draws on larger socio-cultural *topoi*, even as it grounds those differences in a cosmic hierarchy. Indeed, the gender difference Paul evokes in 1 Cor 11 suggests women's speech is not just different, but a source of disorder, even dangerous disorder, for the community. In turn, Paul uses this passage to ground his contention in 1 Cor 14:33-36 that women's speech has no place in the *ekklēsia* context. Ultimately, I argue that Paul seeks to shape Christian identity and community so that full participation and membership is

62. For some of this literature, see Vander Stichele and Penner, "Paul and the Rhetoric of Gender," 287.

63. Fee, *The First Epistle to the Corinthians*, 699–708; Murphy-O'Connor, "Interpolations in 1 Corinthians"; Dautzenberg, *Urchristliche Prophetie*, 253–74. Also see: Conzelmann, *1 Corinthians*, 246. Winsome Munro offers yet another approach to the interpolation theory, suggesting that both 1 Cor 11:2-16 and 1 Cor 14:34-35 are later additions belonging to a "pastoral stratum" that holds much in common with the Pastoral Epistles. Munro, *Authority in Peter and Paul*, 1–15.

64. For instance, Hurley contends that Paul allowed for women's charismatic gifts of prophecy, but drew the line at their verbal participation in judging the prophecy of men within the community. Hurley, "Did Paul Require Veils or the Silence of Women?"

65. Schüssler Fiorenza, *In Memory of Her*, 231; Barrett, *A Commentary on the First Epistle to the Corinthians*, 330–33.

only open to male members. At the same time, Paul's attempt to foreclose women's "citizenship" exposes the potential for their full inclusion according to the radical potential of democratic discourse itself—and the developing theology of the early church.

I will analyze 1 Cor 11:2–16 in light of the preceding discussion over gender and democratic discourse in the Greek East. 1 Cor 11:2–16 connects with the tensions I have explored within democratic discourse regarding women and women's speech. In turn, this tension makes sense in the context of my larger argument that Paul addresses his arguments in 1 Corinthians to a community which understands itself as a democratic assembly—a group in which issues of authority and communal practice, particularly speech, were dependent on the ideals and debates of democratic discourse. The Corinthians, in other words, understood leadership and "citizenship" as determined by the speech and judgment of the assembly. In 1 Cor 11:2–16, Paul asserts women's difference from men in such a way that he questions their reason, their connection to the divine, and thus their equal status and participation in the group. Paul crafts these assertions toward a portrayal of women's speech of prayer and prophecy as essentially different from that of men, requiring the physical marker of the veil. Such an image of women and women's speech undermines women's potential as a "citizen" in ways that are remarkably familiar to the discourse I have examined elsewhere in Greek literature. I argue that Paul crafts this argument regarding women's speech in a "liminal" space that he does not label *ekklēsia*, precisely because he seeks to make women's speech distinct, to show its unsuitability for the assembly in anticipation of his more sustained arguments regarding *ekklēsia* speech in 1 Cor 12–14.

## Cosmology, Creation, and Difference in 1 Cor 11:2–16

Paul's commences his argumentation in 1 Cor 11:2–16 by reminding the Corinthians of their relationship with him, and notably the authority he claims over the community. Thus, Paul introduces an intensive construction of gender difference around prayer and prophecy by commending the Corinthians for maintaining the "traditions"[66] (τὰς παραδόσεις) he has given

---

66. Here, Horrell suggests that these traditions involve men and women praying and prophesying together in worship, while Jervis argues that Paul is referring to his earlier teaching about the unity of men and women in Christ, a teaching similar to Gal 3:28. Both suggest that Paul refers to these traditions as a preparation for correcting the Corinthian interpretations, and their resulting (mis)behavior. Horrell, *Social Ethos*, 169; Jervis, "But I Want You to Know," 234–35.

them.⁶⁷ With this phrasing, Paul awards the weight of custom to his earlier teaching even as he asserts his role of teacher to the Corinthians. Paul indicates that the Corinthians are to be praised for faithfulness to his instruction even as they go wrong by forging their own path. Paul thus seeks to frame his arguments on gender in this passage as a continuation of tradition he himself has imparted in his authoritative role as the Corinthians' formative teacher and leader.⁶⁸

Paul crafts much of 1 Cor 11:2–16 toward the visual, physical differentiation of women's prophecy and prayer through head covering. However, Paul grounds the necessity of that practice in ontological difference and hierarchy between men and women that he introduces in 1 Cor 11:3. With v. 3, Paul claims that "the head of every man is Christ, the head of a woman is her husband, and the head of Christ is God."⁶⁹ For this verse, significant scholarly discussion concerns the meaning of "head" (κεφαλή) in Paul's grouping of man, woman, God, and Christ. The word is alternately argued to mean source, pre-eminence, or authoritative leadership. Those defending the last interpretation cite a range of literature from antiquity that includes Septuagint examples in which κεφαλή translates the Hebrew *rōš* for a human leader.⁷⁰ However, these scholars also cite a larger group of texts describing the relationship of the physical body to the head, recognized as the seat of mind and soul.⁷¹ Plato provides an early example in the *Timaeus* where he calls the head "the most divine part," and that which controls the rest of the body as a servant.⁷² In the first century, Philo likewise calls the head the "best part of the animal,"⁷³ the leader of the rest of the body parts,

---

67. Both Fee and Conzelmann identify this as a *captatio benevolentiae* designed to gain the audience's goodwill. However, Conzelmann also notes the way in which this verse also serves to remind this audience of Paul's role and authority. Fee, *The First Epistle to the Corinthians*, 500; Conzelmann, *1 Corinthians*, 182.

68. While Corrington does not discuss the effect of this framing for Paul's own authority, she recognizes the way it strengthens his instructions over veiling. Corrington, "Paul and the Language of the Body," 225.

69. 1 Cor 11:3. Παντὸς ἀνδρὸς ἡ κεφαλὴ ὁ Χριστός ἐστιν, κεφαλὴ δὲ γυναικὸς ὁ ἀνήρ, κεφαλὴ δὲ τοῦ Χριστοῦ ὁ θεός.

70. Grudem, "Does ΚΕΦΑΛΗ ('Head') Mean 'Source' or 'Authority Over' in Greek Literature?," 54–55; Fitzmyer, "Another Look at ΚΕΦΑΛΗ in 1 Corinthians 11:3," 507–9.

71. Grudem provides the most extensive survey of this material. Ibid.

72 Plato, *Tim.* 44D (Fowler, LCL). τοῦτο δ᾽ νῦν κεφαλὴν ἐπονομάζομεν, ὃ θειότατόν τ᾽ ἐστὶ καὶ τῶν ἐν ἡμῖν πάντων δεσποτοῦν.

73. Philo, *Praem.* 125 (Colson, LCL). ἐν ζῴῳ κεφαλὴ μὲν πρῶτον καὶ ἄριστον.

"which take their life from the faculties in and above the head."[74] In his *On Dreams*, Philo explains his interpretation of the baker's dream in Genesis 40:16, writing, "Head we interpret allegorically to be the ruling part of the soul, the mind on which all things lie."[75] Plutarch for his part, describes the head as "the governor of the senses"[76] and notes, "we affectionately call a person head or soul from his ruling parts."[77] In these and other ancient texts, the head is commonly understood as "the seat of the intellect and emotions, and therefore the director of the body's actions."[78]

Based on such examples, scholars like Wayne Grudem[79] and Richard Cervin[80] have expended considerable energy arguing for head alternately as "preeminence" or "authority." I fear this debate runs the risk of creating a false dichotomy, since I would agree with Joseph Fitzmyer that κεφαλή could have both these connotations.[81] More seriously, this debate obscures the head/body relationship in passages like the ones I have mentioned from Plutarch and Plato. The excellence, the leadership of the head in these examples depends on its associations with mind, soul, and the divine. In

---

74. Ibid., οἷον μέρη σώματος ψυχούμενα ταῖς ἐν κεφαλῇ καὶ ὑπεράνω δυνάμεσιν.

75. Philo, *Somn.* 2.207 (Colson, LCL). κεφαλὴν μὲν τοίνυν ἀλληγοροῦντές φαμεν εἶναι ψυχῆς τὸν ἡγεμόνα νοῦν, ἐπικεῖσθαι δὲ τούτῳ πάντα.

76. Plutarch, *Quaest. conv.* 647 C (Fowler, LCL). Here Plutarch speaks of unmixed wine and how it attacks the head, severing the body from the "governor of the sense." (τομεύσῃ τὰ σώματα πρὸς τὰς τῶν αἰσθήσεων ἀρχάς).

77. Ibid., 692 D. ὥσπερ ψυχὴν καὶ κεφαλὴν τὸν ἄνθρωπον εἰώθαμεν ἀπὸ τῶν κυριωτάτων ὑποκορίζεσθαι.

78. This is the definition that Peter Glare, then editor of the Liddell-Scott lexicon, gives in response to the debate over this term in New Testament studies. In a personal letter sent to Wayne Grudem and reproduced with his permission, Glare argues against source as a definition for this word. At the same time, he suggests that the definition I give above is the one "required" in most cases. Grudem, "The Meaning of κεφαλή ('Head')," 59. For her part, Corrington suggests this word commonly defines, "the governing [leading] part [to hegemonikon] of the soul." Corrington, "Paul and the Language of the Body," 225. Her own examples for this usage: *Stoic. vet. frag.* 111.217.19; Cornutus, *Theol. graec.* 20; Galen, *De rem.* 1, *proem*.

79. Grudem strongly favors the reading of "authority over." Grudem, "Does ΚΕΦΑΛΗ ('Head') Mean 'Source' or 'Authority Over' in Greek Literature?"; and "The Meaning of κεφαλή ('Head')."

80. In conversation with Grudem, Cervin argues for "preeminence" as the meaning for head. Cervin, "Does Κεφαλή Mean 'Source' or 'Authority Over' in Greek Literature? A Rebuttal."

81. Fitzmyer argues that "a Hellenistic Jewish writer such as Paul of Tarsus could well have intended that in 1 Cor 11:3 κεφαλή be understood as 'head' in the sense of authority or supremacy over someone else." Fitzmyer, "Another Look at ΚΕΦΑΛΗ in 1 Corinthians 11:3," 510.

turn, mind, soul, and divinity manifest in intellect, reason, and control.[82] By contrast, the body as the natural servant is home to baser instincts and emotions.[83]

As I showed earlier, Aristotle sets out a similar relationship between the mind-dominated soul and the body: a relationship that Aristotle uses to naturalize gender hierarchy. For Aristotle, the deeply unequal relationship between the ruler soul and servant body helps him to claim a natural hierarchy in every "composite" entity, notably the composite of man/women.[84] At the same time, he asserts the male, free citizen is distinguished from women, slaves, and children by a fully operative, reasoning element of the soul. It is this ability to reason and deliberate that allows Aristotle to define man as a natural ruler superior to woman whose inferiority is revealed in her inherent submissiveness.[85] Women's very lack of reason leaves silence as their most notable virtue.[86]

Paul's own mobilization of the head/body relationship as a metaphor in 11:3 makes a statement about gender difference, and thus capability for men and women to exercise authoritative speech. Gail Corrington points in this direction with her observation that, "The only member of this hierarchy who does not serve as 'head' of anything else is the woman."[87] In this way, Paul defines a woman's identity as entirely in relationship to that of man as "his body."[88] Corrington's insights on this passage take on further weight within the gendered democratic discourse I examined earlier in the chapter.

Paul begins his argument for gendered difference in speech among the Corinthians by placing women at the bottom of a cosmically ordered hierarchy. This construction depicts women as fully body, lacking the head, or mind, which authors like Plato, Philo, and Plutarch all depict as the highest element regulating the body. Such a construction of women as wholly

---

82. The relationship between mind, soul, and body as described by various Greek philosophers resists easy summary. Indeed, a philosopher like Plato provides a slightly different vision of the soul and its functions in the *Phaedo* than he does in the *Republic*. Nevertheless, Laks says that, with Diogenes of Apollonia and Democritus in the fifth century BCE, the soul comes to be seen commonly as the center of intelligence and cognition and thus the ruler of the body—a ruler located by many in the head. Laks, "Soul, Sensation, and Thought," 252–53.

83. For instance, Plato in the *Phaedo* suggests that the body is associated with desires, fears, and passions and requires the soul's wise leadership. *Phaed.* 94A–E.

84. Aristotle, *Pol.* 1254a29–31.

85. Ibid., 1254b13–15.

86. Ibid., 1260a31.

87. Corrington, "Paul and the Language of the Body," 225.

88. Ibid.

"body" in 1 Cor 11:3 questions their possession of mind, of reason—and implies as well an inherent lack of control over themselves or others. Within wider discourse of the Greco-Roman world, this portrayal of women as lacking in controlling reason connects to claims that they are a source of danger—to themselves and to the self-control of men around them. In 1 Cor 11:3, Paul grounds this familiar, essentialized gender difference in a divine, ontological hierarchy that brings together the "order of the household with the order of the natural/created world."[89] Overall, Paul's formulation of a hierarchy based on "heads" and "bodies" in this case intimates women's inability to use reason, and therefore their incapability to speak authoritatively—or even without risk.

Paul's application of the head/body metaphor to men and women in 1 Cor 11:3 sets a tone for the pericope, establishing a "concept of reality" based on gender hierarchy that shapes the rest of the passage.[90] This is a concept of reality that Paul deepens with further appeal to divine order in vv. 7–9. In these verses, Paul gives the creation narratives of Genesis as an origin for the gender difference he fosters. With 1 Cor 11:7–9, Paul combines elements from the two creation stories of Genesis 1–2 to claim a secondary status for women that further separates them from the divine. By speaking of man as the image and glory of God in v.7, Paul first invokes Genesis 1:27 in which God creates human beings in the divine image. However, Paul does not directly quote this verse from the Septuagint. As Wire points out, Paul does not use the Septuagint's ἄνθρωπος with its "generic implications for the human being created according to God's image."[91] Nor does he include the ending of this verse in which God creates humans according to his image, "male and female he created them." Instead, Paul employs the more specific ἀνήρ to connect God's image and glory solely with the male. Meanwhile, he asserts that woman is only the glory of man.[92] In 1 Cor 11:8, Paul underlines the acceptability of this reading by exploiting the second creation story of Genesis 2. By referring to woman's creation from man in v.8, Paul draws on Genesis 2:22. This account of women's secondary creation as man's "helper"

89. Penner and Vander Stichele, "Unveiling Paul," 230.
90. Amador, "Interpretive Unicity," 55.
91. Wire, *Corinthian Women Prophets*, 119.
92. Wire notes here that not only does Paul neglect the more generic term but he also avoids the inclusive ending of this creation story, "male and female he created them." She concludes, "In fact Paul replaces the biblical narrative of God creating according to God's image with a description of the male as God's image and glory." Ibid. Økland notes, "Anyway, woman's possible godlikeness does not fit very well the place Paul attributes to her in the cosmic hierarchy, which is then the reason he leaves it out." Økland, *Women in Their Place*, 182.

furthers the gender difference *and* hierarchy Paul develops from the first creation story.[93] Paul's precise exegetical choices in vv. 7–8 thus reinforce not only women's difference or distinction but also their inferiority which symbolically blocks their access to the divine. As Økland observes, Paul's reading of Genesis in these verses insists on a divinely structured gender hierarchy "that has not collapsed in Christ."[94]

Paul's reading of Genesis in 1 Cor 11:7–8 marks woman as essentially different from man, the afterthought of creation always separated from God's image and glory by the male. In this way, Paul's rhetoric insists upon gender difference and hierarchy. However, this reading does more. Paul's rhetoric in these verses further emphasizes women as a source of danger and disorder. In 1 Cor 11:7, scholars like Fee and Wire interpret "glory" to mean honor and praise, a contrast to the shame Paul invokes elsewhere in the passage.[95] Read in this way, Paul's depiction of glory/honor not only grants to men a divine connection denied to women but also hints at the risk women pose to men. As Wire argues, "If a woman is the glory of a man, her presence reflects honor on him and also makes the man vulnerable to shame through her."[96] Already established as dangerous in 11:3 due to their lack of a controlling head, women here are further targeted as a risk to those above them in Paul's cosmological hierarchy.

With 1 Cor 11:11–12, Paul again applies the creation accounts to the relationship between men and women. At first glance, 1 Cor 11:11–12 appears to interrupt the larger argument of the pericope with a more egalitarian vision of gender and creation. Paul begins v. 11 with a πλὴν that for some signals a departure or new direction in the discussion.[97] Paul follows this πλὴν with the claim that, "in the Lord, woman is not independent of man, or man independent of woman."[98] In v. 12, he further specifies the nature of this interrelationship with another appeal to creation. He states, "For just as woman came from man, so man comes through woman; but all things

---

93. Jervis gives a helpful analysis of Paul's use of the second creation story to shape the meaning of the first toward an insistence on gender distinction. While her analysis is valuable here, Horrell points out that she does not fully acknowledge the hierarchy created through Paul's exegetical use of these passages. Jervis, "'But I want You to Know,'" 241–43; Horrell, *Social Ethos*, 172.

94. Økland, *Women in Their Place*, 183.

95. Wire, *Corinthian Women Prophets*, 120; Fee, *The First Epistle to the Corinthians*, 516.

96. Wire, *Corinthian Women Prophets*, 120.

97. For instance, Fee reads this as a qualification of what comes before in v. 10. Fee, *The First Epistle to the Corinthians*, 522.

98. Πλὴν οὔτε γυνὴ χωρὶς ἀνδρὸς οὔτε ἀνὴρ χωρὶς γυναικὸς ἐν κυρίῳ

come from God."[99] Theissen and Jervis contend that these verses respond to the Corinthian appropriation of Paul's earlier teaching, a teaching similar to Gal 3:28. For these scholars, v.11 is a restating, or "correction" of that earlier teaching in light of Corinthian (mis)interpretation—a correction in which Paul asserts "that in the Lord men and women find harmonious unity"[100] while still maintaining difference in gender roles. For Theissen, v. 11 becomes part of Paul's appeal to the Corinthians who have interpreted this earlier teaching to mean "equality in principle of the sexes."[101] He argues this appeal helps to explain the seeming incongruity between the gender hierarchy of v. 3, 7–8 and the more reciprocal formulation of this verse—even as he notes that v.11 "falls short" of the egalitarian teaching of Gal 3:28.[102]

If 1 Cor 11:11–12 addresses Corinthian practices of gender equality stemming from a theological formulation like Gal 3:28, these verses do not simply "fall short" of the liberative potential of that baptismal formula. Nor would I agree with Fee that these verses ameliorate the gender hierarchy of v. 3, 7–9 by insisting that gender differentiation does not mean women's subordination.[103] Instead, these verses further undermine the potential for gender equality as part of a new life in Christ. These verses reinforce gender hierarchy even as they add a new element of sexual differentiation that strengthens Paul's earlier assertions. Wire notes that although Paul structures these verses as a concession based in an appeal to equivalence in sexual roles, they actually concede "less than appears."[104] V. 11 can be read as a claim for the interdependence of men and women.[105] However,

99. ὥσπερ γὰρ ἡ γυνὴ ἐκ τοῦ ἀνδρός, οὕτως καὶ ὁ ἀνὴρ διὰ τῆς γυναικός· τὰ δὲ πάντα ἐκ τοῦ θεοῦ.

100. Jervis, "'But I Want You to Know,'" 245.

101. Theissen, *Psychological Aspects*, 167.

102. Ibid., 166.

103. Fee makes this argument, claiming, "While it is true that woman is man's glory having been created for his sake (v. 9), Paul now affirms that that does not mean that woman exists for man's purposes, as though in some kind of subordinate position to his aims and will." Fee, *The First Epistle to the Corinthians*, 523. See also Horrell, *Social Ethos*, 173; Delobel, "1 Cor 11,2–16," 386–87.

104. Wire, *Corinthian Women Prophets*, 128.

105. The translation of χωρὶς has been read as a key to the meaning of this verse. Kurzinger argues χωρὶς as "other than" or "different from," thus claiming the verse conveys a meaning of equality. By contrast, the NRSV translates χωρὶς as "without." As Horrell points out, this translation suggests interdependence that does not necessarily include the sense of equality. Horrell, *Social Ethos*, 174. In the larger context of the passage, especially in light of the following verse, I am persuaded by this translation. For interpretation of this verse as suggesting equality, see Kürzinger, "Mann und Frau," 273–75; Byrne, *Paul and the Christian Women*, 47, 57n59; Schüssler Fiorenza,

Paul illustrates this interdependence with two further appeals to gender difference. In v. 12, Paul first reiterates his earlier reference to Genesis 2:22 and woman's secondary creation "from man."[106] In the second half of the verse, man is said to "come through woman," a reference to woman's role in procreation.[107] At once, v. 12 thus reprises Paul's earlier reading of Genesis toward woman's secondary place in creation, even as it suggests that woman's contribution to interdependence "in the Lord" is her ability to bear and birth children. Here, Wire observes that v. 12 is a "shift away" from new life in Christ in which there is no longer "male and female"—and would have particularly serious consequences for those women "practicing this identity through sexual abstinence."[108]

A significant number of scholars, Jervis and Theissen included, read Paul's manipulation of the Genesis creation stories in 1 Cor 11:2–16 in conversation with Corinthian appropriation of the baptismal formula recorded in Gal 3:28—the formula which states that for those baptized into Christ, "There is no longer Jew or Greek, there is no longer slave or free, there is no longer male and female; for all of you are one in Christ Jesus."[109] As a pre-Pauline baptismal formula,[110] Gal 3:28 itself alludes to Genesis 1:27 in negating this last differentiation in Christ of "male and female."[111] Indeed, some contend that the pairing "male and female" as a quotation from Genesis 1:27 was likely the origin of this baptismal formula in the Christian community.[112] I ask here: If the Corinthians did know this formula or some-

---

*In Memory of Her*, 229–30.

106. Brooten contends that this construction not only points to Genesis 2:22 but also to the idea visible in Clement of Alexandria that the male seed contains the entirety of the created person. Brooten, *Love Between Women*, 185.

107. Økland, *Women in Their Place*, 185; Jervis, "'But I Want You to Know,'" 245.

108. Wire, *Corinthian Women Prophets*, 128.

109. Οὐκ ἔνι Ἰουδαῖος οὐδὲ Ἕλλην, οὐκ ἔνι δοῦλος οὐδὲ ἐλεύθερος, οὐκ ἔνι ἄρσεν καὶ θῆλυ· πάντες γὰρ ὑμεῖς εἷς ἐστε ἐν χριστῷ Ἰησοῦ.

110. For a discussion of this verse as part of the tradition Paul quotes, see Betz, *Galatians*, 181–85; Schüssler Fiorenza, *In Memory of Her*, 208; Wire, *Corinthian Women Prophets*, 123–25.

111. As Wire elucidates, several points suggest that Gal 3:28 reformulates Gen 1:27: "[T]he fact that he uses words for 'male' and 'female' that apply to all species rather than his standard terms for human beings of each sex suggests that he is quoting the phrase in the Greek (LXX) text of Genesis 1:27, 'male and female he made them.' This is confirmed by the conjunction between 'and' between these words that breaks the 'neither-nor' pattern Paul just used in speaking of Jew and Greek and slave and free." Wire, *Corinthian Women Prophets*, 124–25. Schüssler Fiorenza, *Rhetoric and Ethic*, 156.

112. Wire, *Corinthian Women Prophets*, 124–25; MacDonald, *There is No Male and*

thing very similar to it, what might such a baptismal formula have meant to a community which also conceived of itself as a democratic *ekklēsia*? Likewise, if the Corinthians embraced not only the theological but also the political, liberative potential of that formula, how does Paul's own exegesis of Genesis in 1 Cor 11:2–16 toward gender difference—toward gendered speech—strategically undermine that potential?

Elisabeth Schüssler Fiorenza's analysis of Gal 3:28 is particularly useful in this case precisely because she has so astutely addressed social and political implications of this formula for the earliest followers of Christ.[113] Schüssler Fiorenza argues that the negation of the three pairings of Gal 3:28 together asserts "the social oneness of the messianic community in which social, cultural, religious, national, and biological gender divisions and status differences are no longer valid. On this reading the pre-Pauline formula Gal 3:28 rejects all structures of domination."[114] She has recognized the last pairing of "male and female" quotes Genesis 1:27, "where humanity created in the image of God is qualified as 'male and female' in order to introduce the theme of procreation and fertility." As she points out, early Jewish exegesis and that in Mark 10:6 read this verse in terms of marriage and family. Against this background, Schüssler Fiorenza contends that "no longer male and female" in the baptismal formula of Gal 3:28

> is best understood, therefore, in terms of marriage and gender realtionships. As such, Gal 3:28c does not assert that there are no longer men and women in Christ, but that patriarchal marriage—and sexual relationships between male and female—is no longer constitutive of the new community in Christ. Irrespective of their procreative capacities and of the social roles connected

*Female*, 17–63, 113–26.

113. A consideration of these political implications sets scholars like Schüssler Fiorenza and Wire apart from other scholars who have emphasized an "eschatological" meaning of the formula, including speculation among Jewish and later Christian groups about "an androgynous first creation." Some scholars have suggested that the Corinthians practice an "over-realized eschatology" that relates to this androgyny and means their transgression of traditional gender boundaries. For examples of this reading: Murphy-O'Connor, "Sex and Logic," 490; Jervis, "'But I Want You to Know.'" For a discussion over androgyny in early Jewish and Christian writings, see Meeks, "The Image of the Androgyne." For her part, Wire recognizes that the place of "male and female" alongside "neither slave nor free" and "neither Jew nor Greek" points away from the hypothesis of androgyny, and toward "overcoming in Christ a division cutting across the whole of society, which privileged one group at the expense of another." Wire, *Corinthian Women Prophets*, 126.

114. Schüssler Fiorenza, *Rhetoric and Ethic*, 155.

with them, persons will be full members of the Christian movement in and through baptism.[115]

If Paul addresses an audience that recognized the radical potential of this baptismal formula toward an end of "all structures of domination," we must further contextualize this potential for a group that also conceived of itself as a democratic "*ekklēsia*." Indeed, the political implications of such a baptismal formula take on new, substantive meaning in the context of ancient democratic discourse. The negation of distinctions based on gender and servitude, not to mention ethnicity, undermine the very boundaries separating the "free" and "equal" citizen from those non-citizens of the *polis* excluded on the basis of gender, slave status, and foreign birth. In these terms, Gal 3:28 appears to have truly radical potential in facilitating a realization of the ideals of democracy toward equality that encompassed not only the free-born male who constituted the "citizen" in the historical practice of Greek democracy—in what Schüssler Fiorenza labels "kyriarchal democracy"[116]—but also the women and slaves ever excluded from full citizenship in that system. As I have discussed, this radical potential appears realized among the Corinthians insofar as this community understands that *all* its members have been enriched through Christ "in speech and knowledge of every kind" (1 Cor 1:5). For a group identifying as a democratic *ekklēsia*, such a transformation indicates that each person has the power and freedom of equal voice, as well as the knowledge necessary for excellence in deliberation and decision.

Paul's rhetoric in 1 Cor 11:2–16 introduces gender difference and hierarchy among the Corinthians in such a way that this very equality of all as wise speakers is brought into question. Paul uses Genesis to establish hierarchy among the Corinthian speakers by naming men alone as the image of God in 1 Cor 11:7, an alteration of the "male and female" image of God in Genesis 1:27. Moreover, Paul twice draws upon the creation story of Genesis 2:2ff to assert woman's secondary status as a creation "for man." These formulations reinforce Paul's earlier appeal to a cosmology that places woman at the bottom of a cosmic hierarchy, separated from Christ and God by the man above her. Together, Paul's use of cosmology and creation emphasize

---

115. Schüssler Fiorenza, *In Memory of Her*, 211.

116. Schüssler Fiorenza, "Introduction for *Prejudice and Christian Beginnings*," 10. Schüssler Fiorenza contrasts this kyriarchal democracy in which "a few select freeborn, propertied, elite male heads of households actually exercised democratic government" with the "theoretical vision of democracy" in which "all those living in the *polis*, the city-state, should be equal citizens, able to participate in government." I largely concur with her analysis, though I note that scholarship on ancient Athens has argued male citizenship, at least theoretically, extended beyond holders of property.

woman's separation from the divine, her place below man in earthly and divine hierarchy, and her lack of controlling "head." This gender differentiation essentially questions women's wisdom and self-control as well as their connection with the divine. In turn, Paul undermines any equality between men and women as wise speakers, especially speakers of the divine speech of prophecy and prayer.

In yet another way, Paul insists on the distinction of men from women. As I have noted, Paul's elaboration of the interdependence of men and women locates that relationship both in women's secondary creation and, perhaps even more significantly, in women's procreative role. Here, I would like to re-examine Wire's contention that v. 12 functions as a "shift away" from the Gal 3:28 claim of a new life in Christ in which there is "no longer male and female." If the baptismal formula of Galatians serves to undermine structures of domination including patriarchal marriage—and thus insists that sexual and procreative roles no longer determine one's place in the community "in Christ"—then Paul's location of women's identity and relationship with men in procreation must be seen not just as a "shift away" from the message of Gal 3:28, but rather as a fundamental challenge to the liberative potential of that formula. Not only does verse 12 reinforce the "traditional phallocentric hierarchy"[117] but, in doing so, it at least implicitly defines "woman" as the "wife" that is procreative partner to her husband in ancient social-political logic. This logic is reinforced by Paul's use of the second creation story, itself linked concretely to marriage in other Christian sources like Mark 10:6 and Matthew 19:4.

Paul's formulation of women's identity in terms of gendered hierarchy and procreation essentially undermines a reading of Gal 3:28 toward an end of the domination associated with patriarchal marriage. As Wire indicates, one casualty of Paul's formulation, if accepted, would be the option for women to choose celibacy. However, this rhetoric has profound implications for other members of the community beyond the free women opting for the celibate life. With the dualistic division of man/woman in these verses directed to the practice of the entire community, and with this definition of "woman" as child-bearing wife, Paul, knowingly or unknowingly, ignores a portion of this community: slave women who might procreate but had no option for marriage.

Jennifer Glancy has pointed out the difficulties for slaves offered by Paul's discussion of *porneia*, a discussion limiting "moral" sex to marriage while claiming that porneia adversely affects the entire community. Without control over their own sexuality—and unable to be married unless they

---

117. Økland, *Women in Their Place*, 186.

were first freed—slaves had little agency to carry out Paul's requirements. Glancy argues that this reality questions the view that, given the baptismal formula of Gal 3:28, "servile status was no impediment to full involvement in the Christian body."[118] Glancy's work encourages us to interrogate the way in which Paul's statements on sexual morality might compromise the baptismal formula's promotion of the free and equal participation of slaves in the Corinthian community. Likewise, we may consider how Paul's formulation of womanhood in 1 Cor 11:2–16 and again in 1 Cor 14:33–36 works to circumscribe full participation, full citizenship in the Corinthian *ekklēsia*, not only for free women but for the enslaved as well. Paul's effective erasure of slaves and their concerns both in these passages, and in his earlier conversation on *porneia*, reinscribes wider political-social patterns of domination in which the concern of elite men's rhetoric with elite women alone obscures the presence of other oppressed people in the *polis*, including the enslaved—effectively reinforcing their lack of citizenship and lack of personhood. In these terms, Paul's rhetoric in 1 Cor 11:2–16 may destabilize not only the Gal 3:28 claim that there is "no longer male and female" for those in Christ but also the claim that there is "neither slave nor free." This function of Paul's rhetoric may be kept in mind as well for the following conversation over women's head covering in these verses since Paul draws on honor/shame distinctions that likewise have differing implications for slave and free members of the community.

## "Let Her Be Covered": Veiled Speech in 1 Cor 11:2–16

Paul mobilizes constructions of gender difference based in creation and cosmology toward a certain vision of community practice. In 1 Cor 11:4–6 and again in 11:13–16 Paul insists that women's heads must be covered while men's are uncovered when they pray or prophesy. Many scholars have located Paul's primary goal for the entire pericope with these verses. Indeed, a dominant understanding of 1 Cor 11:2–16 is that Paul seeks to impose order through proper gender distinction in the gathered community, thus bringing the group into alignment with norms of Greco-Roman propriety. In this reading, Paul combats disorder occasioned by women whose behavior reflects their "overrealized eschatology,"[119] their belief that baptism into Christ has already eliminated traditional boundaries and distinctions between men and women.[120] Paul's attempt to re-establish such boundar-

---

118. Glancy, "Obstacles to Slaves' Participation," 501.
119. Fee, *The First Epistle to the Corinthians*, 498.
120. Allison, "Let Women Be Silent in the Churches," 34.

ies and distinctions by assuring that women are "appropriately attired"[121] reflects his concern for the well-being and honor of the community—honor that will impact the safety and missionary impact of the Corinthians in the wider society.

This interpretation of 1 Cor 11:2–16 as a *response* to disorder helps to mask Paul's rhetorical program in this passage. In fact, the portrayal of the Corinthian women as a risk to the community through their transgression of "norms" takes Paul's representation as reality in this passage, thus replicating the very image that Paul seeks to create.[122] By contrast, I have argued that Paul crafts his rhetoric toward precisely this image of women, including their speech, as disordered. Indeed, Paul's insistence on head covering for women may be interpreted as part of this rhetorical construction. As Caroline Vander Stichele and Todd Penner point out, Greco-Roman socio-cultural *topoi* used to reconstruct the Corinthian situation are often themselves "far from uniform" in ancient discourse and practice. The very mutability of a *topos* like veiling means that its rhetorical deployment in 1 Corinthians may actually be responsible for "obscuring socio-cultural frames of reference."[123] Certainly both hair and veiling, the two *topoi* that appear to be at issue here, have multiple resonances in the ancient world and therefore are effective as rhetorical tools for establishing difference around gender and speech. I contend that it is this very desire to gender speech among the Corinthians that prompts Paul's rhetorical use of both veiling and hair in this passage.

In 1 Cor 11:4–6 and 11:13–15, Paul does not directly address physical location or the nature of the gathering as the concern driving his directives for head covering. Instead, Paul signals that it is the speech of prayer and prophecy in which community members engage that is at issue. During that performance of speech, women must cover their heads or be shamed, while men's heads will be shamed if they apply a covering. Paul's call for women's heads to be covered in 1 Cor 11 has been interpreted variously

---

121. Horrell, *Social Ethos*, 170.

122. Here Schüssler Fiorenza's insights on Pauline rhetoric and its interpretation are valuable. She observes the propensity of scholars to uncritically identify with the "implied author" of 1 Corinthians, an author who is the "image or picture the reader will construct gradually in the process of reading the work." The interpreter then "follows the directives of the inscribed author, who is not identical with the 'real' Paul, as to how to understand the community of Corinth." Schüssler Fiorena critiques such scholarship for failing to assess Paul's rhetoric as political discourse. Schüssler Fiorenza, *Rhetoric and Ethic*, 110–11.

123. Vander Stichele and Penner, "Unveiling Paul," 218.

as an insistence that women veil their heads,[124] or that Paul urges the necessity for particular, gendered hairstyles.[125] With both these arguments, scholars contend that Paul seeks to bring the Corinthian community into conformity with larger cultural "norms" that the Corinthians have betrayed in their newfound spiritual freedom.[126] I favor the more prevalent interpretation of head coverings as veiling in 1 Cor 11:2-16.[127] However, I also see that it is Paul's own rhetorical goals in this passage, rather than cultural norms, that drive his insistence on women's head covering. Gerd Theissen and Cynthia Thompson point out that the archaeological record makes the case for "norms" in Corinth very difficult to establish with regard to women's veiling.[128] Nevertheless, veiling also had a range of associations in the ancient world that rendered it effective "as a site of production of gender difference."[129] These associations meant that Paul could employ veiling

124. In favor of the "veiling" conclusion: MacDonald, "There is No Male and Female," 86-87; Theissen, *Psychological Aspects*, 160; Martin, *The Corinthian Body*, 233.

125. Among those who have argued for hairstyles as Paul's concern: Murphy O'Connor, "Sex and Logic," 484-90; Schüssler Fiorenza, In Memory of Her, 227; Radcliffe, "Paul and Sexual Identity," 68; Padgett, "Paul on Women in the Church," 70.

126. Gundry-Wolf provides a particularly good example of this reasoning. Gundry-Wolf, "Gender and Creation," 169.

127. Martin supports this reading, noting, "Although hairstyles constituted an important symbol system in Greco-Roman society, veiling was a much more common way of indicating the covering of women important for the honor-shame culture of the ancient Mediterranean." Likewise, he recognizes that ancient interpreters nearly universally read this passage as calling for veiling rather than a certain kind of hairstyles. Martin, *The Corinthian Body*, 233. Some of the difficulty with definitively determining the meaning of head covering here lies with 1 Cor 11:15, where the woman's hair "is given to her for (instead) of a covering" (ὅτι ἡ κόμη ἀντὶ περιβολαίου δέδοται [αὐτῇ]). I stand with authors like Delobel and Fee in arguing for hair being used in this verse as an analogy to veiling. Fee favors a translation of ἀντὶ as "that one thing is equivalent to another," thus making possible this reading of analogy even as he avoids forcing "the rigid concept of replacement onto this sentence." Fee also notes the difficulty of understanding the requirement for a certain, upraised hairstyle from this verse over long hair as a covering. Fee, *The First Epistle to the Corinthians*, 529. Delobel points out that in 1 Cor 11:4 it is difficult to read head covering as a hairstyle for men and that "hair" in vv. 5-6, i.e., shaving, is used only to suggest the shame of not having a covering at all. Delobel, "1 Cor 11,2-16," 375-76. For her part, Økland offers the possibility that this passage insists on both hairstyles and veils as a way of marking the gender difference Paul fosters. Økland, *Women in Their Place*, 190-191.

128. Thompson, "Hairstyles, Headcoverings, and St. Paul," 112; Theissen, *Psychological Aspects*, 161-63; and in conversation with Thompson—Økland, *Women in Their Place*, 191-92.

129. Ibid., 190. For further discussion of dress, veiling, and theological construction in early Christianity, see: Daniel-Hughes, *The Salvation of the Flesh*.

to rhetorically mark off as distinct not only women's bodies but also their speech as well.

As Martin explains, veiling in antiquity signaled women's protection from sexual violation even as it symbolized the control of women's own dangerous sexuality. In these terms, a woman's veil could be described as protecting "society from the dangers and chaos represented by her femaleness."[130] However, my earlier discussion attests that women's uncurbed sexuality was only one element in the ancient Greek construction of women as uncontrolled and disordered, and thus unsuited for citizenship. As the veil could be used to symbolize the need for protection against women's uncontrolled sexuality, it could also be used to signify the danger of women's words that were produced without the controlling order of intellect and reason—a danger averted by a veil-imposed silence.

A number of the Greek playwrights witness the veil's usefulness as a symbol of women's silence and praise-worthy remove from the public sphere.[131] For instance, Euripides' Hippolytus claims that women's excessive talking is allied with their unrestrained sexuality, and men's honor can only be protected if women are isolated indoors, deprived of speech.[132] The female character Phaedra substantiates this characterization earlier in the play when she exits her home and unveils her head. Upon removing her veil, Phaedra lets loose a stream of passionate and uncontrolled speech. Phaedra ends this wild speech only when she calls to her nurse, "Cover my head up again! For I am ashamed of my words."[133] Likewise, Aristophanes' *Lysistrata* employs the veil's symbolic power as a humorous element in the women's bid to overturn the social order. When Lysistrata and the other women attempt to intervene in public affairs, Lysistrata, in the heat of her argument, tells the magistrate to be silent. Their following exchange centers on silence and veiling:

> Magistrate: Me, shut up for you? A damned woman, with a veil (κάλυμμα) on your head (κεφαλήν) no less? I'd rather die!

---

130. Martin, *The Corinthian Body*, 235. For further discussion on veiling in ancient literature as a prevention against women's pollution, see Llewellyn-Jones, *Aphrodite's Tortoise*, 262–67.

131. For examples, see Aristophanes, *Frogs* 908–20; Euripides, *Hipp.* 364–439. For more discussion of this use of veiling in drama, see Llewellyn-Jones, *Aphrodite's Tortoise*, 269–73.

132. Euripides, *Hipp.* 645–50. This is part of Hippolytus' impassioned speech against women as he outlines the threats they pose for men.

133. Euripides, *Hipp.* 240. Πάλιν μου κρύψον κεφαλήν, αἰδούμεθα γὰρ τὰ λελεγμένα μοι.

> Lysistrata: If the veil is a problem for you, here, take mine (κάλυμμα), it's yours, put it on your head (κεφαλήν), and then shut up![134]

Thus veiled, the magistrate falls quiet, "overpowered by the silencing, depersonalizing, power of the female veil."[135]

In the first century, Plutarch draws upon this silencing power of the veil in defining "proper" conduct for women in the public sphere. As I have mentioned, Plutarch relates the anecdote of Theano accidentally revealing her arm as she pulls her veiling garment (ἱμάτιον) about her.[136] Upon receiving a compliment on her exposed arm, Theano says, "not for the public."[137] Plutarch uses this story to insist that not only women's exposed bodies but also their speech should not be for the public setting. Instead, women's voices should be reserved for their homes and husbands. According to Plutarch's reasoning, a woman "ought to be modest and guarded about saying anything in the hearing of outsiders, since it is an exposure of herself."[138]

As in these other ancient examples, Paul draws a connection in 1 Cor 11:2–16 between women's speech, honor, and head coverings. Paul's own call for women's veiling suggests that its gender distinction is a matter of honor for the whole community since women will be shamed without this covering, but men gain shame from covering their head during the same speech. As he grounds the necessity for this gender distinction in creation and cosmology, he uses hair and arguments from nature to amplify the honor/shame he attaches to veiling. In 1 Cor 11:6, he asserts an equivalence between the shame of a woman's unveiled speech and the disgrace of a shaved head, insisting "if it is shameful for a woman to have her hair cut off or to be shaved, she should wear a veil."[139] Moreover, in vv. 14–15, the honor/shame of hair as an analogy for veiling is a lesson from nature itself[140] with a man shamed by long hair, even as a woman's long hair is her glory, "given to her as a covering."[141] In these verses, Caroline Vander Stichele and

---

134. Aristophanes, *Lys.* 532–534 (Henderson, LCL).
135. Llewellyn-Jones, *Aphrodite's Tortoise*, 271.
136. Plutarch, *Conj. praec.* 142 C–D.
137. ἀλλ᾽ οὐ δημόσιος.
138. Ibid.
139. Εἰ δὲ αἰσχρὸν γυναικὶ τὸ κείρασθαι ἢ ξυρᾶσθαι, κατακαλυπτέσθω.
140. For a discussion of Paul's use of "nature" in this case, and its relationship to Stoic thought, see Fee, *The First Epistle to the Corinthians*, 526–27; Conzelmann, *1 Corinthians*, 190. Both Conzelmann and Fee conclude that Paul does not use a strongly stoic understanding of nature in this case.
141. These verses provide a logical dilemma for interpreters of Paul, since they can

Todd Penner show that Paul exploits the rhetorical power of hair for naturalizing sex and gender distinctions in the ancient world. As they explain, hair was effective for this rhetorical purpose precisely because it could be associated both with nature as well as with the force of tradition.[142] In fact, the "nature" of hair held a special place in political discourse of citizenship in the Greek world. Ancient authors regularly cite hairiness of face and body as the natural state of the ideal man, a man defined by his participation in the public, political realm.[143] Intellectuals like Dio Chrysostom,[144] Clement of Alexandria,[145] and Epictetus[146] describe hair as a natural sign to be read for the true character, the honor of the individual man. Even as the "correct" hairiness announces, "I am a man,"[147] and therefore moral, shameful dishonor manifests in feminine grooming habits, especially depilation. Depilation, regularly paired with feminine voice in such critiques,[148] renders a man "womanly" and thus unsuited to the practice of citizenship.[149] As Vander Stichele and Penner explain of this depiction, "Hair, or lack thereof, is not only presented as an outward symbol of the inner character (i.e.

---

be argued as suggesting that women's hair acts as their veil. As Amador states, "Only now, womyn's hair is equated with covering, thus undermining any reason for a veil." Amador, "Interpretive Unicity," 57. By contrast, with scholars like Gordon Fee and Delobel, I see this as an analogy that Paul uses to strengthen his argument regarding women's veiling. As stated earlier, I accept Fee's interpretation of ἀντὶ as a sign of equivalence rather than indicating "instead of." Fee, *The First Epistle to the Corinthians*, 529.

142. Vander Stichele and Penner, "Paul and the Rhetoric of Gender," 305.

143. Vander Stichele and Penner call man's role in the civic sphere, "the primary manifestation of male identity in the ancient world." Ibid., 304.

144. *Or.* 33.52.

145. Clement writes that one man can observe another's appearance, and, "Just like a physiognomist, he can divine from their appearance that they are adulterers and effeminates, who go hunting for both kinds of sex . . ." ἀτεχνῶς καθάπερ μετωποσκόπος ἐκ τοῦ σχήματος αὐτοὺς καταμαντεύεται μοιχούς τε καὶ ἀνδρογύνους, ἀμφοτέραν ἀφροδίτην θηρωμένους. *Paid.* 3.15.2. Translation from Gleason, *Making Men*, 68.

146. *Diatr.* 1.16.11–12. Not only does hair in this passage announce manliness but also voice.

147. A quote from Epictetus, who asks, "Does not the nature of each one of us announce from afar: 'I am a man.'" *Diatr.* 1.16.11. οὐκ εὐθὺς μακρόθεν κέκραγεν ἡμῶν ἑκάστου ἡ φύσις ἀνήρ εἰμι. Translation from Gleason, *Making Men*, 69.

148. Dio, *Or.* 33.60.

149. Epictetus provides a particularly good example when he argues that removing the hair on one's body makes one resemble the natural state of a woman and thus renders a man unsuited to such citizen duties as general or superintendent of the *ephebi*—even as one's ability to then father worthy citizens comes into doubt. *Diatr.* 3.1.27–35.

manliness) of the adult male but is also taken, as a consequence, to be a sign of his potential contribution to or impotence within the body politic."[150]

Paul likewise uses hair to assert natural difference between men and women and to assign shame to the transgression of that difference. I suggest this rhetorical deployment has implications for the gendered nature of political participation that Paul envisions. Specifically, Paul uses gender difference associated with hair to further set apart women's vocal participation in a community taking the title, and I argue, the identity of a democratic assembly. In 1 Cor 11:14–15, Paul marks an equivalence between long hair and veiling for women. This equivalence suggests that even as long hair is a natural covering for women, their veiled speech is likewise natural. In this construction, even without the veiled covering Paul requires, women may be seen as naturally veiled, and thus naturally distinguished, from men in their practice of speech.

If Paul's rhetoric in this passage as a whole is designed toward persuading the Corinthians that women must veil during speech, much more is at stake than simply an enforcement of gender difference, or even gender hierarchy. Paul's arguments in this pericope profoundly question women's ability to be credible and authoritative speakers within the Christian *ekklēsia*. His appeals to cosmology render women headless and thus lacking in reason, even as he insists they are the secondary product of creation, separated from the divine by man who is above her both in the order of creation and in the hierarchy of being. Paul finds common cause with Greek writers from Aristotle to Plutarch in questioning women's intellect, and thus their ability to produce rational speech. However, his arguments also render women distant from the divine, and thus handicapped in the performance of the "divine" speech of prophecy. In 1 Cor 11:4–6; 13–15, Paul's call for women's veiling in prayer—and his claim that nature itself distinguishes them physically from men by their hair—further genders speech, thus insisting women should be (are) visibly different in this performance. Moreover, he connects women's honor to this practice and their shame to its abandonment. In these verses, I would suggest that Paul exploits the symbolism of the veil in the ancient world in such a way that he reinforces the sense of women's speech as dangerously different, disordered, and requiring the control—indeed the silencing power—of the veil.

Paul's rhetorical use of the veil in 1 Cor 11:2–16 acts as part of his strategy to foreclose the equal participation of women as speakers in the democratic *ekklēsia* of the community. At the same time, this line of argumentation, like his exegesis of Genesis, has the potential to further divide

150. Vander Stichele and Penner, "Paul and the Rhetoric of Gender," 304.

the community. That exegesis worked toward a definition of woman as wife in these verses, a definition that I argued effectively ignores, even erases, the presence of slave women in the community. Likewise, in his argumentation over veiling, Paul's appeal to the honor of these women, and his insistence that they can choose to protect, to cover, their bodies contradicts the condition of slavery in the ancient world. Indeed, Glancy notes that "[i]nability to maintain corporal integrity . . . characterizes the condition of a slave."[151] Glancy insists that in antiquity "not only modesty but also a sense of shame, chastity, an awareness of what is proper, and attention to propriety—especially sexual propriety in conduct, dress, and speech . . . belongs to the free woman."[152] If Paul's requirements for "women" in 1 Cor 11:2–16 serve to differentiate their bodies and their speech from those of men, these requirements also have the potential to differentiate free women possessed of honor and control regarding dress with slaves whose condition put those things beyond their grasp. Such a differentiation could only help to further align the Corinthian community with the wider social-political hierarchy of the ancient world—in the process moving this community further away from the baptismal promise of Gal 3:28.

## 1 Cor 11:2–16: Speech in the Ekklēsia?

Paul abruptly concludes his argumentation regarding women's head covering with an authoritarian statement that forms something of a full circle with his earlier assertion of authority in 11:2. He states in verse 16, "But if anyone is disposed to be contentious—we have no such custom, nor do the churches of God."[153] This statement ends rather suddenly Paul's complicated and passionate set of arguments regarding gender difference and women's head covering during prophecy and prayer. Indeed, the very abruptness of this last argument from authority signals to scholars like Schüssler Fiorenza and Conzelmann the weakness of Paul's earlier rhetorical construct, and his awareness that his line of reasoning may fail to convince his Corinthian audience.[154] This last verse, a verse J. H. D. Amador labels "a call to silence

---

151. Glancy, "Early Christianity, Slavery, and Women's Bodies," 148.

152. Ibid.

153. Εἰ δέ τις δοκεῖ φιλόνεικος εἶναι, ἡμεῖς τοιαύτην συνήθειαν οὐκ ἔχομεν οὐδὲ αἱ ἐκκλησίαι τοῦ θεοῦ.

154. Schüssler Fiorenza and Conzelmann both make this observation. Schüssler Fiorenza, "1 Corinthians," 1087. Conzelmann, *1 Corinthians*, 191. See also, Amador, "Interpretive Unicity," 57. He suggests this verse is meant to, "stifle all further discussion. It is a power move, pure and simple; the last resort of a weak argument."

*The Gendering of Democratic Participation* 151

and censure," appears to draw on Paul's own authority[155] while it also cites the "custom" (συνήθειαν) of the "*ekklēsia*i of God." In my own analysis of this passage, I find it highly significant that it is only here, at the end of his sustained argument about gender difference and community speech, that Paul introduces the word "*ekklēsia*" into the discussion.

1 Corinthians 11–14 is often held to be a cohesive block of material within the larger context of the letter, united by the theme of "conduct in worship."[156] Indeed, most critics understand Paul's concerns over women's speech and head-covering in 1 Cor 11:2–16 as prompted by the public, communal nature of the church gathering in which this speech takes place. Certainly the appeal to the practice of the *ekklēsiai* of God in 1 Cor 11:16 suggests this context as does Paul's immediate turn in 1 Cor 11:17–18 to the behavior of the Corinthians when they come together in the *ekklēsia* (v. 18, συνερχομένων ὑμῶν ἐν ἐκκλησίᾳ). However, in striking contrast to vv.17–18, and to the later prescriptions regarding women's speech in 1 Cor 14:33–36, Paul does not specify the "*ekklēsia*" as the setting for the behavior at question in 1 Cor 11:2–15. Indeed, he makes no mention of *ekklēsia* or of the gathered community in these verses. Meanwhile, his appeal to the custom (συνήθεια) of the "*ekklēsiai*" in v. 16 is vague as to the custom he references, or whether he uses *ekklēsia* here as the public, community gathering he describes in 1 Cor 14, or as a word denoting, in this case, the overall community of Christ's followers in a certain geographical location.[157] In the case of women's speech in these verses, I ask: Why might Paul fail to locate this speech in the communal gathering—especially given his emphasis on the role of speech for specifically this named *ekklēsia* context in 1 Cor 14?

I would suggest that the very lack of specificity regarding the speakers' context in 1 Cor 11:2–15 serves Paul's larger rhetorical goals in the letter. The combined force of 1 Cor 11–14 indicates that the public practice of the *ekklēsia* drives Paul's interest in speech in these chapters. However, by discussing speech apart from the *ekklēsia* context in 1 Cor 11:2–15, Paul is able to make essential claims about the gendered nature of speech without

155. Wire claims that the "we" in this statement stands for Paul, "who also appears in two other appeals to church practice (4:7; 7:17)." Wire, *Corinthian Women Prophets*, 129.

156. Conzelmann, *1 Corinthians*, 182.

157. In these terms, we may ask whether *ekklēsia* as it is used by Paul and elsewhere in the earliest writings of Jesus' followers has a similar range of meaning as we find with words like *dēmos* or *polis* in Greek democratic discourse. Those words could be used to refer to the citizens of the *polis*, and thus to those who had the right to gather in the *ekklēsia*. However, these words were also used to speak of the entire population of the city, including women and slaves.

explicitly or implicitly suggesting that women's speech has a place in that *ekklēsia* context. In the next chapter, I will show that Paul gradually builds proscriptive arguments regarding *ekklēsia* speech practice in 1 Cor 12–14. In the course of those arguments, he is able to draw upon this earlier portrayal of "male" and "female" speech in 1 Cor 11:2–16 to suggest that only one has legitimacy in the *ekklēsia* he envisions.

## Conclusion

As I have noted, many scholars explain Paul's rhetoric in 1 Cor 11:2–16 by positing that the Corinthians, influenced by their (faulty) interpretation of a formula like Gal 3:28, have broken the bounds of propriety by practicing behavior which blurs gender lines. Such scholarship has hypothesized a range of behaviors which might prompt Paul's arguments in this passage, including the possibility that women have abandoned the veil which the wider society demands, or that these women practice ecstatic worship in which their unkempt hair fails to meet standards of respectability. In this chapter, I have suggested that Paul confronts a far more serious challenge to the construction of gender in the Greek *polis*, and with it the exercise of power in that context.

At issue in 1 Cor 11:2–16 is the practice of speech in the community—specifically the speech of Corinthian women. As I have shown, women's speech occasioned concern and debate in ancient democratic discourse precisely because the freedom, equality, and power of citizenship cohered with the exercise of speech and its discernment in the *ekklēsia* setting. Within democratic discourse, the boundary between citizen and non-citizen was upheld in part by a gendering of women's speech in which their essential lack of reason and control rendered their speech ineligible, and even dangerous, for the public political setting. At the same time, the very tension in the discourse around women's speech attests to the possibility of transgressing that boundary, a possibility engendered by the liberating claims of ancient democracy. The intensity of Paul's arguments in 1 Cor 11:2–16—his own efforts to gender women's speech as disordered and lacking in reason—demonstrates that this tension regarding women's speech is part of the debate between Paul and the Corinthian community. I have argued that this community conceived of itself as a democratic *ekklēsia*. Moreover, it appears that the community understands its transformation in Christ as empowering each member in speech and wisdom—the prerequisites for full citizenship in democratic discourse. In this way, the community may be seen to embrace the social and political potential of the baptismal formula of Gal

3:28 to eradicate the structures of domination that kept citizenship beyond the grasp of women, slaves, and foreigners in the democratic *polis*. Paul's own rhetoric in 1 Cor 11:2–16 and in the following chapters of 1 Cor 12–14 works to foreclose this possibility of citizenship for women, and their counterpart in Greek democratic discourse, slaves. However, that very intensity of Paul's rhetoric regarding women's speech suggests that, in this community, the boundaries separating citizen from non-citizen have already been breached by the speech and active participation of these groups.

# 6

# "As in all the *Ekklēsiai* of the Saints":
# 1 Cor 12–14

## Introduction

1 COR 11:2—14:40 FORMS, AS ELISABETH SCHÜSSLER FIORENZA EXPLAINS, a "ring-composition . . . beginning and ending with a discussion of women's role."[1] More specifically, I argue that the "role" Paul addresses in 1 Cor 11:2-16 and 1 Cor 14:33b-36 is that of women as speakers and, thus, in democratic discourse, their place as leaders, judges, and "citizens" in the gathered *ekklēsia*. Paul's conclusion about women's speech in 1 Cor 14:33b-36—that their speech ultimately has no place in that *ekklēsia*—has been read by many scholars as an interpolation, out of place with the train of Paul's logic in 1 Cor 14, and certainly a contradiction with his discussion over women's speech in 1 Cor 11:2-16. By contrast, I maintain that Paul has thoroughly prepared the rhetorical ground for the prohibition of women's speech in 1 Cor 14. This preparation certainly encompasses the intensive gendering of speech in 1 Cor 11:2-16, gendering which questions women's possession of mind, self-control, and divine connection even as it reifies their identity according to a procreative role. However, the command of 1 Cor 14:33-36 also depends on the preceding arguments of 1 Cor 12—14:33 that enforce difference and require self-limitation in service to the common good.

In this chapter, I consider the requirement for women's silence against the background of this rhetorical preparation. With 1 Cor 12-14, Paul further erodes Corinthian claims to an excellence in speech and wisdom shared equally by all. In these chapters, Paul describes spiritual gifts—notably gifts

---

1. Schüssler Fiorenza, *Rhetoric and Ethic*, 117.

of speech and wisdom—as apportioned differently according to the will of the spirit rather than the will of the individual. Moreover, he differentiates speech gifts themselves according to their place, or value, in the *ekklēsia* setting. This differentiation creates a hierarchy of both *ekklēsia* speech and speakers. Paul establishes this hierarchy, in part, by appealing to the *topoi* of common good, order, and the necessity of "mind,"—*topoi* that have an established place in democratic discourse. In fact, ancient authors regularly deploy these *topoi* not only to strengthen their own rhetorical authority but also to gender *ekklēsia* speech in such a way that free men are left as the only creditable, political speakers of the *polis*.

As I have shown elsewhere, Paul's concern in shaping the community's speech and wisdom is comprehensible within *ekklēsia* discourse, a discourse in which speech and wisdom become the currency of citizenship and thus are bound up with equality, freedom, and power within ancient democracy. Paul's rhetorical construction of *ekklēsia* speech and speakers in 1 Cor 12–14 thus has significant implications for participation and membership in the Corinthian *ekklēsia*. In particular, the very requirements Paul establishes for *ekklēsia* speech in these chapters, notably self-control, and use of the mind, have already been gendered so as to exclude women in the earlier pericope of 1 Cor 11:2–16. In 1 Cor 12, Paul furthers this gender difference and hierarchy with a re-crafting of the baptismal formula that omits the very element, "there is no longer male and female," that facilitates full participation for all, "irrespective of their procreative capacities and of the social roles connected with them."[2] Indeed, Paul's rhetoric in 1 Cor 14:33–36 further naturalizes an identification of "woman" with "wife"—a process that I have argued Paul already initiates in 1 Cor 11:12. As I have suggested in the previous chapter, such a definition of women's roles not only reinforces patriarchal domination but it also furthers the unequal relations occasioned by slavery. Again, I insist that we must contrast Paul's rhetorical construction toward foreclosing women's (and slaves') active citizenship in the gathered *ekklēsia* with signs in the letter that a very different understanding of citizenship existed within the Corinthian community.

## 1 Cor 12: The Gifts which "God has Appointed in the *Ekklēsia*"

With 1 Cor 12, Paul begins an elaboration of spiritual gifts that builds to his instructions regarding the exercise of those gifts in chapter 14. Speech, knowledge, and wisdom occupy the lion's share of Paul's exposition of

2. Schüssler Fiorenza, *In Memory of Her*, 211.

spiritual gifts in chapter 12, and again in chapter 13. These particular gifts form a bridge between the letter's early discussion of speech and wisdom and the coming arguments over prophecy and tongues in chapter 14. In chapter 12, Paul insists that community members *receive* different gifts rather than having equal access or choice as to the gifts they exercise. Moreover, the final verses of the chapter enforce a hierarchy of gifts suitable for the *ekklēsia*—along with an acknowledgment that not all will attain the "greater gifts." Paul explains this differentiation with the analogy of the human body and the variation among its members, explaining that the Corinthians themselves become part of the "body of Christ." Toward this explanation, Paul deploys the early Christian baptismal formula through which the group comes together as that one body. Significant divergences are apparent between the formula Paul cites in 1 Cor 12:13, and the baptismal formula in Galatians 3:27–28. These divergences facilitate difference and hierarchy in 1 Corinthians.

Paul's discussion of spiritual gifts in 1 Cor 12 begins by envisioning the spirit's universal action upon individual members of the community. In 1 Cor 12:4 Paul asserts that only one spirit exists: a spirit responsible for all the gifts the community experiences. Moreover, he explains that each person receives "a manifestation of the spirit for the common good" (φανέρωσις τοῦ πνεύματος πρὸς τὸ συμφέρον. 1 Cor 12:7). This vision of individual, spiritual empowerment echoes the Corinthians' own self-understanding recorded in the *exordium* of 1 Cor 1:5 where experience of Christ Jesus means enrichment of all in "speech and knowledge of every kind" (ἐν παντὶ λόγῳ καὶ πάσῃ γνώσει. 1 Cor 1:5). As I have noted, such claims to individual possession of wisdom and speech in democratic discourse facilitate the argument that all citizens should have freedom and equality. Paul's initial explanation of the spirit's action in 1 Cor 12:4–7 seems designed for an audience that understands the spirit as universally empowering in exactly the qualities necessary for democratic equality. However, in chapter 12, Paul does not ultimately craft his arguments about the spirit's action toward a similar equality of speech and wisdom. Instead, Paul asserts that the spirit, acting upon all, results in differentiated gifts. In turn, this differentiation becomes the necessary prerequisite for the hierarchy of spiritual gifts he describes at the end of the chapter.

In 1 Cor 12:4–6, Paul explains that the spirit creates separate gifts and services and that each receives this expression of the spirit toward τὸ συμφέρον, "the common good." The list Paul sets forth in vv. 8–10 is dominated by the gifts the Corinthians clearly value—distinct acts of speech springing from knowledge and wisdom. Paul's list commences with words of wisdom (λόγος σοφίας) and words of knowledge (λόγος γνώσεως). These two initial gifts recall Corinthian claims to excellence in speech and knowledge in both 1 Cor 1:5 and 8:1, as well as Paul's thorough discussion of wisdom and speech in the first four chapters of the letter. After mentioning the gifts of faith, healing (v. 9), and miracles (v. 10), he resumes his list with the speech of prophecy, tongues, and their discernment (v.10). Out of the nine gifts Paul mentions in these verses, six are gifts that involve speech and the exercise, articulated or implied, of a type of wisdom.

Paul explains the distinct gifts apportioned to community members using the analogy of the human body. The Corinthians have been baptized into one body, Paul tells them, a body in which distinctions of Jew or Greek, slave and free are incorporated. However, bodies are themselves made up of many members. Here again, Paul insists on difference as a defining aspect of this community baptized into the "one Spirit." Not only are there many parts of the body that must work in concert for the overall well-being of the person but Paul also speaks in 1 Cor 12:22-24 of those body parts that seem weaker (ἀσθενέστερα), dishonorable (ἀτιμότερα), and shameful (ἀσχήμονα). While these parts contrast with the "more respectable members," Paul tells the Corinthians that God grants greater honor to the "inferior" parts.

Scholars have frequently read Paul's deployment of the body analogy as affirming the worth of all members of the community,[3] or even, as Dale Martin argues, radically overturning "traditional status expectations" toward empowering those of lower status within the community.[4] For his part, Martin recognizes that the body is commonly used in Greco-Roman rhetoric as an analogy for the social group. He notes that this analogy is commonly mobilized toward *homonoia*, even as it enforces hierarchical difference within society—the idea that certain body parts, like certain members of society, have greater worth.[5] He locates Paul's use of the body analogy in this tradition, but argues that Paul destabilizes the expected hierarchy by insisting that the weaker or shameful body parts are actually due a greater honor.[6] Against this reading, I suggest with Wire that the overall force of chapter 12, including its use of the body analogy, reinforces, rather than unseats, hierarchy within the community.[7] In chapter 12, the body analogy serves to illustrate the differentiation of spiritual gifts. In turn,

3. Conzelmann offers this reading: Conzelmann, *1 Corinthians*, 214. Horrell writes, "The intended result of the reversal of the apparently 'normal' hierarchy is a form of equality—at least an equality in the care and respect accorded to each and every member." Horrell, *Social Ethos*, 182.
4. Martin, *The Corinthian Body*, 102-3.
5. Ibid., 92-93.
6. Ibid., 102.
7. Wire, *Corinthian Women Prophets*, 136-38.

this differentiation is the basis for Paul's ranking of spiritual gifts and their practitioners in the closing verses of the chapter.

Paul ends chapter 12 by claiming that God has appointed spiritual gifts in a particular hierarchy within the "body of Christ." Paul tops this list with the apostles whom God has placed "first" (πρῶτον) in the *ekklēsia* (1 Cor 12:28). Apostles are followed by prophets, teachers, works of power, healing, helpful deeds, forms of leadership—and last, kinds of tongues. From this list, the Corinthians are instructed to "strive for the greater gifts" (1 Cor 12:31. ζηλοῦτε δὲ τὰ χαρίσματα τὰ μείζονα).

Juxtaposing the ranked list of v.28 with the earlier list of vv. 8–10 reveals particularly significant differences between the two. While the Corinthians' own emphasis on wise speech led the earlier list, these two gifts of wise and knowledgeable speech disappear completely in v. 28. In their place, Paul introduces apostleship as "first." This placement speaks directly to Paul's own authority since this is the role he repeatedly claims for himself within the letter.[8] In this latter list, Paul has also ranked prophecy as second only to the gift of apostleship. Meanwhile, the other forms of speech represented by discernment of spirits and of tongues also vanish. Perhaps the most striking point of consistency with the earlier list of 12:8–10 is the place of tongues near, or at the end, in each. In vv. 29–30, Paul reiterates his earlier point from vv.7–11 that gifts are granted individually so that not all can be apostles, prophets or the rest. Yet in tension with this overarching argument, Paul finishes by urging the Corinthians to strive for the higher gifts—advice that helps to reify the hierarchy of gifts Paul has established.[9]

In 1 Cor 12, Paul's rhetoric fosters difference even as it questions individual agency regarding the spiritual gifts that each exercises. Despite urging the Corinthians to seek the "higher" gifts, Paul also establishes the impossibility of all achieving these same gifts. Further, he states in v. 7 that "each is given a manifestation of the spirit," a formulation that emphasizes not choice, but rather a passive acceptance of divine action.

Over the course of this chapter, Paul also narrows the spiritual gifts recognized for communal practice. Paul's later list of these gifts in 12:28 is not only shorter but its elements are also distinguished from the earlier list as gifts "God has appointed in the *ekklēsia*" (ἔθετο ὁ θεὸς ἐν τῇ ἐκκλησίᾳ). Paul's addition here of "in the *ekklēsia*," seems to specify these gifts as divinely sanctioned for the gathered Christian assembly. If this is the case, we can again remark on those gifts that fall away from the earlier list. Most notable here are the words of wisdom and of knowledge—the very speech

---

8. 1 Cor 1:1; 4:9; 9:1–5; 15:8–10.

9. Wire makes a similar observation: Wire, *Corinthian Women Prophets*, 138.

most valued in the Greek civic *ekklēsia*. The absence of these gifts in 12:28, together with the hierarchy Paul constructs in this verse, leaves prophecy and tongues as seemingly the only kinds of speech to be debated for *ekklēsia* practice. Moreover, Paul goes on to argue in chapter 14 that even these two forms of "*ekklēsia*" speech make far-from-equal contributions to the gathered community.

Paul reinforces difference in yet another critical way within this chapter. In 12:13, he references the baptismal formula also appearing in Gal 3:28. The alterations Paul makes in the 1 Corinthians' iteration[10] contribute to his arguments for hierarchical variance within the group. As Wire observes, Paul has dropped the negative particles in this deployment of the formula. In contrast to Gal 3:28, the formula no longer reads that through baptism there is "*no longer* Jew nor Greek, *no longer* slave nor free."[11] Instead, in 1 Cor 12:13, Paul writes that all are baptized into one body "*whether* (εἴτε) Jews or Greeks, *whether* slaves or free." Wire explains that with this change, "The social distinctions are not overcome in Christ but are accepted and integrated in Christ. The principle that distinctions between people are for the common good, which Paul has just claimed in connection with the spirit's differential distribution of gifts, is thus carried over to legitimate social distinctions."[12] In these terms, such a shift in particles significantly alters the radical potential of the baptismal formula to foster not just unity, but equality between all members of the *ekklēsia*. However, Paul makes what is arguably an even more profound change in this formula by omitting the last pair present in Gal 3:27–28.

In his appeal to the baptismal formula in 12:13, Paul completely dispenses with the pairing of "male and female" (ἄρσεν καὶ θῆλυ). His preceding argument regarding gender difference in 1 Cor 11:2–16 throws this omission into high relief—as does Paul's command regarding women's speech in 1 Cor 14:33–36. A number of scholars argue strongly that the Galatians baptismal formula is the "earliest Pauline form of this material."[13]

---

10. Part of the debate over the contrast between the baptismal formula of 1 Cor 12:13 and the one in Gal 3:27–28 revolves around the dating of Galatians. For arguments giving Galatians an early date, and thus contributing to the contention that in 1 Corinthians Paul alters the earlier baptismal formula found in Gal 3:27–28, see Horrell, *Social Ethos*, 84; Fung, *The Epistle to the Galatians*, 9–28; Dunn, *The Epistle to the Galatians*, 1–19.

11. Wire, *Corinthian Women Prophets*, 138. Gal 3:28: Οὐκ ἔνι Ἰουδαῖος οὐδὲ Ἕλλην, οὐκ ἔνι δοῦλος οὐδὲ ἐλεύθερος.

12. Ibid.

13. Horrell, *Social Ethos*, 85; Paulsen, "Einheit und Freiheit," 88; Bruce, *The Epistle of Paul to the Galatians*, 187. For arguments that this formula is also pre-Pauline, see

Moreover, some contend that the pairing "male and female" as a quotation from Genesis 1:27 was itself likely the origin of this baptismal formula in the Christian community and thus not lightly removed.[14] In 1 Corinthians, the omission of this element cannot be explained by indifference toward gender questions on the part of Paul or the Corinthians. 1 Cor 7 and 11:2–16 has already shown gender to be a critical concern for both.[15] Instead, many argue that this element of the formula had great meaning for this particular community[16]—and it is for precisely this reason that Paul removes it.[17]

In the previous chapter, I visited Schüssler Fiorenza's interpretation of Gal 3:28 as challenging the principle structures of domination in antiquity. Within Gal 3:28, Schüssler Fiorenza contends that the "no longer male and female" of the baptismal formula proclaims full and equal membership for

---

MacDonald, *There is no Male and Female*, 5–16; Wire, *Corinthian Women Prophets*, 123–26; Schüssler Fiorenza, *In Memory of Her*, 208. The basis for this argument touches upon the similarity between Gal 3:27-28, 1 Cor 12:12–13, and Col 3:9–11, with all sharing a "common structure," an appeal to a new post-baptismal state, and functioning "in Paul's context as accepted traditions that can validate his arguments." Wire, 123. Further, in Galatians itself, the pairs slave/free and male/female do not contribute to Paul's arguments in the letter, suggesting these pairings were part of an earlier form of the formula that is independent of its present context. Horrell, *Social Ethos*, 85; Schüssler Fiorenza, *In Memory of Her*, 208.

14. Wire, *Corinthian Women Prophets*, 124–25; MacDonald, *There is No Male and Female*, 17–63, 113–26.

15. Wire, *Corinthian Women Prophets*, 137; Økland, *Women in Their Place*, 200.

16. Murphy O'Connor, "Sex and Logic," 490; Theissen, *Psychological Aspects*, 166–67; Meeks, "The Image of the Androgyne," 202; Hurd, *The Origin of 1 Corinthians*, 282; Jervis, "'But I Want You to Know,'" 246.

17. For instance: Horrell, *Social Ethos*, 86; Wire, *Corinthian Women Prophets*, 126; Paulson, "Einheit und Freiheit," 90; Barton, "Paul's Sense of Place," 234. As I discussed in the previous chapter, some scholars like Jervis and Horrell phrase the Corinthian interpretation of the full baptismal formula as problematic, an interpretation that creates "too much misunderstanding and social disruption" as well as producing the "reprehensible practice of disregarding gender-specific cultural norms." Horrell, *Social Ethos*, 86; Jervis, "'But I Want You to Know,'" 246. Such an understanding of the Corinthian situation forms a contrast with that of Wire, who considers the possibility that based on this baptismal understanding, the Corinthians perceive themselves as "a new creation in Christ who is God's image not male and female." Wire, *Corinthian Women Prophets*, 137. And contrasting both these perspectives is that of Schüssler Fiorenza who offers the hypothesis that the Corinthians are productively debating the real-life implications of a formula that suggests "patriarchal marriage was no longer constitutive for the new creation in the spirit." Schüssler Fiorenza, *Rhetoric and Ethic*, 120. While significant differences of tone are apparent in these reconstructions, they all envision the Corinthians as challenging the boundaries of ancient gender construction based on the promise of this baptismal formula.

"As in all the Ekklēsiai of the Saints" 161

all unaffected by procreative roles and patriarchal marriage.[18] I have argued that the radical potential of this formula gains force and substance in conversation with the democratic discourse in evidence within the Corinthian community. Specifically, the baptismal formula of Gal 3:28 undermines the very boundaries separating the truly free and equal male citizen from the *polis'* non-citizens: slaves and women most visible among them. In turn, this opens the possibility for all to practice citizenship through equal voice and equal discernment in the gathered *ekklēsia*. Paul's omission of "no longer male and female" becomes particularly significant in the context of this "ring composition" of 1 Cor 11:2—14:40, a composition which begins and ends by gendering women's speech as unsuitable for just this public context of the *ekklēsia*. I contend that the omission of this element of the baptismal formula serves to strengthen those structures of domination in the ancient *polis* that constructed woman as "wife," and rendered their public speech problematic. Indeed, this omission forms a piece with Paul's location of women's identity and relationship with men in procreation in 1 Cor 11:12, and, as I will show, his call in 1 Cor 14 for women to restrict their speech to home and husband.

## Freedom and Harmony, Self-Interest and the Common Good

Between the hierarchy of gifts "ἐν τῇ ἐκκλεσίᾳ" in 1 Cor 12:28–31, and the longer discussion of tongues, and prophecy in the gathered *ekklēsia* in 1 Cor 14, Paul has placed an extended praise of love that takes all of chapter 13.[19] Margaret Mitchell describes this love in 1 Cor 13 as "the principle of Christian social unity that Paul urges on the Corinthians,"[20] while Fee

18. Schüssler Fiorenza, *In Memory of Her*, 211.

19. There has been significant debate as to whether this "hymn to love" was created independently of 1 Corinthians. Toward this reading, scholars have noted the unity of this passage in itself and the way that it seems to interrupt the imperatives at the end of 12:31 and their resumption at the beginning of 1 Cor 14. (Fee rehearses some of this argumentation in *The First Epistle to the Corinthians*, 626). For the possibility that this passage was composed earlier and then inserted here, see Barrett, *The First Epistle to the Corinthians*, 297; Conzelmann, *1 Corinthians*, 217–20; Wischmeyer, *Der höchste Weg. Das 13. Kapitel des 1 Korintherbriefes*. By contrast, both Fee and Wire argue that the passage is integral to the arguments Paul seeks to make in this passage. It may be labeled a "digression," but it is a digression crafted toward explaining the exercise of spiritual gifts in the community. Fee, *The First Epistle to the Corinthians*, 626; Wire, *Corinthian Women Prophets*, 139.

20. Mitchell, *Paul and the Rhetoric of Reconciliation*, 274.

suggests it is the guide for behavior that will realize the common good, the συμφέρον of 12:7.[21] Within this chapter, Paul repeatedly asserts the value of love, this principle for "social unity," by comparing it to the deficiencies of speech and wisdom. The relationship between such an ideal of social unity, *homonoia*,[22] and individual freedom is one of the critical tensions of democratic discourse in the ancient world. I argue that Paul's juxtaposition of social unity and common good, on the one hand, to freedom and self-interest, on the other, exploits this tension toward a particular vision of *ekklēsia* practice.

In his work on Athenian democracy, Josiah Ober observes the recurring and unresolved tension between the ideals of individual freedom and of civic harmony.[23] As I have stated repeatedly, freedom in ancient democracy was most commonly expressed in terms of the equal opportunity for public, political speech, the *isēgoria* and *parrhēsia* of the *ekklēsia*. Ober explains that Athenians did not see this freedom as being unproblematic or without risk. Indeed, they identified self-interest as a grave danger associated with this expression of freedom. Whenever someone exercised this right, this freedom, the risk existed that the individual might lead the people not to the greater civic interest but to the service of their own greed, ambition, or other form of gain. *Homonoia* was the ideal contrasting to this exercise of freedom and to this risk of self-interest.

As utilized by political orators, Ober defines *homonoia* as "a condition in which all citizens think the same thing, in which their social and political differences are submerged in a unified community of interest."[24] On the face of it, these two ideals of individual freedom and *homonoia* seem completely antithetical and impossible to sustain within the same system. The free speech of *isēgoria* was associated with difference of opinion and contest. Such contest and difference in thought fundamentally clashes with the

---

21. Fee expresses the goal of the chapter in this way, while Wire suggests that here Paul defines the "standard of greatness" which is living for others. Fee, *The First Epistle to the Corinthians*, 628; Wire, *Corinthian Women Prophets*, 139.

22. Mitchell and Welborn have both observed the parallels between Paul's arguments for unity within the Corinthian community and the ancient political ideal of *homonoia*. Both provide ample evidence detailing these parallels. However, while both invoke the "political" context with their discussions of *homonoia*, neither explicitly addresses democracy as part of that context. Moreover, neither confronts the critical tension that exist within democratic discourse between this harmony and the freedom and contest of civic democracy. For examples of their discussions of *homonoia*, see Mitchell, *Paul and the Rhetoric of Reconciliation*, 60–80; Welborn, *Politics and Rhetoric*, 1–42.

23. Ober, *Mass and Elite*, 295–99.

24. Ibid., 297.

*homonoia* definition above, a definition emphasizing sameness and unified interest. Ober himself contends that democracy, as it was constructed in antiquity, required this very contest and diversity of thought associated with free speech. He argues that "a politics of pure consensus" would have led to stagnation and superficiality because it failed to provide a way of revising failed policy. However, Ober points out that the Athenians did not seem to feel the need to resolve these conflicts between the ideals of freedom and *homonoia*.[25] Instead, they held both as critical ideals of the democratic *polis*, taking no steps to legally foster one or the other.[26]

One result of this unresolved tension within democratic discourse is that both ideals were available to orators from the classical period forward, and both are regularly featured as rhetorical themes. In fact, they often are featured together in a productive tension which allows the orator to claim themselves as agents of harmony and the common good, while at the same time appearing to support freedom—albeit, often a freedom limited by that same common good. I suggest that this is the very tension Paul exploits in 1 Cor 13–14.

In 1 Cor 13:1–3 and again in 1 Cor 13:8–12, Paul paints the inadequacy of speech and wisdom in contrast to love. Without love, speech with the "tongues of men and angels" (ἐὰν ταῖς γλώσσαις τῶν ἀνθρώπων λαλῶ) is meaningless, as is prophecy and "all knowledge" (πᾶσαν τὴν γνῶσιν). In verses 1–3, the familiar companions, speech and wisdom, are again found wanting. As Paul questioned speech and wisdom in the community as human and not divine with 1 Cor 1–4, here he suggests that even divine knowledge and speech remain worthless without this further ingredient.

In the last verses of 1 Cor 13, Paul contrasts the eternal endurance of love with all that will pass away in the coming eschatological "wholeness."[27] While love remains forever, prophecies and tongues will end, as will knowledge (γνῶσις). Knowledge and prophecies are only fragmentary (ἐκ μέρους), and thus face sure destruction when "the wholeness" arrives. Paul earlier

25. Ibid., 298–99.

26. Ober explains that this strategy allowed the Athenians to "avoid the conflict between individual rights and the legitimate exercise of majoritarian power which is a major concern of modern democracies." Ibid., 299.

27. For an overview of the debate over the meaning of τὸ τέλειον in this verse, see Fee, 644–45. He notes that it has been common to read this phrase as the fullness or completion of love and thus represents the maturity of the Corinthians into that love. However, Fee argues with Conzelmann that the completion is not of people but of gifts here and that Paul is clearly making an argument between "now" and "then" that requires a reading of this term as eschatological. I agree that this wording points to an eschatological future, though I would debate with Conzelmann whether this may be the *parousia*. Conzemlmann, *1 Corinthians*, 226.

stressed that speech and knowledge lack any worth without love. Now, Paul portrays not only knowledge but also the speech of prophecy and tongues as fragmentary and incomplete—seemingly regardless to their pairing with love. Pre-eschaton knowledge and speech in their fragmentary and temporary state thus become foils for the permanence of love, and the true knowledge that is yet to come.

Paul reinforces the limitations of current speech and wisdom with the metaphor of a child gaining maturity. Thus, he compares the speech, thinking, and reasoning of a child in 1 Cor 13:11 with the superior state of the adult who "has put an end to childish ways."[28] This verse calls to mind Paul's similar use of the maturity trope in 1 Cor 1–4 to emphasize the inadequacy of human speech and wisdom in contrast to divine wisdom. In that earlier conversation, Paul labels the Corinthians "infants" (νηπίοις), implying that their own speech and wisdom is human and thus limited.[29] In 1 Cor 13:11, the word νήπιος again designates the practitioner of deficient speech and knowledge. These parallels, combined with Corinthian claims of excellence in speech and wisdom, strongly suggest that Paul again implicates the Corinthians with this talk of infants. As in the earlier verse, the Corinthians are marked by their exercise of a speech and wisdom that fades to nothing in the presence of the ultimate reality. Their surest path to this ultimate reality in the present resides not with their practice of speech, inescapably inadequate as it is, but with their practice of love.[30]

I suggest that Paul's choice of wisdom, and particularly speech, as the foil for love reaffirms that these elements are central to the identity and practice of his Corinthian audience. For a group viewing their identity through

28. 1 Cor 13:11. "When I was a child, I spoke like a child, I thought like a child, I reasoned like a child; when I became an adult, I put an end to childish ways." ὅτε ἤμην νήπιος, ἐλάλουν ὡς νήπιος, ἐφρόνουν ὡς νήπιος, ἐλογιζόμην ὡς νήπιος· ὅτε γέγονα ἀνήρ, κατήργηκα τὰ τοῦ νηπίου.

29. 1 Cor 3:1. "And so, brothers, I could not speak to you as spiritual people, but rather as people of the flesh, as infants in Christ." Κἀγώ, ἀδελφοί, οὐκ ἠδυνήθην λαλῆσαι ὑμῖν ὡς πνευματικοῖς ἀλλ' ὡς σαρκίνοις, ὡς νηπίοις ἐν Χριστῷ.

30. Other scholars have asserted that Paul targets Corinthian practice in his description of love and its contrasts. For instance, Fee reads in this description of love a further critique of the Corinthians that echoes Paul's earlier admonishments of the community. In this vein, Paul cites the Corinthians for jealousy and strife, boasting of their wisdom and selfishness to the detriment of the group—all behaviors that preclude their attainment of this greatest gift of love. Fee, *The First Epistle to the Corinthians*, 637–38. In a more positive vein, Wire also sees this passage as giving insights on Corinthian practice and belief. She understands Paul's love discussion here as aimed toward a people that understands themselves as newly empowered in the spirit, concerned less for the common good, and more for "striving to embody divine forces." Wire, *Corinthian Women Prophets*, 139.

the lens of ancient democratic discourse, speech and wisdom form the basis not only for individual freedom but also for the corporate authority of the group *as ekklēsia*. Paul's efforts to destabilize Corinthian speech and wisdom throughout the letter signal his attempt to shape and circumscribe this freedom and authority. In 1 Cor 13 and 14, Paul uses the pervasive tension in democratic discourse between freedom through the exercise of speech, and its antithesis, the ideal of harmony and the common good, to qualify Corinthian "performance" of freedom. Toward that end, Paul imbues his superior love with many of those characteristics that also accompany the ideal of *homonoia* in ancient democratic discourse.

Paul defines the love he requires for the community in verses 4–7 mainly with negative contrasts of what love is *not*. Love is not "envious, or boastful or arrogant or rude. It does not seek its own benefit; it is not irritable or resentful; it does not rejoice in wrongdoing."[31] In these verses, Paul catalogs the very kinds of negative self-interest seen as the risk of freedom in democratic discourse. In common with other ancient orators, Paul asks his audience to reject such self-interest in the favor of a common good that is realized in patience, kindness, and self-less concern for others. Indeed, Paul's definition of love strongly resembles other ancient descriptions of *homonoia* and its pre-requisites.

Dio's thirty-fourth oration to Tarsus provides one instructive parallel to Paul's description of love. In this oration, Dio seeks to persuade the civic assembly to maintain a recent, fragile harmony among its citizens. Dio asserts that the only way to sustain citizen unity, *homonoia*, is to eradicate the evils of jealousy (φθόνος), greed (πλεονεξία), rivalry (φιλονεικία), and especially, "the striving in each case to promote one's own welfare at the expense of both one's native land and the common good."[32] Here, Dio's own list of evils closely resembles love's opposites in 1 Cor 13:4–6. In both cases, the greatest good is achieved only when such negative, selfish inclinations are completely abandoned. Strikingly, Dio also illustrates the lack of harmony, the discord created by self-interest, with a metaphor that also dominates Paul's arguments regarding *ekklēsia* speech in the following chapter 14. Thus, Dio compares civic unity to instruments playing in harmony, and its opposite, civic discord, to those same instruments playing clashing, dissonant notes.[33]

---

31. 1 Cor 13:4–6. Οὐ ζηλοῖ, [ἡ ἀγάπη] οὐ περπερεύεται, οὐ φυσιοῦται, οὐκ ἀσχημονεῖ, οὐ ζητεῖ τὰ ἑαυτῆς, οὐ παροξύνεται, οὐ λογίζεται τὸ κακόν, οὐ χαίρει ἐπὶ τῇ ἀδικίᾳ . . .

32. *Or*. 34.19. τοῦ ζητεῖν ἕκαστον αὔξειν ἑαυτόν, καὶ τὴν πατρίδα καὶ τὸ κοινῇ συμφέρον ἐάσαντα . . .

33. Ibid., 34.18.

## The Gathered *Ekklēsia* of 1 Cor 14

In 1 Cor 14, Paul makes his most sustained argument regarding Corinthian practice in the *ekklēsia* setting.[34] As in the civic sphere, Paul's own meditation on the *ekklēsia* in this chapter is dominated by the speech and discernment of the group. Paul crafts an ideal *ekklēsia* that is built on contrasts, an *ekklēsia* in which prophecy is privileged over tongues, order over disorder, speech of the mind over that employing only the spirit—and men's speech over that of women. Paul's arguments in this chapter are strongly tied to what has come before in chapters 11, 12, and 13. Paul's differentiation of spiritual gifts in 1 Cor 12, and his assertion of a hierarchy of gifts appointed "for the *ekklēsia*," sustain his contention in 1 Cor 14 that certain types of speech and speakers have greater value in the gathered assembly. In chapter 14, the speech of greatest value (prophecy) gains this distinction as the instrument of "upbuilding." In this chapter, prophecy is a form of speech associated with order, and by implication, with the mind. In these terms, prophecy serves the harmony which secures the common good and thus performs as the representative of love which Paul has described in 1 Cor 13. Against the backdrop of 1 Cor 11:2–16, Paul's arguments regarding ideal *ekklēsia* behavior in chapter 14 are deeply gendered, prioritizing as they do mind, order, and the limitation of freedom. This gendering of *ekklēsia* practice then provides the foundation for Paul's command to the Corinthian women in 1 Cor 14:33–36.

The first verse of 1 Cor 14 immediately brings to bear the conclusions of both chapters 12 and 13. Paul commands the Corinthians to "[p]ursue love and strive for the spiritual gifts, and especially that you may prophesy."[35] With this wording, Paul reminds the Corinthians he has named self-sacrificing love as the highest good, and their best opportunity to take part in the eternal reality of the eschatological future. However, Paul's command to "strive" (ζηλοῦτε) for the spiritual things also recalls the command of 1 Cor 12:31 where the Corinthians are also told to strive (ζηλοῦτε) for the greater gifts. In the ranking of spiritual gifts "God has appointed in the *ekklēsia*," prophecy comes second in Paul's hierarchy of 1 Cor 12:28. In 1 Cor 14:1, Paul again privileges prophecy among the spiritual gifts exercised

---

34. As with the civic assembly, the *ekklēsia* of 1 Cor 14 does not seem to a particular place but instead the gathering when the community comes together in one place. See especially 1 Cor 14:23, where Paul speaks of the whole church coming together. "If therefore, the whole church comes together . . ." ἐὰν οὖν συνέλθῃ ἡ ἐκκλησία ὅλη ἐπὶ τὸ αὐτό.

35. Διώκετε τὴν ἀγάπην, ζηλοῦτε δὲ τὰ πνευματικά, μᾶλλον δὲ ἵνα προφητεύητε.

in the *ekklēsia*, thus reinforcing his conclusion that all spiritual gifts are not equal—nor, we may infer, are their practitioners.

Much of 1 Cor 14 sets prophecy up against tongues as that speech which will best serve the gathered community.[36] Paul outlines the terms of the prophecy-tongues comparison in 1 Cor 14:2–4 where he declares that those who prophesy "build up the *ekklēsia*."[37] Meanwhile, tongues are directed to God alone. Because they are intelligible only to God, tongues build up only the individual who uses them. In the following verses, Paul insists that intelligible speech alone can profit others. By contrast, speaking in tongues is comparable to the indistinct notes of instruments played badly[38] or to the speech of foreigners.[39] Through these characterizations, prophecy shines as the instrument of "upbuilding and encouragement and consolation" for the *ekklēsia*.[40] On the other hand, Paul portrays tongues as the source of chaos and misunderstanding—a gift that can only benefit the individual. Thus, Paul gives tongues only a very limited role in an *ekklēsia* in which "all things should be done decently and in order."[41] Paul claims such order is itself divine when he writes in 1 Cor 14:33, "God is a God not of disorder, but of peace."

Paul's demands for order in the assembly, and his contrast of prophecy and tongues, has led scholars to describe the Corinthian gatherings as disorderly, chaotic, and confused.[42] Moreover, scholars have located the

---

36. The very forcefulness of the dichotomy Paul creates between prophecy and tongues implies these are the *only* forms of speech truly at issue for the *ekklēsia* context. Notably, the "word of wisdom" and "word of knowledge" from 1 Cor 12:8 have largely faded into the background here.

37. 1 Cor 14:4. "Those who speak in a tongue build up themselves, but those who prophesy build up the *ekklēsia*." ὁ λαλῶν γλώσσῃ ἑαυτὸν οἰκοδομεῖ· ὁ δὲ προφητεύων ἐκκλησίαν οἰκοδομεῖ.

38. Mitchell notes that the *topos* for civic discord of people speaking at the same time and not listening is often accompanied by a discussion of musical instruments. She gives the example of Dio Chrysostom for this phenomenon (*Or.* 34.18; 48:7). Mitchell, *Paul and the Rhetoric of Reconciliation*, 172.

39. Such language can only make people strangers to each other since, "If then I do not know the meaning of a sound, I will be a foreigner to the speaker and the speaker a foreigner to me." 1 Cor 14:11. ἐὰν οὖν μὴ εἰδῶ τὴν δύναμιν τῆς φωνῆς, ἔσομαι τῷ λαλοῦντι βάρβαρος καὶ ὁ λαλῶν ἐν ἐμοὶ βάρβαρος.

40. 1 Cor 14:3. "Those who prophesy speak to other people for their upbuilding and encouragement and consolation." ὁ δὲ προφητεύων ἀνθρώποις λαλεῖ οἰκοδομὴν καὶ παράκλησιν καὶ παραμυθίαν.

41. 1 Cor 14:40. Πάντα δὲ εὐσχημόνως καὶ κατὰ τάξιν γινέσθω.

42. For representative examples, see Fee, *The First Epistle to the Corinthians*, 684–98; Witherington III, *Conflict and Community*, 275.

disorder in "the apparently unbridled use of tongues in the assembly."[43] In this reading, the Corinthians' appreciation for both their own spiritual gifts and their understanding results in their insistence on individual rather than communal advantage. Betz represents this interpretation of the Corinthian situation when he writes in sympathy with Paul, "To the apostle, the congregation offered a rather distressing picture: so-called spiritual experiences justifying excesses and abuses of freedom in complete disregard for the life of the community, all of them certain signs of a community falling apart."[44] Such a portrayal fails to recognize the strong rhetorical argument that Paul constructs toward just this image of the community. As Laura Nasrallah explains regarding Paul's rhetoric, "1 Corinthians deliberately constructs the individual over and against the community and insists the inscribed audience is concerned with the former and Paul with the latter."[45] I argue that in 1 Cor 14, Paul achieves such a portrayal by deploying elements of democratic *ekklēsia* discourse that include the tension between harmony, and individual freedom I examined with regard to 1 Cor 13. In 1 Cor 14, Paul exploits this tension by suggesting that one form of *ekklēsia* speech, tongues, is purely in the service of self-interest and is an exercise of freedom that damages the cohesion of the group. The contrasting speech of prophecy contributes instead to the common good, harmony, and order.

Paul's own deployment of *ekklēsia* discourse in 1 Cor 14 is revealed in part by his characterization of tongues through the metaphors of discordant music and foreign languages. Margaret Mitchell has recognized that the metaphor of discordant instruments has a place in political discourse in the ancient world, asserting that it is one of the *topoi* used to describe divided groups.[46] However, Mitchell neither connects this *topos* with democratic discourse nor recognizes its usefulness in contrasting the dangers of individual freedom to the ideal of harmony. Mitchell cites Dio Chrysostom for evidence of this *topos* in ancient literature, noting that it occurs in *Or.* 34.18 and 48.7. In *Or.* 34, I have observed Dio's use of this *topos* in tandem with his list of those types of negative self-interest that must be eliminated to achieve harmony—a list with remarkable similarities to Paul's catalogue of love's opposites in 1 Cor 13. However, another example of this discordant music *topos* in Dio's writing proves especially illuminating for 1 Cor 14.

In his thirty-ninth oration to the Nicaeans, Dio praises his audience for "wearing the same costume, speaking the same language, and desiring

---

43. Ibid., 652.
44. Betz, "The Problem of Rhetoric," 26.
45. Nasrallah, *An Ecstasy of Folly*, 78.
46. Mitchell, *Paul and the Rhetoric of Reconciliation*, 172.

the same things."⁴⁷ Regarding such "singleness of purpose," Dio asks, "What city is wiser in council than that which takes council together?"⁴⁸ Dio advises such unity because, "as many citizens as there are, so many are the eyes with which to see that city's interest (τὸ ἐκείνης συμφέρον), so many the ears with which to hear, so many the tongues to give advice, so many the minds concerned in its behalf (τοσαῦται δὲ διάνοιαι φροντίζουσιν)."⁴⁹ Dio compares this city unified around a common interest with citizens at odds, suggesting that such citizens do not even hear one another properly. Instead, they are like a chorus that is out of harmony (τῶν ἀσυμφώνων χορῶν).⁵⁰

In this oration, citizens' accord manifests in shared language and their commitment to the common good of the city. Their contrasting discord means that they are unable to understand each other and thus can neither hear nor act upon the wise advice audible in the harmonious city. This oration illustrates well the tension in democratic discourse between the ideals of freedom and harmony, even as it provides important parallels for Paul's rhetoric in 1 Cor 14. Here, Dio, like Paul, uses the *topoi* of music and languages to persuade his audience to achieve harmony. Dio argues that they must pursue this harmony in order that the contribution of each individual, their wisdom and speech, may be audible and thus serve the common good of the city. Here, the unresolved tension is apparent between harmony and individual freedom manifested in speech and wisdom. Dio calls for harmony so that citizens may productively exercise free speech. However, he fails to acknowledge that this expression of individual thought must produce the differing opinions, the debates, that Ober suggests are the very foundation of ancient democracy. Like his classical predecessors, Dio dispenses with neither the freedom nor harmony so highly valued in democratic discourse, instead keeping both together in an uneasy but productive tension.⁵¹

Paul employs this same tension in his discussion of *ekklēsia* speech and wisdom in 1 Cor 14 when he identifies tongues as a negative freedom—one that enriches only the individual to the detriment of the group. In this way, tongues act as a foreign language or discordant music that is a barrier to the group forming a productive, harmonious *ekklēsia*. By contrast, Paul portrays prophecy as the key for successful *ekklēsia* participation. In fact, prophecy facilitates an interaction that is very similar to the one Dio describes as the

47. *Or.* 39.3. ὡς ἔγωγε ἥδομαι νῦν ὁρῶν ὑμᾶς ἓν μὲν σχῆμα ἔχοντας, μίαν δὲ φωνὴν ἀφιέντας, ταὐτὰ δὲ βουλομένους.
48. Ibid. Ποία μὲν βουλεύεται πόλις ἄμεινον τῆς ἅμα βουλευομένης;
49. Ibid., 39.9.
50. Ibid., 39.4.
51. Ober, *Mass and Elite*, 299.

product of harmony. As intelligible speech, prophecy allows the Corinthians to understand each other and in this way "builds ups" the *ekklēsia*. Moreover, this intelligibility also makes possible the partner of *ekklēsia* speech in the democratic *polis*, audience discernment. Paul mentions this discernment regarding the outsider entering the Corinthian *ekklēsia*. Instead of considering the Corinthians mad[52] as he might on entering an *ekklēsia* of tongue speakers, the outsider may himself be judged (ἀνακρίνεται) and persuaded if he encounters the intelligible speech of prophecy (1 Cor 14:24–25). In his model *ekklēsia*, Paul further suggests that orderly prophecy will be accompanied by "others discerning" (οἱ ἄλλοι διακρινέτωσαν), even as such orderly prophecy allows all "to learn" (1 Cor 14:29–31). Like Dio, Paul claims that the restrictions he counsels in the name of the common good results in the very ability of the Corinthians to profitably exercise their own freedom in speech and wisdom.

Paul's ideal *ekklēsia* speech has yet another element in common with the productive harmony in Dio's thirty-ninth oration. For Dio, harmony means that not only voices, eyes, and ears of the citizens will be active in the common interest of the city but that the citizens' minds will also be engaged on its behalf. Paul likewise claims that for *ekklēsia* speech to benefit, to "build up" the other person, it must employ the mind (ὁ νοῦς, 14:14–19). This requirement again marks tongues as inadequate for the *ekklēsia* context. Paul claims that tongues are a form of speech that employs only the spirit but does not use the mind.[53] In 1 Cor 14:14–19, where Paul describes the necessity of engaging the mind in *ekklēsia* speech, intelligibility again drives his argument. If one does not use the mind in giving thanks, the outsider (ἰδιώτος) will not be able to understand or respond (1 Cor 14:16). The person employing only the spirit may be able to "give thanks well enough," but the other person does not gain, they are not built up (1 Cor 14:17). Instead, Paul advises that "ἐν ἐκκλησίᾳ" the speaker must employ both spirit and mind. Paul offers thanks that he speaks in tongues "more than all of you" (14:18), while insisting that in the *ekklēsia* he would rather "speak five words with my mind, in order to instruct others also, than ten thousand words in a tongue."[54]

---

52. The Greek is μαίνεσθε. For some discussion of this word and its significance in the Greek world, see Fee, *The First Epistle to the Corinthians*, 685.

53. 1 Cor 14:14. "For if I pray in a tongue, my spirit prays but my mind is unproductive." ἐὰν [γὰρ] προσεύχωμαι γλώσσῃ, τὸ πνεῦμά μου προσεύχεται, ὁ δὲ νοῦς μου ἄκαρπός ἐστιν.

54. 1 Cor 14:19. ἀλλὰ ἐν ἐκκλησίᾳ θέλω πέντε λόγους τῷ νοΐ μου λαλῆσαι, ἵνα καὶ ἄλλους κατηχήσω, ἢ μυρίους λόγους ἐν γλώσσῃ.

Paul's insistence in 1 Cor 14:14–19 that correct *ekklēsia* speech employs both spirit and mind has led scholars like Dale Martin and C. K. Barrett to conclude that Paul's contrast to tongues in these verses is also a form of inspired speech[55]—and likely the prophecy that elsewhere in the chapter is also described as building up the community (14:3–4) and facilitating learning (14:31). At first blush, it might seem that Paul makes a departure from Greek democratic discourse in arguing that a form of divination not only has a place in the *ekklēsia* but itself could also facilitate audience discernment in that setting. However, the scholar Jean-Pierre Vernant has observed that the Greeks of the classical period preferred oral divination over other forms, such as augury, precisely because this speech found a place in "the field of the new rationality of discourse" that characterized "political, historical, medical, philosophical and scientific thought." As Vernant explains of this divination,

> By contrast to the interpretation of signs or procedures of technical divination that require the services of a specialized seer, the god's oracular word, once formulated, is, like every other word accessible to each individual. In order to understand it, there is no need for a particular competence in divination; it is sufficient that whoever piously comes to consult the oracle has the same qualities of sane reflection, levelheadedness, and moderation that characterize the good citizen and, with the addition of shrewdness and acuity, serve political ends. In the different explanations the oracular response elicits, it can even become the object of the same kind of argumentative debate used in assemblies and law courts.[56]

In these terms, divination itself becomes a democratizing force, since in an intelligible form it could be understood by all, and if necessary, even debated in an *ekklēsia* setting. As Vernant points out, Herodotus gives a vivid example of this kind of debate during the Persian War. During this time, the Athenians consulted the oracle at Delphi and received the response that they would be saved by a wooden rampart.[57] The resulting debate over the meaning of the oracle and the action to be taken appealed "to the same order of argumentation as every other question debated in the Assembly."[58]

---

55. Martin, *The Corinthian Body*, 100–103; Barrett, *The First Epistle to the Corinthians*, 319; Horrell, *Social Ethos*, 183.

56. Vernant, "Speech and Mute Signs," 311.

57. Herodotus 7.140–45.

58. Vernant, "Speech and Mute Signs," 313.

This connection of oral divination to Greek civic discourse and practice makes sensible Paul's insistence that inspired speech in the *ekklēsia* context must be intelligible precisely in order that it may be judged and debated. However, Paul does not ask only that *ekklēsia* speech be intelligible but also insists that the speakers utilize their minds in performing spiritual speech in the *ekklēsia*. Dale Martin has observed that Paul's direction to prophets that they use both spirit *and* mind in their inspired speech sets Paul apart from the common descriptions of such speech in platonic philosophy. In the authors he examines, Plato, Philo, and Iamblicus, the mind becomes inactive, or even briefly absent, when the person's body is acted upon by a higher divine mind or spirit.[59] Martin demonstrates that in the case of Philo and Iamblicus, the human mind is understood to be below the divine spirit or πνεῦμα. For Martin, Paul's call for prophets to use both mind and spirit challenges the received hierarchy in which divine spirit was understood to be superior to the human mind—a mind with no place in mantic activity. In turn, Martin understands Paul's uncommon insistence on "mindful" prophecy to be part of a larger pattern in 1 Corinthians, a pattern in which Paul repeatedly seeks to challenge status hierarchies within the Corinthians' "social body" so as to achieve greater equality in the community.[60] I agree that Paul's inclusion of the mind as an element of inspired speech is unusual. However, Paul's rhetorical strategy in making this inclusion comes into better focus when one recognizes that the mind, literally out of place when it comes to the action of prophesy as described by some platonic philosophers, was understood as essential in the *ekklēsia* context for both speakers and their audiences.

Aristotle, Dio, and Plutarch illustrate well the place of the νοῦς in Greek democratic discourse from the classical period forward. Aristotle uses the body's (σῶμα) relationship to the soul (ψυχή), and desire's (ὄρεξις) relationship to the mind (νοῦς) to demonstrate that the hierarchies between men and women, masters, and slaves, are "natural." Even as the soul naturally controls the body, the mind likewise rules over the emotions because it possesses reason (λόγος).[61] As I explained in the last chapter, the possession of a fully functioning reasoning capacity or mind belongs only to the free male in Ariostotle's construction, and thus only the free man is capable of citizenship which entails rule over others. By contrast, the deliberative (τὸ Βουλευτικόν) portion of the soul associated with reason and the mind is absent in the slave and inoperative in the woman, leaving both naturally and

---

59. Martin, *The Corinthian Body*, 97–100.
60. Ibid., 103.
61. Aristotle, *Pol.* 1254b5–10.

permanently ruled by the male citizen.⁶² Without the fully realized mind that allows reason and deliberation, women and slaves can neither fully control body or desire nor can they participate in the most critical political activity in the democratic *polis*, the speech and debate of the *ekklēsia*.

Dio and Plutarch likewise identify the νοῦς as a necessity for carrying out civic politics with any chance of success. In his first speech to the Tarsus assembly, Dio councils his audience that it is the νοῦς combined with prudence (σωφροσύνη) that saves a city—that makes blessed the citizens that use these properties.⁶³ This insistence that citizens concerned for the common good of their cities must use the faculty of the mind (often with accompanying σωφροσύνη) is a thread running through many of Dio's speeches.⁶⁴ Likewise, Plutarch's names the mind as an essential tool for statesman in his advice for civic politics. To the elder statesman, Plutarch explains that politics do not require "deeds of hands and feet"⁶⁵ but "of counsel, foresight, and speech."⁶⁶ This speech must not be disruptive, but instead it must have sense or mind (νοῦν), prudent thought (φροντίδα πεπνυμένην), and caution (ἀσφάλειαν). In advising the younger politician, Plutarch again combines a discussion of speech and the mind. The politician must use well-crafted and persuasive speech (λόγον . . . συμπείθοντα) to lead others, but he must also "have in himself the mind (νοῦν) that steers."⁶⁷

Like Aristotle, Dio shows that conversations regarding the mind could be deeply gendered in Greek political and philosophical discourse. In his first speech to Tarsus, Dio chides the citizens for corrupting their minds⁶⁸ with the indecent snorting that takes place among them.⁶⁹ Dio compares this impolite sound, and the resulting corruption of mind, with men that go entirely against their natures by becoming effeminate. After a time, these men learn to make a sound that is utterly shameful, being neither male nor

---

62. Ibid., 1260a12–15.

63. Dio, *Or.* 33.28. ἀλλὰ σωφροσύνη καὶ νοῦς ἐστι τὰ σῴζοντα. Ταῦτα ποιεῖ τοὺς χρωμένους μακαρίους . . .

64. Among the examples: Dio, *Or.* 32.5; 34.13; 34.39; 40.20, 26; 50.5.

65. Plutarch, *An seni* 789 D.

66. Ibid. βουλῆς καὶ προνοίας καὶ λόγου.

67. Plutarch, *Praec. ger. rei publ.* 801F. ὁ δὲ πολιτικὸς ἐν ἑαυτῷ μὲν ὀφείλει τὸν κυβερνῶντα νοῦν ἔχειν.

68. Dio, *Or.* 33.59. He claims, "The mind of the men of Tarsus has been the very first thing to be ruined and utterly corrupted." τούτων δὲ ὁ νοῦς πρῶτος ἀπόλωλε καὶ διέφθαρται.

69. Much of this oration is taken up with Dio's critique of the citizens for some kind of snorting, a habit he designates with the term ῥέγκειν. For instance, see *Or.* 33.33.

female.⁷⁰ In this example, those male citizens that betray gender boundaries can no longer maintain an uncorrupted mind, and their speech, the currency of citizenship in the democratic *polis*, becomes utterly debased and no longer fit for the public setting.

Dio again genders the mind and its performance in his thirtieth discourse, a philosophical dialogue on the nature of human life. In one part of this dialogue, Dio compares human life to a banquet thrown by the gods. At this banquet, Dio explains that pleasure (ἡδονή) is the intoxicating beverage offered. Two cup-bearers serve at this banquet, and each diner must choose how to utilize them. One cup-bearer is male and represents the mind (νοῦς), while the other, a female cup-bearer, stands for intemperance (Ἀκράτεια). The wise take drink only from the male cup-bearer who very sparingly mixes in the intoxicating ingredient, a contrast to the female cup-bearer who gives the full strength of pleasure to guests. This metaphor of male and female cup-bearers indicates that the mind, the faculty determining self-control, is itself male. Meanwhile, the female personifies the utter inability to control one's passions or pleasures. It is but a short logical jump from this metaphor to Aristotle's earlier conclusion that only men could exercise the mind in its fullness.

Paul's requirement that speakers exercise their minds as well as spirits in the assembly renders these speakers and their spiritual speech valued and valuable according to the logic of democratic discourse. In that discourse, the mind connotes reason, power of deliberation, wisdom, and not least, self-control. All these elements have a critical place in the construction of productive and beneficial *ekklēsia* speech and speakers in democratic discourse. Moreover, these elements are frequent partners with another element of this discourse present in 1 Cor 14, the contrast between common good and individual benefit. In 1 Cor 14, Paul suggests that the common good depends on speakers whose use of the mind not only makes their speech sensible but also shows their restraint and self-control so that "the spirits of prophets are subject to the prophets" (1Cor 14:32).⁷¹

I have argued that Paul crafts his rhetoric in 1 Corinthians for an audience that identifies itself as a democratic *ekklēsia* and highly values the wise speech and deliberation at the heart of democratic discourse. Together with his deployment of the tension between freedom and harmony, common good and individual gain, Paul's call for *ekklēsia* speech to use both mind and spirit is designed for just such an audience. Paul's rhetoric presents prophecy, his preferred form of *ekklēsia* speech, as the agent of the common good

---

70. Ibid., 33.60.
71. Καὶ πνεύματα προφητῶν προφήταις ὑποτάσσεται . . .

"As in all the Ekklēsiai of the Saints" 175

which makes possible audience discernment, learning, and encouragement. Moreover, Paul urges that the Corinthians' spiritual, *ekklēsia* speech also employs the mind—the necessary ingredient to valued political speech in democratic discourse. Paul's inclusion of this element might be expected to appeal to the Corinthians who themselves value not only democratic discourse but also their own claims to wisdom in Christ.

Rhetorically, Paul suggests that the kind of *ekklēsia* speech he favors, performed according to his direction, provides the best avenue toward an *ekklēsia* in which all are built up and "all" are able to speak as they prophesy "one by one." However, this presentation masks the ways in which Paul's arguments continue to divide and limit, rather than unify and empower the Corinthian community. Throughout 1 Cor 14, Paul sets one type of speech against another with the assertion that one builds up and benefits the *ekklēsia*, while the other damages this body. For much of the chapter, this contrast is between prophecy and tongues. However, Paul also makes a contrast between speech utilizing the mind and speech drawing on the spirit alone, even as he implies the distinction between orderly and disorderly *ekklēsia* speech. In each case, Paul approves one form of speech and its practitioners while suggesting the other has little if any role in the gathered *ekklēsia*. Not only do these dichotomies devalue certain types of speech but they also help to obscure the full range of possibilities for *ekklēsia* expression.

While Paul mentions teaching, revelation, hymns, and knowledge in 1 Cor 14:6 and 26,[72] the contrast of prophecy and tongues dominates most of the chapter with the implication that these are the only forms of speech truly at issue for the *ekklēsia* context. Notably, the "word of wisdom" and "word of knowledge" from 1 Cor 12:8 have all but disappeared[73]—as have Corinthian claims that all have wisdom or excellence in speech. Instead, Paul advocates prophecy in most of 1 Cor 14, a form of speech that he denied was available to all members of the community in 12:29. This narrowing of correct *ekklēsia* speech in turn limits those speakers who can be recognized as worthwhile contributors to the *ekklēsia*. This is a limitation that serves Paul's own authority as someone who in earlier chapters asserted

---

72. Wire reads in these verses an expression of the Corinthians' own engagement of "the many kinds of speaking that characterize the spiritual." Wire, *Corinthian Women Prophets*, 142.

73. Paul does ask in 1 Cor 14:6, "Now, brothers, if I come to you speaking in tongues, how will I benefit you unless I speak to you in some revelation or knowledge (γνώσει) or prophecy or teaching?" Wire reads this verse together with 1 Cor 14:26 as an indication of Corinthian practice rather than Pauline preferences, an indication of "the many types of speech that characterize the spiritual" in this community. Wire, *Corinthian Women Prophets*, 142.

his superiority in spiritual speech.[74] In 1 Cor 14, he reaffirms his value as a speaker, someone who chooses to exercise the mind in his spiritual, *ekklēsia* speech—while claiming to speak in tongues "more than all of you" outside the *ekklēsia*.

If 1 Cor 14 limits speech and speakers by narrowing the ideal to orderly, intelligible prophecy, I have noted that this chapter also narrows correct *ekklēsia* speech by arguing that it must utilize the mind. Again, this is a limitation that builds Paul's own authority since he presents himself as an exemplar for this type of *ekklēsia* speech. However, Paul's assertion that assembly speech must engage the mind serves his program for the Corinthian *ekklēsia* in another way. As I have shown, the mind's role in political speech took part in the portrayal of reason, self-control, and wisdom as masculine attributes in ancient democratic discourse. In conjunction with the arguments gendering speech and speakers in 1 Cor 11:2–16, Paul's requirement of mindful *ekklēsia* speech is essential to his contention in 1 Cor 14:33–36 that women's speech has no place in the Corinthian assembly.

## 1 Cor 14:33–36

> As in all the *ekklēsiai* of the saints, ³⁴women should be silent in the *ekklēsiai*. For they are not permitted to speak, but should be subordinate, as the law also says. ³⁵If there is anything that they desire to know, let them ask their husbands at home. For it is shameful for a woman to speak in church. ³⁶Or did the word of God originate with you? Or are you the only ones it has reached?

Starting in 1 Cor 14:34, Paul demands that women's voices be entirely silenced in the ideal *ekklēsia* he has envisioned in this chapter. In these verses, Paul requires not only women's silence in all "the *ekklēsiai* of the saints" but also their matching subordination. He portrays women's *ekklēsia* speech as shameful and suggests their only opportunity to speak comes through their men/husbands ἐν οἴκῳ. In contrast to those who have argued these verses as an interpolation which contradict Paul's earlier arguments in the letter,[75] I contend that Paul's rhetorical preparation for this command has

---

74. For instance, 1 Cor 2:13, where Paul states that, "We speak of these things in words not taught by human wisdom but taught by the Spirit, interpreting spiritual things to those who are spiritual."

75. For helpful summaries of the arguments for and against parts or all of vv. 33b–36 as interpolations in 1 Corinthians, see Fee, *The First Epistle to the Corinthians*, 699–708; Brooten, "Paul and the Law," 77–80; Horrell, *Social Ethos*, 184–95; Wire, *Corinthian Women Prophets*, 149–52, 229–32. The two strongest arguments for

been thorough. This preparation includes the arguments throughout the letter questioning the speech and wisdom of the Corinthians as a corporate entity—arguments that pick away at the *exordium* assertion that all in the community have been enriched in "speech and knowledge of every kind." However, this command silencing the Corinthian women gains its strength and logic most directly from the gendering of speech in 1 Cor 11:2–16 and from the very requirements for *ekklēsia* speech that Paul develops in the earlier verses of chapter 14.

In 1 Cor 11:2–16, I have shown that Paul's arguments gender women's speech as both lacking in wisdom and also as a source of disorder. Paul builds these arguments with theological appeals to creation and cosmology, even as he exploits socio-cultural *topoi* such as the veiling used widely to express gender difference and hierarchy. Paul's exegetical choices regarding Genesis leave women the secondary product of creation, even as he places them in a cosmic hierarchy in which they alone are left "headless." This lack of "head," commonly associated with the mind, reason, and self-control in Greek literature, suggests women are likewise missing those very faculties necessary for the speech and discernment of the able democratic citizen. Likewise, Paul's requirement for women's veiling during the speech of prayer and prophecy undermines women as productive and authoritative speakers. In the Greek world, veiling evoked the danger and disorder posed by women's speech and the necessity to control, to silence that speech in the public context. Paul's use of the creation narratives and of cosmic hierarchy also separates woman from the divine, and thus I suggest, undermines their performance of the spirit-filled speech of prophecy. Finally, Paul asserts that the maintenance of gender difference and hierarchy, represented by women's veiling during speech, is itself a matter of honor. Its abandonment shames these women and, by association, can cause shame to those above them in the hierarchy Paul presents.

---

interpolation are the seeming disagreements of these verses with 1 Cor 11:2–16 and the placement of these verses in some witnesses, mostly Western, after 14:40 (D, F, G, 88*, itar[61], b[89], d, e, f, g, vgms, Ambrosiaster, Seledulius-Scotus). In the following pages, I argue that 1 Cor 14:33b–36 does not pose a contradiction with 1 Cor 11:2–16 or with its context in 1 Cor 14. With regard to the movement of these verses in the (mostly) Western text, I emphasize with Wire and Brooten that there is no surviving manuscript that lacks these words—nor is there a text that puts them in a third location. As Brooten points out, "If the verses were an interpolation, one might expect to find greater regional distribution of those witnesses indicating a problem" (78). Wire argues that this transposition of the verses may go back to a single witness that is the origin of the Western tradition. For the hypotheses she offers regarding the original transposition of these witnesses, see pp. 151–52.

In the previous chapter, I located this construction of women's speech in the democratic discourse of the ancient world. In that discourse, women's lack of citizenship, their literal lack of public voice, finds justification in a construction of women as naturally lacking in reason and self-control. As such, their voice does not productively contribute to the common good of the *polis* and must be contained both within the private space of the home and within the enveloping, silencing veil. In this construction, women's virtue springs from their public silence and, ideally, their location in the home. As I have noted, women and slaves are similarly marked in this discourse in their lack of reason and their subservient nature—both of which prevent them acting out political citizenship. However, this question of honor serves to divide these groups since slaves, unlike free women, possess no honor and, consequently, no shame according to the ancient understanding of slavery. In this way, evocation of honor/shame serves not only to maintain free women's place in a hierarchy of power topped by the free, male citizen but it also contributes to the power differential related to ancient slavery.

In 1 Cor 14, Paul deploys democratic discourse in his assertion that the speech of the gathered *ekklēsia* must employ the mind, and in his call for each member of the *ekklēsia* to exercise self-control in performing speech that builds the common good rather than individual benefit. I have shown that the ability to fulfill these requirements—the ability to perform mindful and restrained speech—is regularly gendered male and attributed to the free, male citizen. Paul himself has evoked these associations with gender in 1 Cor 11:2–16. With the verses of 1 Cor 14:33–36, Paul reasserts gendered difference in speech and the inability of women to perform "correct" *ekklēsia* speech.

Within the immediate context of 1 Cor 14, Paul grounds the command for women's *ekklēsia* silence in an appeal to self-control and divine order. Directly preceding his prohibition of women's speech in 1 Cor 14:34, Paul links the divine with the restrained *ekklēsia* speech he champions throughout chapter 14. In v. 33, he claims that God has nothing to do with confusion or disorder. This statement acts as connective tissue between Paul's detailed instructions for those performing *ekklēsia* speech of prophecy and tongues in vv. 26–31, and his injunction against women raising their voices in that context. In vv. 26–31, Paul allows two or three tongue speakers at most in the *ekklēsia*, and those only with interpreters. Otherwise, they must be silent in the assembly. Likewise, prophecy is limited to "two or three" speakers at a time, while others occupy themselves by discerning that speech. All may prophesy, but only "one by one." Paul constructs this model of *ekklēsia* speech as a matter of self-control that is itself in line with the nature of the divine since, "[t]he spirits of the prophets are subject to the prophets, for

God is a God not of disorder but of peace" (1 Cor 14:32–33a).⁷⁶ Immediately thereafter, Paul tells the Corinthians, "As in all the *ekklēsiai* of the saints, women should be silent in the *ekklēsiai*."⁷⁷

Wire contends that after Paul asserts that "God is a God not of disorder but of peace" in 1 Cor 14:33, his subsequent call for women's *ekklēsia* silence "associates women with such disruption of the divine peace without having to give sex-specific evidence."⁷⁸ By contrast, I recognize that as an introduction to silencing women in vv. 33b-36, the assertion of divine order and prophetic self-control serves to reaffirm the gender difference around speech Paul has already created. In particular, Paul builds here on the arguments in 1 Cor 11:2–16 that women's speech occasions the risk of disorder, and thus requires the control and the containment of the veil. In those verses, I have argued that Paul locates this risk of disorder, and the concomitant need for the containment of the veil, in woman's lack of "head" and thus their lack of self-control. In vv. 27–36, Paul underscores this gender difference necessitating women's *ekklēsia* silence with the "equivalence" he establishes between the commands given to tongue speakers and prophets in 1 Cor 14:27–31, and the command given to women in vv. 33b-36.

There is general scholarly agreement that strong convergences exist between Paul's commands to tongue speakers and prophets for correct *ekklēsia* speech in 1 Cor 14:26–31 and the silencing of women that starts in 1 Cor 14:33b-34. Together, 1 Cor 14:27–36 contains a set of instructions given to three separate groups regarding speech in the gathered *ekklēsia*: tongue speakers, prophets, and women. These instructions feature similar structures with a third-person imperative (vv. 27,29, 34a) "followed by a conditional clause (vv. 28, 30, 35a) and, in the last two cases, by a motivation (vv.31–33; vv. 34b, 35b)."⁷⁹ These verses also share critical vocabulary. The verb "to speak" (λαλέω) appears in vv. 27, 28, 29, 34, 35, while Paul uses the verb "to be silent" (σιγάω) in vv. 28, 30, 34. Likewise, the verb "subject" (ὑποτάσσω) is used to describe the correct relationship between both the prophet and prophet's spirit (v. 32) and between men and women (v. 34). Both sets of verses include the verb "to learn" (Μανθάνω) in vv. 31 and 35, and together they contain four references to the *ekklēsia* (vv. 28, 33, 34, 35).

76. Καὶ πνεύματα προφητῶν προφήταις ὑποτάσσεται, οὐ γάρ ἐστιν ἀκαταστασίας ὁ θεὸς ἀλλὰ εἰρήνης.

77. 1 Cor 14:33b-34. ὡς ἐν πάσαις ταῖς ἐκκλησίαις τῶν ἁγίων αἱ γυναῖκες ἐν ταῖς ἐκκλησίαις σιγάτωσαν

78. Wire, *Corinthian Women Prophets*, 154.

79. Vander Stichele, "Is Silence Golden," 245. Dautzenberg lays out a similar structure with imperative, explanatory sentence and conditional further detailing the proscribed behavior. Dautzenberg, *Unchristliche Prophetie*, 253–88.

If significant convergences exist between vv. 27–33a and vv. 34b–36,[80] there is an equally significant contrast to be drawn between these sets of verses. Verses 27–33 detail a protocol for orderly speech, requiring only temporary silence for the sake of that order. Ultimately, these verses state that "you can all prophesy one by one" (1 Cor 14:31; δύνασθε γὰρ καθ᾽ ἕνα πάντες προφητεύειν). However, vv. 34- 35 commands a large segment of the population, the women in the assembly, to "absolute" silence.[81] For some scholars, these contrasts buttress arguments for vv. 34b–36 as an interpolation that shows a fundamental break in tone and intention with the earlier commands to prophets and tongue speakers. By contrast, I contend that Paul himself has crafted this equivalence between the commands of vv. 27–33a and vv. 33b–36 precisely because it serves his rhetorical goals in this letter regarding women's participation in the Corinthian *ekklēsia*.

By grouping his commands to prophets and tongue speakers with that given to women, and by linking all three commands to an ideal *ekklēsia* governed by divine order and self-control, Paul suggests that the overall aim driving vv. 27–36 is his concern for this order and common good of the community. Prophets and tongue speakers, presumably male, foster this common good by practicing restraint—speaking only in turn or with interpreters. By contrast, when women are constructed as lacking in the self-control that allows them to exercise similar restraint, any speech they perform can be portrayed as a threat to order and thus to the common good of the group. Paul solidifies this conclusion in vv. 34–35 with further appeals to the gendered construction of women's speech within this discourse.

In v. 34, Paul links women's *ekklēsia* silence with their necessary subordination according to the law.[82] He goes on to illuminate the nature

---

80. Schüssler Fiorenza suggests that the similarity of structure for the commands for all three groups suggests a church order—and also speaks to vv. 33b–36 as Pauline. Schüssler Fiorenza, *In Memory of Her*, 230.

81. Horrell, *Social Ethos*, 191.

82. Vander Stichele points out that Paul argues women's subordination in both 1 Cor 11:2–16 and 1 Cor 14:33b–36 with a theological appeal. As Paul engaged creation in 1 Cor 11:7–9, here in 1 Cor 14:34, he evokes the "law" in order to show women's place in the gender hierarchy. Vander Stichele, "Silence is Golden," 246. While some scholars have argued that this very general appeal to the law is "un-Pauline," and thus further evidence for v. 34 as part of an interpolation (for example, Fee, *The First Epistle to the Corinthians*, 707), Brooten shows that Paul's own writings are not without general appeals to the law, as can be seen in Rom 3:18, 3:31 and 7:12. Further, Brooten argues that even without direct commands silencing or subjecting women, portions of the Torah contribute to an overall impression of gender hierarchy and women's subordination—not least in the marriage law of the Pentateuch. Like his near contemporary Josephus (*Contra Apionem* 2.24), Paul may be making a general appeal to the force of

"As in all the Ekklēsiai of the Saints"  181

of that subordination in v. 35. If women want to learn, they should save their questions for home, for their own ἄνδρας. Women's *ekklēsia* speech is shameful, Paul insists. Thus, the only honorable exercise of women's speech is located in the home and runs through their husbands. This characterization of women's speech strongly recalls a text I briefly discussed in the last chapter: Plutarch's *Advice to Bride and Groom*. In that text, Plutarch likewise argues that women's speech is not for the public context. Instead, Plutarch holds forward the ideal of women "keeping at home and keeping silence."[83] In these terms, "a woman ought to do her speaking either to her husband or through her husband."[84]

In the following lines of his *Advice*, Plutarch directly connects the honor associated with women's lack of public speech, the preservation of their voices for home and husband, with the rightful subordination of the woman to that same husband. Plutarch compares husbands' control of their wives with another familiar pairing. Plutarch likens the husband to the soul which controls the body. Plutarch argues that this comparison shows that, "As it is possible to exercise care over the body without being a slave to its pleasures and desires, so it is possible to govern a wife, and at the same time to delight and gratify her."[85] As in Paul's description of cosmological hierarchy in 1 Cor 11:3, this is a comparison which intimates that women are fully body, containing only "pleasures and desires," and thus requiring the controlling guidance of the man. In his *Advice*, Plutarch also, like Paul, offers a vision in which this governance of man over woman manifests in at-home instruction. Plutarch counsels that the man should teach philosophy to his wife, enriching her understanding and helping her to avoid the "unnatural growths" that result if she tries to learn on her own. In this treatise, Plutarch, like Paul, deems women's speech unsuitable for the public context and channels their voice and "learning" to the private context where both come under the control of the husband.

---

the Torah regarding gender difference and hierarchy. While some have proposed that Paul makes reference to the Greek or Roman secular law in this verse (see Hollander, "The Meaning of the Term 'Law,'" 130; Blampied, "Paul and Silence,"158), Brooten contends that that it makes the most sense for Paul to be speaking of the Jewish law here since he does not elsewhere make "direct and unmistakable reference to the Roman or Greek law." Brooten, "Paul and the Law," 73–78.

83. Plutarch, *Conj. praec.* 142 D (Fowler, LCL).

84. Ibid. δεῖ γὰρ ἢ πρὸς τὸν ἄνδρα λαλεῖν ἢ διὰ τοῦ ἀνδρός. Plutarch contends that a marriage is successful when the woman subordinates herself to the man, and the man exercises control over the woman like the soul controls the body. Ibid., 142 E.

85. Plutarch, *Conj. praec.* 142 E (Fowler, LCL). ὥσπερ οὖν σώματος ἔστι κήδεσθαι μὴ δουλεύοντα ταῖς ἡδοναῖς αὐτοῦ καὶ ταῖς ἐπιθυμίαις, οὕτω γυναικὸς ἄρχειν εὐφραίνοντα καὶ χαριζόμενον.

The convergences between Plutarch's depiction of the ideal relationship between husband and wife in his *Advice to Bride and Groom* and Paul's statements about women's speech in 1 Cor 14:33b–36 provides grounding for Schüssler Fiorenza's argument that Paul addresses "wives" in these verses.[86] However, I want to nuance that argument in several critical respects. In contrast to Schüssler Fiorenza, I do not visualize these verses directed only to married women in the community as a contrast to 1 Cor 11:2–16 which concern unmarried women alone. I believe that in both cases, Paul's rhetoric is directed to a corporate group we may call the "women of the community." However, Paul rhetorically constructs this group with signifiers that equate "woman" with "wife" in both passages.

As I have stated, 1 Cor 11:11 bases the relationship between men and women in women's procreative role—a role certainly linked in the wider Greco-Roman discourse with the marriage relationship. With his erasure of "no longer male and female" from the baptismal formula in 1 Cor 12:13, Paul signals that this traditional marriage continues to structure a hierarchical relationship between men and women in the community. Meanwhile, the command of 1 Cor 14:33b–36 not only forbids women's public voice entirely but also places the woman under the governance and tutelage of the husband in the context of the home. By naturalizing "woman" in 1 Cor 11:2–16 and in 1 Cor 14:33b–36 as the subordinate partner of patriarchal marriage, Paul indicates that the power structure of the community will likewise be determined by this particular "pattern of domination." I wish to reformulate here Wire's observation regarding 1 Cor 11:11 and argue that Paul's rhetorical constructs obstruct not only other choices for women in the community, including the option for celibacy, but also other relationships based in equality.

As is the case with 1 Cor 11:2–16, the verses of 1 Cor 14:33b–36 have the potential to further other patterns of hierarchy and domination in this community. As I have noted, the common practice of elite authors to concern themselves primarily with the lives and practices of elite women, and to universalize "womanhood" as synonymous with that group, serves to

---

86. Schüssler Fiorenza has argued forcefully that 1 Cor 14:33b–36 is directed to wives in particular, while the earlier verses of 1 Cor 11:2–16 target the unmarried, pneumatic women in the community. In these terms, Schüssler Fiorenza understands αἱ γυναῖκες as "wives," and τοὺς ἰδίους ἄνδρας, as "their own husbands." This reading seeks to reconcile the seeming conflict between 1 Cor 11:2–16 and 1 Cor 14:33b–36, even as it takes into account the indication from 1 Cor 7 that not all Corinthian women would be married and able "to ask their husbands." Schüssler Fiorenza, *In Memory of Her*, 230–33. For a similar argument, see Ellis, "The Silenced Wives of Corinth," 216–18.

erase the presence of women who do not belong to that category. I have suggested that Paul's rhetoric, by equating the category of women with wives, performs a similar erasure of other women in the Corinthian community—both unmarried and slave women in this case. As in the Greek *polis*, this erasure has serious implications for the value, the personhood, assigned to these groups. However, in another way, Paul's rhetoric in 1 Cor 14:33b–36 compromises the voices and thus the citizenship of women who are not wives.

Paul, like Plutarch, indicates that women's voices have no place in the public but find expression through their husbands. In Plutarch's case, he urges that when a woman speaks "through" her husband, she "should not feel aggrieved if, like the flute-player, she makes a more impressive sound through a tongue not her own."[87] In 1 Cor 14:35, Paul provides a similar path for women to speak "through" their husbands, and thus in Plutarch's terms, a chance for women's voice to find its way to the public context. If this formulation compromises the public voice, and thus the full citizenship of free, married women, it even more thoroughly silences other women in the community. Slaves, unable to marry and having no claim to the honor Paul deploys in this passage, also have no one to speak to or through in the scenario Paul has crafted.[88] We may ask also about two other groups: unmarried women—including those who have indeed chosen celibacy—and those married to "unbelieving" husbands. In both cases, we might expect that these women would have no husband to whom they might speak to or "through" about matters of the *ekklēsia*. These verses thus leave the unmarried, the slave, and those married to unbelievers "doubly" silenced—possessing a voice neither in the public setting nor in the private. In turn, such a reading suggests a reexamination of the implications for women in Paul's insistence that a believing wife must not divorce her disbelieving husband in 1 Cor 7:13.

Paul's composition in 1 Cor 14:33b–36 ends, like that of 1 Cor 11:2–16, with rhetorical questions (1 Cor 11:13 and 1 Cor 14:36) and appeals to

---

87. Plutarch, *Conj. praec.* 142 D (Fowler, LCL). μὴ δυσχεραίνουσαν εἰ δι' ἀλλοτρίας γλώττης ὥσπερ αὐλητὴς φθέγγεται σεμνότερον.

88. Wire argues that one could translate τοὺς ἰδίους ἄνδρας as "their own men," meaning that the command of v. 35 requires women to pose their questions to those men in authority over them, whether it be husbands, fathers, or masters. Interpreted in this way, the command of v. 35 to ask "their men" not only locates women's speech entirely in the home but it also reinforces gender hierarchy by suggesting that all women require the authoritative teaching of a man. Wire, *Corinthian Women Prophets*, 156. I argue that this reading does not entirely account for the markers of patriarchal marriage that are present in 1 Cor 11:2–16 and 1 Cor 14:33b–36 and thus must be questioned as an explanation for this verse.

authority (11:16 and 14:36)—here combined.⁸⁹ As in 11:16, the appeal to authority in 14:36 seeks to enforce the practice that Paul has just outlined for the Corinthian community. In the case of 14:36, Paul's appeal to authority is immediately strengthened by the subsequent verses of 37–38. Paul's rhetorical questions of 1 Cor 14:36 ("Or did the word of God originate with you? Or are you the only ones it has reached?") may be intended to contrast Paul's "active, worldwide role in bringing the gospel to Corinth" to the Corinthians' "initially receptive role and local impact."⁹⁰ However, in conjunction with vv. 37–38, these questions more broadly highlight Paul's authority as a spiritual speaker and arbiter of the community's speech practice. These questions recall Paul's assertions that he originally proclaimed "God's wisdom" to the Corinthians with "a demonstration of the Spirit and of power" (1 Cor 2:4–7)—a contrast to persuasive words of human wisdom.

As I noted, Paul reasserts his authority as a spiritual speaker in 1 Cor 14:18–19 where he claims to speak in tongues "more than all of you" even as he chooses to exercise correct speech for the *ekklēsia* context that engages both mind and spirit. Following his rhetorical questions about the "word of God," Paul brings to bear in 14:37–38 the full force of the authority he has constructed for himself around speech. Paul writes, "Anyone who claims to be a prophet, or to have spiritual powers, must acknowledge that what I am writing to you is a command of the Lord. Anyone who does not recognize this is not to be recognized."⁹¹ In these verses, Paul makes the Corinthians' own spiritual speech—their very identity as spiritual people—contingent on their acceptance of his vision for *ekklēsia* practice in 1 Cor 14. In the case of the Corinthian women, this acceptance and proof of their spirituality would mean that their own spiritual gift of speech would entirely disappear from the *ekklēsia*.

## Conclusion

In this chapter, I have shown that Paul uses a variety of rhetorical strategies to differentiate and establish hierarchy regarding the practice of speech and wisdom. In 1 Cor 12–13, Paul crafts this rhetoric toward 1 Cor 14 and his

---

89. Vander Stichele observes these similarities between the passages, adding that they also have a common appeal to practice in other communities. Vander Stichele, "Silence is Golden," 246. Wire also observes the common characteristics of these passages. Wire, *Corinthian Women Prophets*, 154.

90. Wire, *Corinthian Women Prophets*, 157.

91. 1 Cor 14:37. Εἴ τις δοκεῖ προφήτης εἶναι ἢ πνευματικός, ἐπιγινωσκέτω ἃ γράφω ὑμῖν ὅτι κυρίου ἐστὶν ἐντολή· εἰ δέ τις ἀγνοεῖ, [ἀγνοεῖται.]

ideal of the gathered *ekklēsia*. This ideal *ekklēsia* builds on the differentiation of spiritual gifts in 1 Cor 12 and Paul's insistence that these gifts—apportioned by the will of the spirit—have differing value for the *ekklēsia* context. Likewise, Paul draws in 1 Cor 14 on the elaboration of love as the agent of the common good, an elaboration that itself exploits the tension between harmony and freedom in democratic discourse. In this case, love means the limitation of freedom, the practice of self-control, in favor of common good and harmony. I have argued that Paul's rhetoric in 1 Cor 14 is also deeply indebted to a gendering of speech that reflects tension in democratic discourse over women's speech, and thus their citizenship, in the democratic *polis*. Paul's gendering of women's speech as lacking in self-control and intellect in 1 Cor 11:2–16 registers this tension. This construction of women's speech, together with his insistence that "correct" *ekklēsia* speech utilizes both mind and self-control, provides the foundation for Paul's command silencing women's voices in the *ekklēsia* context. In turn, Paul's rhetoric on both ends of this "ring composition," 1 Cor 11:2–16 and 1 Cor 14:33b–36, constructs "women" as wives. This construction provides further justification for the silencing of women and thus the denial of their "citizenship" even as it compromises the voice of other women in the community.

The very limits that Paul seeks to impose upon Corinthian speech practice in 1 Cor 14, and elsewhere in the letter, reveals the radical potential of that practice. In 1 Corinthians, Paul confronts an audience that vocalizes its experience of the risen Christ as enrichment of all its members in "speech and knowledge of every kind." Schüssler Fiorenza locates this empowerment of the Corinthian community in their baptismal understanding—an understanding she argues is revealed throughout the letter.[92] In this, I do not disagree. As I wrote earlier, 1 Corinthians reveals at different points an audience that knew and embraced a baptismal formula like Gal 3:27–28. However, I have also argued that this was an audience that deployed democratic discourse toward a construction of their own identity as a democratic *ekklēsia*. The emphasis of both Paul and the Corinthians on speech, wisdom, and discernment are sensible according to that discourse. Indeed, I argue that the Corinthians interpreted their new, post-baptismal status through the lens of *ekklēsia* discourse—that they understood their empowerment in terms of the speech and wisdom that meant freedom and equality. Here the radical potential of democratic discourse comes together with a baptismal formula that "can be understood as challenging deeply ingrained elite male status prerogatives"[93] of the ancient world. The assertion that the Corin-

---

92. Schüssler Fiorenza, *Rhetoric and Ethic*, 122.
93. Ibid., 170.

thians as individuals—including women and slaves—all possess the excellence in speech and wisdom required for citizenship in an *ekklēsia* setting profoundly challenges the limitations and exclusions of ancient democracy. Paul's own rhetoric directed to women's speech—his intense efforts to gender that speech to silence in the *ekklēsia*—gives the clearest witness of that challenge. Paul's rhetoric towards women's speech make little sense unless Corinthian women were vocally participating, and through that participation claiming full citizenship in the group's *ekklēsia*.

# Conclusion

IN RECENT DECADES, MANY SCHOLARS HAVE EXAMINED THE APOSTLE PAUL as a political actor within the wider context of ancient politics. This scholarship, in the main, investigates imperial power dynamics and describes Paul's rhetoric and leadership in relationship to the Roman Empire. In this last task, much of the scholarly debate centers on Paul's letters as offering resistance to—or reinforcement of—the domination and hierarchy associated with Roman imperial power. These recent "political" interpretations of Paul can reinforce the perception that the imperial power hierarchy was the primary, or even the only, viable political model in the early empire. Likewise, such studies often further the impression of Paul himself as a paternal/imperial figure whose letters attest his command of, and unique responsibility for, the theology found in those letters.

This monograph shows that during the first century CE another political model conditioned peoples' expectations of leadership and community interaction. Democracy, with the *ekklēsia* as its central institution, had its origins in classical Athens. By the first century CE, however, democratic discourse permeated the Greek East. Replicated and reinforced by a number of practices and institutions, not least Greek *paideia*, this discourse was intimately intertwined with constructions of citizenship, freedom, and even *polis* itself, in the eastern Empire. Indeed, I have shown that the powerful conception of "Greekness" had tight connections with democratic discourse and practice during this period.

From the classical period forward, this democratic discourse centered on freedom and equality realized in free speech open to all citizens in the *ekklēsia* setting. In that setting, leadership likewise cohered with speech, with the ability to persuade a powerful audience composed of equals. In this way, the power of each leader, each speaker, was always negotiated with an audience composed of individuals with the right not only to speak in agreement or disagreement but also to discern and to vote. Democratic discourse thus offers a marked contrast to imperial discourse characterized by hierarchy and domination through force. In turn, the presence of this discourse in the Pauline letter 1 Corinthians suggests new possibilities for understanding both the early Christian community and the nature of Paul's own leadership.

Cynthia Kittredge points out that among New Testament scholars the dominant approach to interpreting Paul's letters centers on Paul as "original author and single authority."[1] With other feminist biblical scholars and theologians, Kittredge argues that such an approach means "the dialogical aspects of theologizing, such as response to other voices, discussion, and dispute, are bounded and contained."[2] By analyzing *ekklēsia* discourse in 1 Corinthians, my study reveals ways in which the dynamic between Paul and the Corinthians is determined by democratic discourse—and thus by just such a multiplicity of voices and debates. In this dynamic, Paul's leadership plays out in persuasive speech to the Corinthians as a powerful *ekklēsia*. While Paul seeks to persuade the Corinthians to a particular vision of community, his rhetoric reveals debates that signal the presence of other visions and other leaders within this authoritative assembly. In this assembly, Paul's rhetoric is carefully designed to further his own leadership claims—not least by undermining the Corinthians' speech and wisdom, the currency of their own authority as an *ekklēsia*.

This monograph addresses speech and wisdom as *topoi* of democratic discourse in 1 Corinthians. However, this study also investigates the particular debate evident in this letter around women's speech. This debate illuminates a struggle over the nature of women's participation—their citizenship—in this Corinthian *ekklēsia*. As I have observed, ancient democratic discourse constructed the full citizen—the free, adult, native-born male—over and against the non-citizens of the *polis*, the women, children, slaves, and foreigners who shared the ancient city with these citizens. The very ideals of democracy promising freedom and equality to the many necessitated assertions of essential difference between citizen and non-citizen to justify these exclusions from full citizenship. Meanwhile, the potential of democracy to promote radical equality meant these exclusions occasioned tensions and struggles in democratic discourse from the classical period forward. As democratic citizenship cohered with speech, and ideally with wisdom, this foreclosure of political citizenship for women played out in assertions of their inability to successfully perform such wise speech. As I have shown, Paul's own rhetoric around women's speech in 1 Corinthians participates in this attempt to foreclose women's speech, even as his

1. Kittredge, "Rethinking Authorship," 327.
2. Ibid., 322.

formulations demonstrate an ongoing debate around women's participation through speech—and thus their citizenship.

Paul's rhetoric in 1 Cor 11:2–16 and again in 1 Cor 14 resonates with the assertions of other ancient writers that women's lack of reason, virtue, and divine connection prohibit their successful, political participation in the democratic *polis*. However, Paul's argumentation also reveals that there is within his audience an understanding that their transformation and empowerment in Christ facilitates full citizenship for both men and women in the Corinthian *ekklēsia*. Indeed, the Corinthian *ekklēsia* seems familiar with the baptismal transformation promised in Gal 3:28. I have argued that this baptismal promise takes on new, substantive meaning in light of the Corinthian engagement with democratic discourse. This baptismal formula offers a new life in Christ in which critical markers of difference establishing the boundary between citizen and non-citizen in the democratic *polis*—gender, status as slave or free, and ethnicity—are named irrelevant. The political potential of this formula for radical empowerment of the full range of Jesus' followers is realized in the claim that all the Corinthians have been enriched through Christ in "speech and knowledge of every kind" (1 Cor 1:5). Indeed, much of Paul's rhetoric in 1 Corinthians seems designed to qualify, question, and undermine this rather breathtaking claim to the speech and wisdom grounding equality, freedom, and full citizenship for all within the Corinthian *ekklēsia*—for women, men, and slaves alike.

As this monograph asserts the first century CE knew a contrast to imperial politics in the discourse and practice of democracy, my work also suggests that some of the earliest followers of Jesus participated in the struggles and debates inherent to democratic discourse. In 1 Corinthians, Paul's own rhetoric, his very leadership in this *ekklēsia*, is both constrained and enabled by this discourse. While an appreciation of democratic discourse in 1 Corinthians offers striking insights into Paul's exercise of authority in relationship to his audience, the mobilization of this discourse by the Corinthians also suggests that early Christian theology could combine with this discourse to initiate an equality that strained, even eliminated, the boundary between citizen and non-citizen in ancient democracy.

# Bibliography

Aalders, Gerhard Jean Daniël. *Plutarch's Political Thought*. New York: North-Holland, 1982.

Adams, Edward. "First-Century Models for Paul's Churches: Selected Scholarly Developments since Meeks." In *After the First Urban Christians: The Social-Scientific Study of Pauline Christianity Twenty-Five Years Later*, edited by Todd D. Still and David G. Horrell, 60–78. New York: T. & T. Clark, 2009.

*Aeschines*. Translated by C. D. Adams. LCL. Cambridge, MA: Harvard University Press, 1919.

*Aeschylus*. 2 vols. Translated by H. W. Smyth. LCL. Cambridge, MA: Harvard University Press, 1922–1926.

Alcock, S. E. "Greece: A Landscape of Resistance?" In *Dialogues in Roman Imperialism: Power, Discourse, and Discrepant Experience in the Roman Empire*, edited by D. J. Mattingly, 103–16. Ann Arbor, MI: Journal of Roman Archaeology, 1997.

Alexander, Loveday. "Paul and the Hellenistic Schools: The Evidence of Galen." In *Paul in His Hellenistic Context*, edited by Troels Engberg-Pederson, 60–83. Minneapolis: Fortress, 1995.

Allison, Robert W. "Let Women Be Silent in the Churches (1 Cor 14:33b–36): What Did Paul Really Say, and What Did It Mean?" *Journal for the Study of the New Testament* 32 (1988) 27–60.

Amador, J. David Hester. "Interpretive Unicity: The Drive toward Monological (Monotheistic) Rhetoric." In *The Rhetorical Interpretation of Scripture*, edited by Stanley M. Porter and Dennis L. Stamps, 48–62. JSNTSupp 180. Sheffield: Sheffield Academic, 1999.

———. *Academic Constraints in Rhetorical Criticism of the New Testament*. Sheffield: Sheffield Academic, 1999.

Anderson, Graham. *The Second Sophistic: A Cultural Phenomenon in the Roman Empire*. New York: Routledge, 1993.

*Aristides: Orations*. Vol. 1. Translated by C. A. Behr. LCL. Cambridge, MA: Harvard University Press, 1973.

Aristotle. *Politics*. Translated by H. Rackham. LCL. Cambridge, MA: Harvard University Press, 2005.

Ascough, Richard S. *Paul's Macedonian Associations: The Social Context of Philippians and 1 Thessalonians*. Tübingen: Mohr/Siebeck, 2003.

Attridge, Harold W. *The Interpretation of Biblical History in the Antiquitates Judaicae of Flavius Josephus*. Harvard Dissertations in Religion. Missoula, MT: Scholars, 1976.

———. "Josephus and His Works." In *Jewish Writings of the Second Temple Period*, edited by Michael E. Stone, 185–232. Philadelphia: Fortress, 1984.
Aune, David. *The New Testament in Its Literary Environment*. Philadelphia: Westminster, 1987.
———. *Prophecy in Early Christianity and the Ancient Mediterranean World*. Grand Rapids, Mich.: Eerdmans, 1983.
Barrett, C. K. *A Commentary on the First Epistle to the Corinthians*. Harper's New Testament Commentaries. New York: Harper & Row, 1968.
———. *The First Epistle to the Corinthians*. New York: Harper & Row, 1968.
Bartchy, S. Scott. *First-Century Slavery and 1 Corinthains 7:21*. Missoula: University of Montana Press, 1973.
Barton, S. C. "Paul's Sense of Place: An Anthropological Approach to Community Formation in Corinth." *New Testament Studies* 32 (1986) 225–46.
Belleville, Linda L. "ΚΕΦΑΛΗ and the Thorny Issue of Head Covering in 1 Corinthians 11:2–16." In *Paul and the Corinthians: Studies on a Community in Conflict*, edited by Trevor J. Burke and J. Keith Elliott, 215–31. Supplements to Novum Testamentum 109. Boston: Brill, 2003.
Berger, Klaus. "Volksversammlung und Gemeinde Gottes: Zu den Anfängen der christlichen Verwendung von 'ekklesia.'" In *Tradition und Offenbarung: Studien zum frühen Christentum*, edited by Matthias Klinghardt und Günter Röhser, 173–206. Tübingen: Francke, 2006.
Betz, H. D. *Galatians: A Commentary on Paul's Letter to the Churches in Galatia*. Philadelphia: Fortress, 1979.
———. "The Problem of Rhetoric and Theology According to the Apostle Paul." In *L'apôtre Paul: Personnalité, Style et Conception Du Ministère*, edited by A. Vanhoye, 16–48. Leuven: Leuven University Press, 1989.
Bilde, Per. *Flavius Josephus Between Jerusalem and Rome: His Life, His Works and Their Importance*. Journal for the Study of the Pseudepigrapha Supplement 2. Sheffield: JSOT Press, 1988.
Blampied, Anne B. "Paul and Silence for 'the Women' in 1 Cor 14:34–35." *Studia Biblica et Theologica* 13 (1983) 143–65.
Blumenfeld, Bruno. *The Political Paul: Justice, Democracy and Kingship in a Hellenistic Framework*. New York: Sheffield Academic, 2001.
Bookidis, Nancy. "Religion in Corinth: 146 B.C.E.–100 C.E.." In *Urban Religion in Roman Corinth*, edited by Daniel N. Schowalter and Steven J. Friesen, 141–64. Cambridge, MA: Harvard University Press, 2005.
Botha, Jan. "On the 'Reinvention' of Rhetoric." *Scriptura* 31 (1989) 14–31.
Bowie, E. L. "Hellenism in the Writers of the Early Second Sophistic." In *Hellenismos. Quelques Jalons Pour Un Histoire De L'identité Grecque*, edited by S. Said, 183–204. Leiden: Brill, 1991.
———. "Portrait of the Sophist as a Young Man." In *The Limits of Ancient Biography*, edited by Brian C. McGing and Judith Mossman, 141–53. Swansea, Wales: Classical Press of Wales, 2006.
Boyarin, Daniel. *Dying for God: Martyrdom and the Making of Christianity and Judaism*. Stanford, CA: Stanford University Press, 1999.
Briggs, Sheila. "Paul on Bondage and Freedom in Imperial Society." In *Paul and Politics: Ekklesia, Israel, Imperium, Interpretation*, edited by Richard A. Horsley, 110–23. Harrisburg, PA: Trinity, 2000.

Brooten, Bernadette J. *Love between Women: Early Christian Responses to Female Homoeroticism*. Chicago: University of Chicago Press, 1996.

———. "Paul and the Law: How Complete Was the Departure?" *Princeton Seminary Bulletin* 11 (1990) 71–89.

Brown, C. "Church, Synagogue, Ekklēsia." In *The New International Dictionary of New Testament Theology*. edited by Colin Brown, 291–306. Exeter: Paternoster Press, 1975.

Bruce, F. F. *The Epistle to the Galatians: A Commentary on the Greek Text*. The New International Greek Testament Commentary. Grand Rapids: Eerdmans, 1982.

Butler, Judith. *Bodies That Matter: On the Discursive Limits of "Sex."* New York: Routledge, 2011.

Byrne, Brendan. *Paul and the Christian Woman*. Collegeville, MN: Liturgical, 1988.

Campbell, J. Y. "The Origin and Meaning of the Christian Use of the Word Ekklesia." *Journal of Theological Studies* 49, nos. 195–96 (1948) 130–42.

Castelli, Elizabeth A. *Imitating Paul: A Discourse of Power*. Literary Currents in Biblical Interpretation. Louisville, KY: Westminster John Knox, 1991.

———. "Interpretations of Power in 1 Corinthians." In *Michel Foucault and Theology: The Politics of Religious Experience*, edited by James Bernauer and Jeremy Carrette, 19–38. Aldershot, VT: Ashgate, 2004.

Cervin, Richard S. "Does *Kephalē* Mean 'Source' or 'Authority over' in Greek Literature? A Rebuttal." *Trinity Journal* 10 (1989) 85–112.

Chester, Stephen J. "Divine Madness? Speaking in Tongues in 1 Corinthians 14:23." *Journal for the Study of the New Testament* 27 (2005) 417–46.

Coenen, Lothar. "Church, Synagogue." In *The New International Dictionary of New Testament Theology*, edited by Colin Brown, 1:291–306. Exeter, UK: Paternoster, 1975.

Cohen, Shaye J. D. *Josephus in Galilee and Rome: His Vita and Development as a Historian*. Columbia Studies in the Classical Tradition 8. Leiden: Brill, 1979.

Conacher, D.J. "Rhetoric and Relevance in Euripidean Drama." In *Euripides*, edited by Judith Mossman, 79–102. Oxford: Oxford University Press, 2003.

Connolly, Joy. "Problems of the Past in Imperial Greek Education." In *Education in Greek and Roman Antiquity*, edited by Yun Lee Too, 339–72. Boston: Brill, 2001.

Conzelmann, Hans. *1 Corinthians: A Commentary on the First Epistle to the Corinthians*. Hermeneia. Philadelphia: Fortress, 1975.

Corrington, Gail Paterson. "The "Headless Woman": Paul and the Language of the Body in 1 Cor 11:2–16." *Perspectives in Religious Studies* 18 (1991) 223–31.

Cribiore, Raffaella. "The Grammarian's Choice: The Popularity of Euripides' *Phoenissae* in Hellenistic and Roman Education." In *Education in Greek and Roman Antiquity*, edited by Yun Lee Too, 241–60. Leiden: Brill, 2001.

———. *Gymnastics of the Mind: Greek Education in Hellenistic and Roman Egypt*. Princeton: Princeton University Press, 2001.

———. *Writing, Teachers, and Students in Greaeco-Roman Egypt*. American Studies in Papyrology. Atlanta: Scholars, 1996.

Crossan, John Dominic, and Jonathan L. Reed. *In Search of Paul: How Jesus's Apostle Opposed Rome's Empire with God's Kingdom: A New Vision of Paul's Words & World*. San Francisco: HarperSanFrancisco, 2004.

Crüsemann, Marlene. "Irredeemably Hostile to Women: Anti-Jewish Elements in the Exegesis of the Dispute About Women's Right to Speak (1 Cor. 14:34–35)." *Journal for the Study of the New Testament* 79 (2000) 19–36.

D'Angelo, Mary Rose. "Veils, Virgins, and the Tongues of Men and Angels: Women's Heads in Early Christianity." In *Women, Gender, Religion: A Reader*, edited by Elizabeth A. Castelli, 389–419. New York: Palgrave, 2001.

Dahl, Nils Alstrup, and Paul Donahue. *Studies in Paul: Theology for the Early Christian Mission*. Minneapolis: Augsburg, 1977.

Daniel-Hughes, Carly. *The Salvation of the Flesh in Tertullian of Carthage: Dressing for the Resurrection*. New York: Palgrave Macmillan, 2011.

Dautzenberg, Gerhard. *Urchristliche Prophetie: Ihre Forschung, ihre Voraussetzungen im Judentum und ihre Struktur im ersten Korintherbrief*. Stuttgart: Kohlhammer, 1975.

Delobel, Joel. "1 Cor 11, 2–16: Towards a Coherent Interpretation." In *L'apôtre Paul: Personnalité, Style Et Conception Du Ministère*, edited by A. Vanhoye, 369–89. Leuven: Leuven University Press, 1986.

*Demosthenes*. 7 vols. Translated by J. H. Vince and C. A. Vince et al. LCL. Cambridge, MA: Harvard University Press, 1930–1949.

Desideri, Paolo. "City and Country in Dio." In *Dio Chrysostom: Politics, Letters, and Philosophy*, edited by Simon Swain, 93–107. New York: Oxford University Press, 2000.

*Dio Chrysostom*. 5 vols. Translated by J. W. Cohoon and H. L. Crosby. LCL. Cambridge, MA: Harvard University Press, 1932–1951.

*Dio Chrysostom Orations: VII, XII and XXXVI*. Translated by D. A. Russell. Cambridge: Cambridge University Press, 1992.

*Dionis Prusaensis, Quem Vocant Chrysostomum, Quae Exstant Omnia*. Edited by J. De Arnim. Berlin: Weidmannos, 1962.

Dixon, Suzanne. *Reading Roman Women: Sources, Genres, and Real Life*. London: Duckworth, 2001.

Dubois, Page. *Centaurs and Amazons: Women and the Pre-History of the Great Chain of Being*. Ann Arbor: University of Michigan Press, 1982.

Dunn, Francis M. *Tragedy's End: Closure and Innovation In Euripidean Drama*. New York: Oxford University Press, 1996.

Dutch, Robert. *The Educated Elite in 1 Corinthians: Education and Community Conflict in Graeco-Roman Context*. New York: T & T Clark International, 2005.

Dunn, J. D. G. *The Epistle to the Galatians*. London: A. & C. Black, 1993.

Elliott, Neil. *The Arrogance of Nations: Reading Romans in the Shadow of Empire*. Paul in Critical Contexts. Minneapolis: Fortress, 2008.

Ellis, E. E. "The Silenced Wives of Corinth (1 Cor. 14.34–35)." In *New Testament Textual Criticism: Its Significance for Exegesis: Essays in Honour of Bruce M. Metzger*, edited by E. J. Epp and Gordon Fee, 213–20. Oxford: Clarendon, 1981.

*Euripides*. 8 vols. Translated by David Kovacs. LCL. Cambridge, MA: Harvard University Press, 1994–2008.

Fantham, Elaine. *Women in the Classical World: Image and Text*. New York: Oxford University Press, 1994.

Fatum, Lone. "Image of God and Glory of Man: Women in the Pauline Congregations." In *The Image of God: Gender Models in Judaeo-Christian Tradition*, edited by K. E. Børresen, 50–133. Minneapolis: Fortress, 1995.

Fee, Gordon D. *The First Epistle to the Corinthians*. New International Commentary on the New Testament. Grand Rapids: Eerdmans, 1987.
Feldman, Louis H. *Josephus and Modern Scholarship, 1937–1980*. Berlin: de Gruyter, 1984.
———. *Josephus's Interpretation of the Bible*. Berkeley: University of California Press, 1998.
———. *Judaism and Hellenism Reconsidered*. Supplements to the Journal for the Study of Judaism. Leiden: Brill, 2006.
Feldman, Louis H., and Gohei Hata. *Josephus, the Bible, and History*. Detroit: Wayne State University Press, 1989.
Fitzmyer, Joseph A. "Another Look at ΚΕΦΑΛΗ in 1 Corinthians 11:3." *New Testament Studies* 35 (1989) 503–11.
*Flavii Josephi: Opera*. Translated by Benedictus Niese. 7 vols. Berlin: Weidmann, 1995.
Foucault, Michel. *The Archaeology of Knowledge and the Discourse on Language*. Translated by A.M. Sheridan Smith. New York: Pantheon, 1972.
———. *The History of Sexuality*. Vol. 1, *An Introduction*. Translated by Robert Hurley. New York: Vintage, 1990.
Foxhall, Lin. "Foreign Powers: Plutarch and the Discourses of Domination in Roman Greece." In *Plutarch's Advice to the Bride and Groom and a Consolation to His Wife*, edited by Sarah B. Pomeroy, 138–50. New York: Oxford University Press, 1999.
Friesen, Steven J. "Poverty in Pauline Studies: Beyond the So-Called New Consensus." *Journal for the Study of the New Testament* 26 (2004) 323–61.
Fung, Ronald Y. K. *The Epistle to the Galatians*. New International Commentary on the New Testament. Grand Rapids: Eerdmans, 1988.
Garland, David E. "The Dispute over Food Sacrificed to Idols (1 Cor. 8:1–11:1)." *Perspectives in Religious Studies* 26 (2003) 173–97.
Gauthier, P. "Les cités Hellénistiques." In *The Ancient City-State*, edited by Mogens Herman Hansen, 211–31. Copenhagen: Munksgaard, 1993.
Gebhard, Elizabeth R., and M. W. Dickie. "The View from the Isthmus: Ca. 200–44 B.C." In *Corinth: The Centenary, 1896–1996*, edited by Charles K. Williams and Nancy Bookidis, 261–78. Princeton: ASCSA, 2003.
Georgi, Dieter. "The Interest in Life of Jesus Theology as a Paradigm for the Social History of Biblical Criticism." *Harvard Theological Review* 85 (1992) 51–83.
———. *The Opponents of Paul in Second Corinthians: A Study of Religious Propaganda in Late Antiquity*. Philadelphia: Fortress, 1986.
Glancy, Jennifer. "Early Christianity, Slavery, and Women's Bodies." In *Beyond Slavery: Overcoming Its Religious and Sexual Legacies*, edited by Bernadette J. Brooten, 143–58. Black Religion/Womanist Thought/Social Justice. New York: Palgrave Macmillan, 2010.
———. "Obstacles to Slaves' Participation in the Corinthian Church." *Journal of Biblical Literature* 117 (1998) 481–501.
———. *Slavery in Early Christianity* Oxford: Oxford University Press, 2002.
Gleason, Maud W. *Making Men: Sophists and Self-Presentation in Ancient Rome*. Princeton: Princeton University Press, 1995.
Goldhill, Simon. "Representing Democracy: Women at the Great Dionysia." In *Ritual, Finance, Politics: Athenian Democratic Accounts Presented to David Lewis*, edited by Robin Osborne and Simon Hornblower, 347–69. Oxford: Clarendon, 1994.

Goulder, Michael Douglas. "Libertines? (1 Cor. 5–6)." *Novum Testamentum* 41 (1999) 334–48.

Grudem, Wayne A. "Does ΚΕΦΑΛΗ ("HEAD") Mean "Source" or "Authority Over" in Greek Literature? a Survey of 2,336 Examples." *Trinity Journal* 6 (1985): 38–59.

———. "The Meaning of κεφαλή ("Head"): An Evaluation of New Evidence, Real and Alleged." *Journal of the Evangelical Theological Society* 44 (2001) 25–65.

———. "The Meaning of κεφαλή ("Head"): A Response to Recent Studies." In *Recovering Biblical Manhood and Womanhood: A Response to Evangelical Feminism*, edited by Wayne A. Grudem and John Piper, 425–68. Wheaton, IL: Crossway, 1991.

Gruen, Erich. "The Polis in the Hellenistic World." In *Nomodeiktes: Greek Studies in Honor of Martin Ostwald*, edited by Ralph M. Rosen and Joseph Farrell, 339–54. Ann Arbor: University of Michigan Press, 1993.

Gundry-Volf, Judith M. "Gender and Creation in 1 Corinthians 11:2–16: A Study in Paul's Theological Method." In *Evangelium Schriftauslegung Kirche: Festschrift Für Peter Stuhlmacher Zum 65. Geburtstag*, edited by Jostein Ådna, Scott J. Hafemann and Otfried Hofius, 151–71. Göttingen: Vandenhoeck & Ruprecht, 1997.

Hamilton, Charles D. "The Politics of Revolution in Corinth, 395–386 BC." *Zeitschrift fur alte Geschichte* 21 (1972) 21–37.

Hansen, Mogens Herman. *The Athenian Democracy in the Age of Demosthenes: Structure, Principles, and Ideology*. Translated by J. A. Crook. Norman: University of Oklahoma Press, 1999.

———. "Review 'What's Wrong with Democracy? From Athenian Practice to American Worship.'" *Bryn Mawr Classical Review* 32 (2006).

Harland, Philip A. *Associations, Synagogues, and Congregations: Claiming a Place in Ancient Mediterranean Society*. Minneapolis: Fortress, 2003.

Harrill, J. Albert. *The Manumission of Slaves in Early Christianity*. Tübingen: Mohr, 1995.

Harris, William V. *Ancient Literacy*. Cambridge, MA: Harvard University Press, 1989.

Hays, R. B. *First Corinthians*. Louisville: John Knox, 1997.

Hedrick, Charles. "The Zero Degree of Society: Aristotle and the Athenian Citizen." In *Athenian Political Thought and the Reconstruction of American Democracy*, edited by J. Peter Euben, John R. Wallach and Josiah Ober, 289–318. Ithaca: Cornell University Press, 1994.

Heinrici, C. F. Georg. *Der erste Brief an die Korinther*. Göttingen: Vandenhoeck & Ruprecht, 1896.

Helmbold, William Clark, and Edward N. O'Neil. *Plutarch's Quotations*. Philological Monographs 19. Baltimore: American Philological Association, 1959.

Héring, J. *The First Epistle of Saint Paul to the Corinthians*. Translated by A. W. Heathcote and P. J. Allcock. London: Epworth, 1962.

Hill, David. *New Testament Prophecy*. London: Marshall, Morgan & Scott, 1979.

Holl, K. "Der Kirchenbegriff des Paulus in seinem Verhälnis zu dem der Urgemeinde." *Ges. Aufs.* II (1928) 44–67.

Hollander, Harm W. "The Meaning of the Term 'Law' (Νομός) in 1 Corinthians." *Novum Testamentum* 40 (1998) 117–35.

Homer. *Illiad*. 2 vols. Translated by A. T. Murray. LCL. Cambridge, MA: Harvard University Press, 1993–1999.

Horrell, David G. *The Social Ethos of the Corinthian Correspondence: Interests and Ideology from 1 Corinthians to 1 Clement*. Studies of the New Testament and Its World. Edinburgh: T. & T. Clark, 1996.

Horrell, David G., and Edward Adams. "Introduction, the Scholarly Quest for Paul's Church at Corinth: A Critical Survey." In *Christianity at Corinth: The Quest for the Pauline Church*, edited by Edward Adams and David G. Horrell, 1–43. Louisville: Westminster John Knox, 2004.

Horsfall, Nicholas. "Statistics or States of Mind?" In *Literacy in the Roman World*, edited by Mary Beard et al., 59–76. Ann Arbor: Journal of Roman Archaeology, 1991.

Horsley, Richard A. "Rhetoric and Empire- and 1 Corinthians." In *Paul and Politics: Ekklesia, Israel, Imperium, Interpretation: Essays in Honor of Krister Stendahl*, edited by Richard A. Horsley, 72–102. Harrisburg, PA: Trinity, 2000.

Hunt, Allen. *The Inspired Body: Paul, the Corinthians and Divine Inspiration*. Macon, GA: Mercer University Press, 1996.

Hurd, John. *The Origin of 1 Corinthians*. Macon, GA: Mercer University Press, 1983.

Hurley, James B. "Did Paul Require Veils or the Silence of Women: A Consideration of 1 Cor 11:2–16 and 14: 33b-36." *Westminster Theological Journal* 35 (1973) 190–220.

*Isocrates*. 3 vols. Translated by G. Norlin and L. Van Hook. LCL. Cambridge, MA: Harvard University Press, 1928–1945.

Jervis, L. Ann. "'But I Want You to Know. . .': Paul's Midrashic Intertextual Response to the Corinthian Worshipers (1 Cor 11:2–16)." *Journal of Biblical Literature* 112, no. 2 (1993) 231–46.

———. "1 Corinthians 14:34–35: A Reconsideration of Paul's Limitation of the Free Speech of Some Corinthian Women." *Journal for the Study of the New Testament* 58 (1995) 51–74.

Jones, A. H. M. *Athenian Democracy*. Oxford: Blackwell, 1964.

———. *The Greek City from Alexander to Justinian*. Oxford: Clarendon, 1971.

Jones, C. P. *Plutarch and Rome*. Oxford: Clarendon, 1971.

———. *The Roman World of Dio Chrysostom*. Cambridge, MA: Harvard University Press, 1978.

*Josephus*. 10 vols. Translated by H. St. J.Thackeray et al. LCL. Cambridge, MA: Harvard University Press, 1926–1965.

Kahl, Brigitte. *Galatians Re-Imagined: Reading with the Eyes of the Vanquished*. Minneapolis: Fortress, 2010.

Ker, Donald P. "Paul and Apollos—Colleagues or Rivals." *Journal for the Study of the New Testament* 77 (2000) 75–97.

King, Karen L. "Prophetic Power and Women's Authority: The Case of the *Gospel of Mary* (Magdalene)." In *Women Preachers and Prophets through Two Millennia of Christianity*, edited by Beverly Mayne Kienzle and Pamela J. Walker, 21–41. Berkeley: University of California Press, 1998.

———. *What Is Gnosticism?* Cambridge, MA: Belknap, 2003.

Kittredge, Cynthia Briggs. "Corinthian Women Prophets and Paul's Arguments in 1 Corinthians." In *Paul and Politics: Ekklesia, Israel, Imperium, Interpretation*, edited by Richard A. Horsley, 103–9. Harrisburg, PA: Trinity, 2000.

———. "Rethinking Authorship in the Letters of Paul: Elisabeth Schüssler Fiorenza's Model of Pauline Theology." In *Walk in the Ways of Wisdom: Essays in Honor of Elisabeth Schüssler Fiorenza*, edited by Shelly Matthews, Cynthia Briggs Kittredge, and Melanie Johnson-Debaufre, 318–33. Harrisburg, PA: Trinity, 2003.

Klauck, H. J. *1. Korintherbrief*. Würzburg: Echter, 1984.
Kloppenborg, John S. "Edwin Hatch, Churches and Collegia." In *Origins and Method: Towards a New Understanding of Judaism and Christianity*, edited by Bradley H. McLean, 212–38. Sheffield: Sheffield Academic, 1993.
Kloppenborg, John S., and S. G. Wilson. *Voluntary Associations in the Graeco-Roman World*. London: Routledge, 1996.
König, Jason. "Favorinus' *Corinthian Oration* in Its Corinthian Context." *Proceedings of the Cambridge Philological Society* 47 (2001) 141–71.
Korenjak, Martin. *Publikum Und Redner: Ihre Interaktion in der sophistischen Rhetorik der Kaiserzeit*. Zetemata. Münich: Beck, 2000.
Kürzinger, J. "Mann Und Frau nach 1 Kor 11, 11f." *Biblische Zeitschrift* 22 (1978) 270–75.
Laks, André. "Soul, Sensation, and Thought." In *The Cambridge Companion to Early Greek Philosophy*, edited by A. A. Long, 250–70. Cambridge: Cambridge University Press, 1999.
Lamberton, Robert. *Plutarch*. New Haven: Yale University Press, 2001.
Levine, Baruch A. *Numbers 1–20: A New Translation with Introduction and Commentary*. Anchor Bible 4A. New York: Doubleday, 1993.
Levine, Lee I. *Judaism and Hellenism in Antiquity: Conflict or Confluence?* Seattle: University of Washington Press, 1998.
Lévy, I. "Études sur la vie municipale de l'Aie Mineure sous Les Antonins. I." *REG* 8 (1895) 203–50.
*Libanius: Opera*. 12 vols. Edited by R. Foerster. 1903–1923. Reprint, Hildesheim: Olms, 1963.
*Libanius's Progymnasmata: Model Exercises in Greek Prose Composition and Rhetoric*. Translated by Craig Gibson. Writings from the Greco-Roman World. Atlanta: SBL, 2008.
Lightfoot, Joseph Barber. *Notes on the Epistles of St. Paul*. Grand Rapids: Zondervan, 1957.
Litfin, A. Duane. *St. Paul's Theology of Proclamation: 1 Corinthians 1–4 and Greco-Roman Rhetoric*. Society for New Testament Studies Monograph. Cambridge: Cambridge University Press, 1994.
Livingstone, Niall. "The Voice of Isocrates and the Dissemination of Cultural Power." In *Pedagogy and Power*, edited by Yun Lee Too and Niall Livingstone, 263–81. Cambridge: Cambridge Unviersity Press, 1998.
Llewellyn-Jones, Lloyd. *Aphrodite's Tortoise: The Veiled Woman of Ancient Greece*. Swansea, Wales: Classical Press of Wales, 2003.
*Lysias*. Translated by W. R. M. Lamb. LCL. Cambridge, MA: Harvard University Press, 1930.
Ma, John. "Public Speech and Community in the *Euboicus*." In *Dio Chrysostom: Politics, Letters, and Philosophy*, edited by Simon Swain, 108–24. New York: Oxford University Press, 2000.
MacDonald, Dennis Ronald. *There Is No Male and Female: The Fate of a Dominical Saying in Paul and Gnosticism*. Harvard Dissertations in Religion. Philadelphia: Fortress, 1987.
Magie, David. *Roman Rule in Asia Minor, to the End of the Third Century after Christ*. 2 vols. Princeton: Princeton University Press, 1950.

Manville, Phillip. *The Origins of Citizenship in Ancient Athens*. Princeton: Princeton University Press, 1990.
Marchal, Joseph. *The Politics of Heaven: Women, Gender and Empire in the Study of Paul*. Minneapolis: Fortress, 2008.
Marrou, Henri Irénée. *A History of Education in Antiquity*. Translated by George Lamb. New York: Sheed and Ward, 1956.
Martin, Dale B. *The Corinthian Body*. New Haven: Yale University Press, 1995.
———. *Slavery as Salvation: The Metaphor of Slavery in Pauline Christianity*. New Haven: Yale University Press, 1995.
———. "Tongues of Angels and Other Status Indicators." *Journal of the American Academy of Religion* 59 (1991) 547–89.
Mason, Steve. "Should Any Wish to Enquire Further (*Ant.* 1.25): The Aim and Audience of Josephus's *Judean Antiquities/Life*." In *Understanding Josephus: Seven Perspectives*, edited by Steve Mason, 64–104. Sheffield: Sheffield Academic, 1998.
McCready, Wayne O. "*Ekklesia* and Voluntary Associations." In *Voluntary Associations in the Graeco-Roman World*, edited by John S. Kloppenborg and S. G. Wilson, 59–73. New York: Routledge, 1996.
McNamara, Jo Ann. "Gendering Virtue." In *Plutarch's Advice to the Bride and Groom and a Consolation to His Wife*, edited by Sarah B. Pomeroy, 151–61. New York: Oxford University Press, 1999.
Meeks, Wayne A. "'And Rose up to Play': Midrash and Paraenesis in 1 Cor 10:1–22." *Journal for the Study of the New Testament* 16 (1982) 64–78.
———. *The First Urban Christians: The Social World of the Apostle Paul*. 2nd ed. New Haven: Yale University Press, 2003.
———. "The Image of Androgyne: Some Uses of the Symbol in Earliest Christianity." *History of Religions* 13 (1974) 165–208.
Meggitt, Justin J. *Paul, Poverty and Survival*. Edinburgh: T. & T. Clark, 1998.
Millar, Fergus. "The Greek City in the Roman Period." In *The Ancient Greek City-State*, edited by Mogens Herman Hansen, 232–60. Copenhagen: Munksgaard, 1993.
Millis, Benjamin W. "The Social and Ethnic Origins of the Colonists in Early Roman Corinth." In *Corinth in Context: Comparative Studies on Religion and Society*, edited by Steven J. Friesen, Daniel N. Schowalter, and James C. Walters, 13–35. Leiden: Brill, 2010.
Mitchell, Margaret M. *Paul and the Rhetoric of Reconciliation: An Exegetical Investigation of the Language and Composition of 1 Corinthians*. Tübingen: Mohr, 1991.
———. "Response: The Politics of the Assembly in Corinth." In *Paul and Politics: Ekklēsia, Israel, Imperium, Interpretation*, edited by Richard A. Horsley. Harrisburg, PA: Trinity, 2000.
Mitchell, Stephen. *Anatolia: Land, Men, and Gods in Asia Minor*. Vol. 1. Oxford: Clarendon, 1993.
Morgan, Teresa. *Literate Education in the Hellenistic and Roman Worlds*. Cambridge: Cambridge University Press, 1998.
Mulgan, Richard G. "Liberty in Ancient Greece." In *Conceptions of Liberty in Political Philosophy*, edited by Z. Pelczynski, 7–26. London: Athlone, 1984.
———. "Aristotle's Analysis of Oligarchy and Democracy." In *A Companion to Aristotle's Politics*, edited by David Keyt and Fred D. Miller, 307–22. Cambridge: Blackwell, 1991.

Munro, Winsome. *Authority in Peter and Paul: The Identification of a Pastoral Stratum in the Pauline Corpus and 1 Peter*. London: Cambridge University Press, 1983.

Murphy-O'Connor, Jerome. "Sex and Logic in 1 Corinthians 11:2–16." *Catholic Biblical Quarterly* 42 (1980) 482–500.

Nasrallah, Laura Salah. *An Ecstasy of Folly: Prophecy and Authority in Early Christianity*. Harvard Theological Studies 52. Cambridge, MA: Harvard University Press, 2003.

Ober, Josiah. *The Athenian Revolution: Essays on Ancient Greek Democracy and Political Theory*. Princeton: Princeton University Press, 1996.

———. "The Debate over Civic Education in Classical Athens." In *Education in Greek and Roman Antiquity*, edited by Yun Lee Too, 175–207. Boston: Brill, 2001.

———. *Mass and Elite in Democratic Athens: Rhetoric, Ideology, and the Power of the People*. Princeton: Princeton University Press, 1989.

———. "Political Conflicts, Political Debates, and Political Thought." In *Classical Greece: 500–323 BC*, edited by R. Osborne, 111–38. Oxford: Oxford University Press, 2000.

———. *Political Dissent in Democratic Athens: Intellectual Critics of Popular Rule*. Princeton: Princeton University Press, 1998.

———. "Power and Oratory in Democratic Athens: Demosthenes 21, against Meidias." In *Persuasion: Greek Rhetoric in Action*, edited by Ian Worthington, 85–108. New York: Routledge, 1994.

Økland, Jorunn. *Women in Their Place: Paul and the Corinthian Discourse of Gender and Sanctuary Space*. London: T. & T. Clark, 2004.

Padgett, Alan. "Paul on Women in the Church: The Contradictions of Coiffure in 1 Corinthians 11.2–16." *Journal for the Study of the New Testament* 20 (1984) 69–86.

Parker, Holt. "Aristotle's Unanswered Questions: Women and Slaves in the Politics 1252a–1260b." *Eugesta* 2 (2012).

Paulsen, H. "Einheit und Freiheit der Söhne Gottes—Gal 3.26–29." *ZNW* 71 (1980) 74–95.

Peterson, Eric. *Ekklesia: Studien zum Altkirchlichen Kirchenbegriff*. Stuttgart: Echter, 2010.

Philo. 12 vols. Translated by F. H. Colson et al. LCL. Cambridge, MA: Harvard University Press, 1929–1962.

Plato. 10 vols. Translated by H. N. Fowler, W. R. M. Lamb, and R. G. Bury. LCL. Cambridge, MA: Harvard University Press, 1914–1929.

Plutarch. *Moralia*. 17 vols. Translated by H. N. Fowler et al. LCL. Cambridge, MA: Harvard University Press, 1927–2004.

*Plutarque Oevres Morales*. Edited by Marcel Cuvingy. Paris: Société d'édition, 1984.

Pogoloff, Stephen M. *Logos and Sophia: The Rhetorical Situation of 1 Corinthians*. Atlanta: Scholars, 1992.

*Progymnasmata: Greek Textbooks of Prose, Composition, and Rhetoric: Writings from the Greco-Roman World*. Edited by G. A. Kennedy. Atlanta: SBL, 2003.

Pseudo-Xenophon. *Constitution of the Athenians*. Translated by G. W. Bowersock. LCL. Cambridge, MA: Harvard University Press, 1984.

Quass, Friedemann. *Die Honoratiorenschicht in den Städten des griechischen Ostens: Untersuchungen zur politischen und sozialen Entwicklung in hellenistischer und römischer Zeit*. Stuttgart: Steiner, 1993.

Raaflaub, Kurt A. *Die Entdeckung der Freiheit: zur historischen Semantik und Gesellschaftsgeschichte eines politischen Grundbegriffes der Griechen*, Vestigia 37. Münich: Beck, 1985.
Radcliffe, T. "Paul and Sexual Identity: 1 Corinthians 11.2–16." In *After Eve: Women, Theology and the Christian Tradition*, edited by J. M. Soskice, 66–72. London: Collins, Marshall Pickering, 1990.
Rajak, Tessa. "The *Against Apion* and the Continuities in Josephus' Political Thought." In *The Jewish Dialogue with Greece and Rome: Studies in Cultural and Social Interaction*, edited by Tessa Rajak, 195–217. Boston: Brill, 2001.
———. "Greeks and Barbarians in Josephus." In *Hellenism in the Land of Israel*, edited by John J. Collins and Gregory E. Sterling, 244–62. Notre Dame: University of Notre Dame, 2001.
———. *The Jewish Dialogue with Greece and Rome: Studies in Cultural and Social Interaction*. Leiden: Brill, 2001.
———. "Josephus and the Archaeology of the Jews." *Journal of Jewish Studies* 33 (1982) 465–77.
———. *Josephus: The Historian and His Society*. London: Duckworth, 1983.
Rhodes, P. J. *The Athenian Boule*. Oxford: Clarendon, 1972.
Rhodes, P. J., and David M. Lewis. *The Decrees of the Greek States*. Oxford: Oxford University Press, 1997.
Rogers, Guy MacLean. "The Assembly of Imperial Ephesos." *ZPE* 94 (1992) 224–28.
Romano, David Gilman. "Urban and Rural Planning in Roman Corinth." In *Urban Religion in Roman Corinth*, edited by Daniel N. Schowalter and Stephen J. Friesen, 25–59. Cambridge, MA: Harvard Theological Studies, 2005.
Rost, Leonhard. *Die Vorstufen von Kirche und Synagoge im Alten Testament; eine wortgeschichtliche Untersuchung*. Beiträge Zur Wissenschaft vom Alten und Neuen Testament, Begründet von Rudolf Kittel 4/24 (der ganzen sammlung, Hft. 76). Stuttgart: Kohlhammer, 1938.
Russell, D. A. *Greek Declamation*. Cambridge: Cambridge University Press, 1983.
———. "Introduction." In *Dio Chrysostom Orations: VII, XII and XXXVI*, edited by D. A. Russell, 1–25. Cambridge: Cambridge University Press, 1992.
———. *Libanius: Imaginary Speeches*. London: Duckworth, 1996.
———. "On Reading Plutarch's *Moralia*." *Greece and Rome* 15 (1968) 130–46.
Salmeri, Giovanni. "Dio, Rome, and the Civic Life of Asia Minor." In *Dio Chrysostom: Politics, Letters, and Philosophy*, edited by Simon Swain, 53–92. Oxford: Oxford University Press, 2000.
Saxonhouse, Arlene. "Another Antigone: The Emergence of the Female Political Actor in Euripides' *Phoenician Women*." *Political Theory* 33 (2005) 472–94.
———. *Athenian Democracy: Modern Mythmakers and Ancient Theorists*. Notre Dame: University of Notre Dame Press, 1996.
———. *Free Speech and Democracy in Ancient Athens*. Cambridge: Cambridge University Press, 2006.
Schmidt, K. L. "*Ekklēsia*." In *Theological Dictionary of the New Testament*, edited by Geoffrey W. Bromiley, 501–36. Grand Rapids: Eerdman's, 1964.
Schouler, Bernard. "La Tradition Hellenique Chez Libanios." PhD diss., Université de Paris, 1977.
Schrage, Wolfgang. *Der erste Brief an die Korinther*. Evangelisch-Katholischer Kommentar Zum Neuen Testament. Zürich: Neukirchener, 1991.

———. "'Ekklēsia' Und 'Synagoge': Zum Ursprung Des Urchristlichen Kirchenbegriffs." *Zeitschrift fur Theologie und Kirche* 60 (1963) 178–202.

Schüssler Fiorenza, Elisabeth. "1 Corinthians." In *Harpercollins Bible Commentary*, edited by James L. Mays, 1074–92. San Francisco: HarperOne, 2000.

———. *Bread Not Stone: The Challenge of Feminist Biblical Interpretation*. Boston: Beacon Press, 1984.

———. *In Memory of Her: A Feminist Theological Reconstruction of Christian Origins*. New York: Crossroad, 1994.

———. "Introduction for *Prejudice and Christian Beginnings*." In *Prejudice and Christian Beginnings: Investigating Race, Gender, and Ethnicity in Early Christian Studies*, edited by Elisabeth Schüssler Fiorenza and Laura Salah Nasrallah, 1–26. Minneapolis: Fortress, 2010.

———. *The Power of the Word: Scripture and the Rhetoric of the Empire*. Minneapolis: Fortress, 2007.

———. *Rhetoric and Ethic: The Politics of Biblical Studies*. Minneapolis: Fortress, 1999.

Smit, Joop. "Argument and Genre of 1 Corinthians 12–14." In *Rhetoric and the New Testament: Essays from the 1992 Heidelberg Conferences*, edited by Stanley M. Porter and Thomas H. Olbricht, 211–30. Sheffield: JSOT, 1993.

Spawforth, A. J. S. "Roman Corinth: The Formation of a Colonial Elite." In *Roman Onomastics in the Greek East*, edited by A.D. Rizakis, 167–82. Athens: Research Center for Greek and Roman Antiquity, 1996.

Spicq, Ceslas. *Théologie Morale du Nouveau Testament*. 2 vols. Études Bibliques. Paris: Lecoffre, 1965.

Ste Croix, G. E. M. de. *The Class Struggle in the Ancient Greek World*. Ithaca: Cornell University Press, 1981.

Stein, O. "Menemachos." RE 15 (1931) 836–38.

Sterling, Gregory E. *Historiography and Self-Definition: Josephos, Luke-Acts and Apologetic Historiography*. New York: Brill, 1992.

Stichele, Caroline Vander. "Is Silence Golden? Paul and Women's Speech in Corinth." *Louvian Studies* 20 (1995) 241–53.

Stichele, Caroline Vander, and Todd C. Penner. "Paul and the Rhetoric of Gender." In *Her Master's Tools? Feminist and Postcolonial Engagements of Historical-Critical Discourse*, edited by Caroline Vander Stichele and Todd C. Penner, 287–310. Atlanta: SBL, 2005.

Stichele, Caroline Vander and Todd Penner. "Unveiling Paul: Gendering Ethos in 1 Corinthians 11:2–16." In *Rhetoric, Ethic, and Moral Persuasion in Biblical Discourse*, edited by Thomas H. Olbricht and Anders Eriksson, 214–237. New York: T & T Clark International, 2005.

Stowers, Stanley K. "Does Pauline Christianity Resemble a Hellenistic Philosophy?" In *Redescribing Paul and the Corinthians*, edited by Ron Cameron and Merrill P. Miller, 219–44. Atlanta: SBL, 2011.

———. *Letter Writing in Greco-Roman Antiquity*. Library of Early Christianity. Philadelphia: Westminster Press, 1986.

———. "Paul on the Use and Abuse of Reason." In *Greeks, Romans and Christians*, edited by David Balch, Everett Ferguson, and Wayne A. Meeks, 253–86. Minneapolis: Fortress, 1990.

Swain, Simon. *Hellenism and Empire: Language, Classicism and Power in the Greek World, AD 50–250*. Oxford: Clarendon, 1996.

Thackeray, H. St J. *Josephus, the Man and the Historian*. New York: Ktav, 1968.
Theissen, Gerd. *Psychological Aspects of Pauline Theology*. Philadelphia: Fortress, 1987.
———. *The Social Setting of Pauline Christianity: Essays on Corinth*. Philadelphia: Fortress, 1982.
Theon. *Progymnasmata*. Translated by M. Patillon and Giancarlo Bolognesi. Paris: Les Belles Lettres, 1997.
Thomas, Christine M. "Greek Heritage in Roman Corinth and Ephesos: Hybrid Identities and Strategies of Display in the Material Record of Traditional Mediterranean Religions." In *Corinth in Context: Comparative Studies on Religion and Society*, edited by Steven J. Friesen, Daniel N. Schowalter, and James C. Walters, 117–47. Leiden: Brill, 2010.
Thompson, Cynthia. "Hairstyles, Headcoverings and St. Paul: Portraits from Roman Corinth." *Biblical Archaeologist* 51 (1988) 99–115.
*Thucydides*. 4 vols. Translated by C. F. Smith. LCL. Cambridge, MA: Harvard University Press, 1919–1923.
Trebilco, Paul. "Why Did the Early Christians Call Themselves ἡ ἐκκλησία?" *New Testament Studies* 57 (2011) 440–60.
Van Kooten, George H. "Ἐκκλησία τοῦ θεοῦ: The Church of God and the Civic Assemblies." *New Testament Studies* 58 (2012) 522–48.
Van Nijf, Onno M. "Local Heroes: Athletes, Festivals and Elite Self-Fashioning in the Roman East." In *Being Greek under Rome*, edited by Simon Goldhill, 306–34. Cambridge: Cambridge University Press, 2001.
Vernant, Jean Pierre. "Speech and Mute Signs." In *Mortals and Immortals: Collected Essays*, edited by Froma I. Zeitlin, 303–33. Princeton: Princeton University Press, 1991.
Walbank, Mary E. Hoskins. "The Foundation and Planning of Early Roman Corinth." *JRA* 10 (1997) 95–130.
Walters, James. "Civic Identity in Roman Corinth and Its Impact on Early Christians." In *Urban Religion in Roman Corinth*, edited by Daniel N. Schowalter and Steven J. Friesen, 397–417. Cambridge: Harvard Theological Studies, 2005.
Webb, Ruth. "The *Progymnasmata* as Practice." In *Education in Greek and Roman Antiquity*, edited by Yun Lee Too, 289–316. Boston: Brill, 2001.
Weiss, Johannes. *Der erste Korintherbrief*. Göttingen,: Vandenhoeck & Ruprecht, 1910.
Welborn, L. L. "A Conciliatory Principle in 1 Cor 4:6." *Novum Testamentum* 29 (1987) 320–46.
———. "On the Discord in Corinth: 1 Corinthians 1–4 and Ancient Politics." *Journal of Biblical Literature* 106 (1987) 85–111.
———. *Politics and Rhetoric in the Corinthian Epistles*. Macon, GA: Mercer University Press, 1997.
Whitmarsh, Tim. *The Second Sophistic*. New York: Oxford University Press, 2005.
Winter, Bruce W. *Roman Wives, Roman Widows: The Appearance of the New Women and the Pauline Communities*. Grand Rapids: Eerdmans, 2003.
Wire, Antoinette Clark. *The Corinthian Women Prophets: A Reconstruction through Paul's Rhetoric*. Minneapolis: Fortress, 1990.
Wischmeyer, Oda. *Der Höchste Weg: Das 13. Kapitel Des 1. Korintherbriefes*. Gütersloh: Gütersloher Mohn, 1981.
Witherington, Ben, III. *Conflict and Community in Corinth: A Socio-Rhetorical Commentary on 1 and 2 Corinthians*. Grand Rapids: Eerdmans, 1995.

———. *Women in the Earliest Churches*. Cambridge: Cambridge University Press, 1988.

Wolff, Christian. *Der erste Brief des Paulus an die Korinther Zweiter Teil, Kap 8–16*. THKNT 7. Leipzig: Evangelische, 1996.

Wolin, Sheldon. "Transgression, Equality and Voice." In *Demokratia: A Conversation on Democracies, Ancient and Modern*, edited by Josiah Ober and Charles Hedrick, 63–90. Princeton: Princeton University Press, 1996.

Woolf, Greg. "Becoming Roman, Staying Greek: Culture, Identity and the Civilizing Process in the Roman East." *PCPS* 40 (1995) 116–43.

Wyke, Maria. "Woman in the Mirror: The Rhetoric of Adornment in the Roman World." In *Women in Ancient Societies: An Illusion of the Night*, edited by Léonie J. Archer, Susan Fischle and Maria Wyke, 136–47. New York: Routledge, 1994.

*Xenophon*. 7 vols. Translated by C. L. Brownson, O. J. Todd et al. LCL. Cambridge, MA: Harvard University Press, 1918–1925.

Zamfir, Korinna. "Is the *ekklēsia* a Household (of God)? Reassessing the Notion of οἶκος θεοῦ in 1 Tim 3.15." *New Testament Studies* 60 (2014) 511–28.

Ziegler, K. "Plutarckos von Chaironeia." RE 21 (1951) 636–962.

# Ancient Sources Index

## HEBREW BIBLE

### Genesis
| | |
|---|---|
| 1–2 | 115, 140 |
| 1:27 | 139, 140, 141, 160 |
| 2 | 136 |
| 2:2ff | 141 |
| 2:22 | 136, 139 |
| 40:16 | 134 |

### Exodus
| | |
|---|---|
| 4:10 | 80 |
| 5:1 | 80n50 |
| 6:12 | 80 |

### Numbers
| | |
|---|---|
| 16 | 11, 68–69, 73, 75, 75–78, 78, 79, 88, 89 |
| 16:3 | 71n10, 78, 79 |
| 16:5–6 | 78 |
| 16:6–7 | 82–83 |
| 16:12 | 86 |
| 16:28–30 | 86–87 |
| 27:17 | 71n10 |

### Deuteronomy
| | |
|---|---|
| 4:10 | 71n9 |
| 5:22 | 71n9 |
| 9:10 | 71n9 |
| 23:1–8 | 70, 92–93 |
| 23:2 | 71n10, 93n12 |
| 23:3 | 93 |
| 23:4 | 93 |

### Judges
| | |
|---|---|
| 20:2 | 93n12 |

### 1 Samuel
| | |
|---|---|
| 19:19 | 72 |

### 2 Chronicles
| | |
|---|---|
| 28:14 | 72 |

### Psalm
| | |
|---|---|
| 26:5 | 71 |

### Ezekiel
| | |
|---|---|
| 27:27 | 71 |

## NEW TESTAMENT

### Matthew
| | |
|---|---|
| 16:18 | 99n41 |
| 18:17 | 99n41 |
| 19:4 | 142 |

### Mark
| | |
|---|---|
| 1:27 | 107n79 |
| 8:11 | 107n79 |
| 10:6 | 142 |

### Luke
| | |
|---|---|
| 22:23 | 107n79 |
| 24:15 | 107n79 |

## Acts

| | |
|---|---|
| 19:29ff | 78n44 |
| 19:35 | 108 |

## Romans

| | |
|---|---|
| | 100n43 |
| 3:18 | 180n82 |
| 3:31 | 180n82 |
| 7:12 | 180n82 |

## 1 Corinthians

| | |
|---|---|
| | 1, 3, 6, 7–8, 11, 69, 90, 96, 100, 105, 108, 110–11n88, 112, 113, 117, 144n127, 153, 172, 182n86, 188 |
| 1–2 | 115 |
| 1–4 | 90–91, 102n53, 163, 164 |
| 1:1 | 158 |
| 1:1–9 | 102 |
| 1:4–9 | 102n53 |
| 1:5 | 90, 100n43, 102, 103, 109, 141, 156, 157, 189 |
| 1:17 | 103, 107 |
| 1:18 | 106 |
| 1:20 | 107, 108 |
| 1:20–21 | 106 |
| 1:23 | 106 |
| 1:24 | 106 |
| 1:26 | 105 |
| 1:26–28 | 106 |
| 1:27–28 | 106 |
| 2:1 | 103, 107 |
| 2:2 | 106 |
| 2:3 | 107 |
| 2:4 | 90, 107 |
| 2:4–5 | 103, 106 |
| 2:4–7 | 184 |
| 2:5 | 107 |
| 2:6 | 107, 108 |
| 2:7 | 106 |
| 2:8 | 108 |
| 2:13 | 176 |
| 2:14 | 112 |
| 2:15 | 111 |
| 3:1 | 109, 164 |
| 3:1–4 | 107 |
| 3:4 | 109 |
| 4:3–4 | 112 |
| 4:7 | 151n155 |
| 4:8 | 110 |
| 4:8–10 | 106 |
| 4:8–13 | 110 |
| 4:9 | 158 |
| 7 | 160, 182n86 |
| 7:13 | 183 |
| 7:17 | 151n155 |
| 8 | 102n53 |
| 8:1 | 157 |
| 9:1–5 | 158 |
| 11 | 116, 131, 144, 166 |
| 11–14 | 151 |
| 11:2 | 150 |
| 11:2—14:40 | 154, 161 |
| 11:2–15 | 151 |
| 11:2–16 | 12, 115–16, 130–53, 154, 155, 159, 160, 166, 176, 176–177n75, 177, 178, 179, 180n82, 182, 183, 185, 189 |
| 11:3 | 133, 134, 135, 136, 137, 138, 181 |
| 11:4 | 144n127 |
| 11:4–6 | 143, 144, 149 |
| 11:6 | 147 |
| 11:7 | 141 |
| 11:7–8 | 137 |
| 11:7–9 | 136, 138 |
| 11:11 | 138 |
| 11:11–12 | 137 |
| 11:12 | 139, 142, 155, 161 |
| 11:13–15 | 144, 149 |
| 11:13–16 | 143 |
| 11:14–15 | 147, 149 |
| 11:15 | 144n127 |
| 11:16 | 150, 151, 184 |
| 11:17–18 | 151 |
| 11:18 | 100 |
| 12 | 103n55, 155–66, 156, 166, 185 |
| 12–13 | 184 |
| 12–14 | 12, 102n53, 132, 152, 153, 154, 155 |
| 12—14:33 | 154 |
| 12:1–3 | 163 |
| 12:4–7 | 156 |
| 12:7 | 156, 158, 162 |

| | |
|---|---|
| 12:7–11 | 158 |
| 12:8 | 167n36, 175 |
| 12:8–10 | 158 |
| 12:9 | 157 |
| 12:10 | 157 |
| 12:12–13 | 159–60n13 |
| 12:13 | 156, 159 |
| 12:22–24 | 157 |
| 12:28 | 158, 159, 166 |
| 12:28–31 | 161 |
| 12:29 | 175 |
| 12:29–30 | 158 |
| 12:31 | 158, 166 |
| 13 | 156, 161, 164, 165, 166, 168 |
| 13–14 | 163 |
| 13–15 | 107 |
| 13:1–3 | 163 |
| 13:4–7 | 165 |
| 13:8–12 | 163 |
| 13:11 | 164 |
| 14 | 151, 154, 155–56, 159, 161, 165, 166–76, 184, 185 |
| 14:2–4 | 167 |
| 14:3 | 167n39 |
| 14:3–4 | 171 |
| 14:4 | 167 |
| 14:6 | 175, 175n73 |
| 14:11 | 167n39 |
| 14:14–19 | 170, 171 |
| 14:18–19 | 184 |
| 14:23 | 166n36 |
| 14:24–25 | 170 |
| 14:26 | 175, 175n73 |
| 14:26–31 | 178, 179 |
| 14:27–33 | 180 |
| 14:27–33a | 180 |
| 14:27–36 | 179, 180 |
| 14:29–31 | 170 |
| 14:31 | 171, 180 |
| 14:32 | 174 |
| 14:32–33a | 179 |
| 14:33 | 167, 179 |
| 14:33–36 | 12, 143, 151, 155, 159, 166, 176–84 |
| 14:33b–34 | 179 |
| 14:33b–36 | 131, 154, 179, 180n82, 182, 183, 185 |
| 14:34–35 | 131, 180 |
| 14:34b–36 | 180 |
| 14:35 | 181 |
| 14:36 | 184 |
| 14:37 | 184 |
| 14:37–38 | 184 |
| 14:40 | 167n39 |
| 15:8–10 | 158 |

## 2 Corinthians

| | |
|---|---|
| | 100 |
| 11:6 | 106 |

## Galatians

| | |
|---|---|
| 3:27–28 | 12, 156, 159, 159–60n13, 185 |
| 3:28 | 116, 132n66, 138, 139, 140, 141, 142, 143, 150, 152–53, 159, 160–61, 189 |

## Ephesians

| | |
|---|---|
| | 100 |
| 18:1 | 107n79 |

## Philippians

| | |
|---|---|
| 1:9 | 102 |

## Colossians

| | |
|---|---|
| | 100 |
| 3:9–11 | 159–60n13 |
| 14:1 | 166 |

## 1 Thessalonias

| | |
|---|---|
| 1:3 | 102 |

## 2 Timothy

| | |
|---|---|
| | 99n41 |

## Titus 1

| | |
|---|---|
| | 99n41 |

## 2 Peter

| | |
|---|---|
| | 99n41 |

## Ancient Sources Index

**1 John**
99n41

**2 John**
99n41

**Revelation**
99–100n41

# SEPTUAGINT
70–71, 92, 133

# GREEK TEXTS

## Aeschines
| | |
|---|---|
| 1.173 | 104 |
| 1.30–31 | 105 |
| 2.4 | 78n44 |
| 3.233 | 104n61 |

*Timarchus*
| | |
|---|---|
| 185 | 121 |

## Aeschylus

*Seven Against Thebes*
| | |
|---|---|
| 200–204 | 122 |
| 230–32 | 122 |

## Aristides

*Hieroi logoi*
| | |
|---|---|
| I.16 | 33 |

## Aristophanes

*Ekklesiazusae*
| | |
|---|---|
| 18 | 126 |
| 105–10 | 125 |
| 151 | 124 |
| 155 | 124 |
| 189 | 124 |
| 208–10 | 125 |
| 245 | 125 |
| 598 | 127 |

*Frogs*
| | |
|---|---|
| 908–20 | 146 |

*Lysistrata*
| | |
|---|---|
| 532–34 | 147 |

## Aristotle
121, 121–22

*Politics*
| | |
|---|---|
| | 127 |
| 1252a32 | 119 |
| 1253a1–5 | 118 |
| 1253a10–35 | 118 |
| 1254a29–31 | 120, 135 |
| 1254b5–10 | 172 |
| 1254b13–15 | 120, 135 |
| 1254b22–25 | 120 |
| 1259b35–40 | 119 |
| 1260a12–15 | 120 |
| 1260a23 | 120 |
| 1260a31 | 120, 135 |
| 1279 B–1280 A | 110–11n88 |
| 1281b5 | 96 |
| 1303b5 | 75 |
| 1318b10–15 | 123 |
| 1319b27–31 | 123 |

*Rhetoric*
| | |
|---|---|
| 1355a2–3 | 78n44 |
| 1372a11–17 | 104 |

## Chariton

*Chaereas and Callirhoe*
| | |
|---|---|
| 8.7.1 | 78n44 |

## Clement of Alexandria
139

*Paedagogus*
| | |
|---|---|
| 3.15.2 | 148n145 |

## Cornutus

*Theol. graec.*
| | |
|---|---|
| 20 | 134 |

## Ancient Sources Index

**Demosthenes**

| | |
|---|---|
| | 74, 101n49 |
| 1.10 | 96–97 |
| 1.19–20 | 104 |
| 2.29–31 | 86 |
| 4.26 | 83n65 |
| 5.19 | 76 |
| 6.24 | 57 |
| 6.25 | 79n45 |
| 8.71 | 96–97 |
| 18.61 | 74n27 |
| 18.109 | 83n66 |
| 18.138 | 85, 105 |
| 18.154 | 76 |
| 18.273 | 84 |
| 18.278 | 84 |
| 18.320 | 83n66 |
| 18.321 | 84 |
| 19.246–50 | 104 |
| 21.124–27 | 31n76 |
| 21.141–42 | 105n69 |
| 31.1–2 | 75 |
| 35.40–43 | 104 |
| 45.2 | 96–97 |
| 46.16 | 121 |
| 51.22 | 104 |
| 55.2 | 104 |

*On the Crown*

| | |
|---|---|
| | 33–35, 34 |

*False Legation*

| | |
|---|---|
| | 33, 35 |

*Second Olynthiac*

| | |
|---|---|
| | 33–34, 35 |
| 2.29–31 | 85n78 |

**Dio Chrysostom**

| | |
|---|---|
| | 10, 21, 95, 105, 172 |

*Euboicus*

| | |
|---|---|
| | 40–43, 46, 48, 49–50, 52, 57 |
| 7.23 | 40 |
| 7.25–6 | 40 |

*Oration*

| | |
|---|---|
| 3.44–48 | 77n40 |
| 3.46ff | 64n108 |
| 3.47 | 85n78 |
| 3.127 | 108n81 |
| 7.23ff | 78n44 |
| 7.30 | 58 |
| 7.33 | 58 |
| 12.15–16 | 105 |
| 13.33 | 108 |
| 18.8 | 19 |
| 20.9–10 | 17n10 |
| 30 | 174 |
| 31.125 | 64n109 |
| 32 | 46n26, 52n53, 53n53 |
| 32.5 | 173n64 |
| 32.11 | 84–85n74 |
| 32.26–27 | 52, 53, 85 |
| 32.27–28 | 110–111n87 |
| 33.28 | 173 |
| 33.33 | 173 |
| 33.52 | 148 |
| 33.59 | 173 |
| 33.60 | 148, 174 |
| 34.5 | 5n12 |
| 34.13 | 173n64 |
| 34.18 | 165, 167n38, 168 |
| 34.19 | 165 |
| 34.23 | 64n107 |
| 34.38–39 | 64n110 |
| 34.39 | 173n64 |
| 35.1 | 105n69 |
| 37.1 | 99 |
| 37.7 | 99 |
| 37.16 | 99, 99n39 |
| 37.17–20 | 99n39 |
| 37.26 | 99, 99n37 |
| 37.27 | 99n37 |
| 38 | 46n26 |
| 38.2 | 52 |
| 38.4 | 52 |
| 39.3 | 169 |
| 39.4 | 169 |
| 39.9 | 169 |
| 40.13–15 | 47n27 |
| 40.20 | 173n64 |
| 40.26 | 173n64 |
| 40.5 | 46n26 |
| 41 | 46n26 |
| 41.3 | 54 |
| 42.1–3 | 97n29, 105 |

### Ancient Sources Index

*Oration (continued)*

| | |
|---|---|
| 43.3 | 97 |
| 43.11 | 54 |
| 43.12 | 54 |
| 43.46 | 54n58 |
| 44.3–5 | 52 |
| 44.6–7 | 47n29 |
| 44.12 | 46n26 |
| 45 | 51 |
| 45.3 | 47n29 |
| 46.2–6 | 47n27, 52 |
| 47.1 | 97n29, 105 |
| 47.3 | 108n81 |
| 47.13 | 46n26 |
| 47.18 | 55 |
| 47.19 | 108n84 |
| 47.23 | 55 |
| 48.1 | 62 |
| 48.1–2 | 51 |
| 48.2 | 62, 78n44 |
| 48.3 | 62, 63 |
| 48.6 | 52 |
| 48.7 | 167n38, 168 |
| 48.9 | 62 |
| 48.10 | 62 |
| 49.11 | 108 |
| 49.15 | 47n27 |
| 50 | 55 |
| 50.10 | 47n27 |
| 50.5 | 173n64 |
| 52.11–12 | 108n81 |
| 56.2 | 108 |

*"Reply to Diodorus"*

    25–26

*Second Discourse on Kingship*

    21–22

## Epictetus

*Dissertationes*

| | |
|---|---|
| 1.16.11 | 148n147 |
| 1.16.11–12 | 148 |
| 3.1.27–35 | 148 |

## Euripides

    22–26

*Antiope*

    97

*Children of Hercules*

| | |
|---|---|
| 475 | 122 |

*Hippolytus*

| | |
|---|---|
| 240 | 146 |
| 364–439 | 146 |
| 645–50 | 146 |
| 966–70 | 121 |

*Orestes*

    22n37

*Phoenissae (Phoenician Woman)*

    22–26, 50, 54

*Suppliant Women*

| | |
|---|---|
| 410–35 | 77n41 |
| 435 | 49n34 |

## Galen

*De rem 1*

| | |
|---|---|
| proem. | 134n78 |

## Herodotus

| | |
|---|---|
| 7.140–45 | 171 |

## Homer

    19–22

*Iliad*

| | |
|---|---|
| | 21 |
| 2.215–20 | 36 |
| 2.245–325 | 36 |

*Odyssey*

    21

## Iamblicus

    172

## Isocrates

    21, 101n49

| | |
|---|---|
| 4 | 33 |

*Antidosis*
                    20n24, 58
235                    57n82

*De Pace*
8.128              110–11n88

*To Nicocles*
                    20n24

*Panathenaicus*
                    20n24

*Panegyricus*
51                    20

*Philip*
                    20n24

# Josephus

*Antiquities of the Jews*
                5n12, 11, 68
1.10              71
1.5              68n2, 73n23
2.281            80n50
3.13              80
3.316            81
3.317            81
4                68–69
4.12              73
4.14              76
4.15–16          76
4.17              77
4.20              84
4.22              78
4.23          79n45, 80
4.24              79
4.25–26          81
4.29              82
4.30–31          82
4.32              82
4.34          83, 83n65
4.35              83
4.35–36          84
4.36              85
4.40              86
4.42              86
4.46              86
4.50              87
4.54              87
4.223            88
4.328            80
4.329–30         81
6.222            72
9.250            72
14.150          72
14.252          72
15.346          71
19.300–305     72

*Jewish War*
2.285            72
2.289            72
2.490            72
4.162ff          72
7.44              72
7.47              72

# Libanius

*Progymnasmata*
*Anecdotes*
3                  29
13                  29

*Common Topics*
4                  31
5                  31
7                  31

*Encomium*
4.1                36

*Thesis*
1                 29–31
11               29–31

# Lycurgus
1.79         104n61, 108

# Lysias
                  74
2                  33
2.19            50
12.43–45        76
17.1            104
18.6–17         75
19.2          105n69

## Lysias (continued)

| | |
|---|---|
| 28.14 | 83n65 |
| 31.2 | 104 |
| 31.4 | 104 |

## Thucydides

| | |
|---|---|
| 2.35–46 | 33 |
| 2.37 | 31 |

## Philo of Alexandria

172

### On Dreams

| | |
|---|---|
| 2.207 | 134 |

### On Rewards and Punishments

| | |
|---|---|
| 125 | 133 |

## Plato

133, 172

### Phaedo

| | |
|---|---|
| 94A–E | 135 |

### Respublica

| | |
|---|---|
| 8.557 A | 110–11n88 |
| 8.557 B | 110–11n88 |

### Timaeus

| | |
|---|---|
| 44D | 133 |

## Plutarch

10, 22–23, 40–41, 46, 52, 95, 172

### Advice to the Bride and Groom

127

| | |
|---|---|
| 139 C | 129 |
| 140 A | 128 |
| 142 C–D | 129, 147 |
| 142 D | 181, 183 |
| 142 E | 128, 181–82, 181n84 |
| 145 D | 128 |

### A Consolation to His Wife

127

| | |
|---|---|
| 609 A | 128 |
| 609 D | 128 |

### De vitando aere alieno

| | |
|---|---|
| 829 A | 46–47n26 |

### The Dinner of the Seven Wise Men

| | |
|---|---|
| 149 A | 108 |
| 151 A | 108 |

### On Exile

| | |
|---|---|
| 602 C | 47n27 |

### Old Men in Political Affairs

60

| | |
|---|---|
| 783 B | 60n87 |
| 784 F | 64n108 |
| 784 F–785 A | 60n88 |
| 785 A–C | 60 |
| 789 D | 5n12, 173 |
| 790 A | 97 |
| 796 E5 | 108 |

### Political Advice

55–56, 60n87

| | |
|---|---|
| 798 A–B | 51, 60n87 |
| 799 B | 56 |
| 799 C | 56 |
| 799 D | 56 |
| 799 F | 56 |
| 800 A | 56 |
| 801 A | 56 |
| 801 C | 51 |
| 801 E | 51n44 |
| 801 F | 173 |
| 802 D | 51 |
| 802 F | 97 |
| 804 C | 60, 61 |
| 805 A | 47n27 |
| 811 C | 47n28 |
| 813 A | 61 |
| 813 B | 62 |
| 813 C | 61, 108n84 |
| 814 A | 65 |
| 814 F | 65 |
| 815 A | 65 |
| 816 C | 47n27 |
| 816 F | 108n84 |
| 820 D | 60n91 |
| 821 B | 57 |
| 821 C | 57 |

| | |
|---|---|
| 822 F | 57 |

*On the Pythian Oracles*

| | |
|---|---|
| 408 B–C | 64n108 |

*Quastionum convivialum*

| | |
|---|---|
| 628 A | 46–47n26 |
| 647 C | 134 |
| 692 D | 134 |
| 700 E | 47n27 |

## Pseudo-Xenophon

*Athenaion Politeia*

| | |
|---|---|
| | 57–58, 110–11n88 |
| 1.6 | 122, 123 |
| 1.10 | 122 |
| 1.11 | 122 |

## Sophocles

| | |
|---|---|
| | 116 |

*Ajax*

| | |
|---|---|
| | 122 |
| 293 | 120 |

## Theon, Aelius

*Progymnasmata*

| | |
|---|---|
| | 10, 21n29, 25–26, 26–32 |
| 2.30 | 35 |
| 2.214 | 36 |
| 2.215 | 36 |
| 2.222 | 36 |
| 18.86 | 34 |
| 18.102 | 34 |
| 18.109 | 34 |
| 18.138 | 35 |
| 18.273 | 35 |
| 18.278 | 34 |
| 18.320 | 34 |
| 18.322 | 34 |
| 19.34 | 35 |
| 61.15–16 | 33 |
| 63.3–7 | 33 |
| 68.2 | 33 |
| 68.27–28 | 33 |
| 72.24–25 | 33 |
| 79.4 | 28 |
| 92.5–15 | 33 |
| 101 | 31–32 |
| 106.1–2 | 36n101 |
| 106.5–6 | 30n67 |
| 106.14–15 | 30, 30n68 |
| 116.9–10 | 28 |
| 120.21–24 | 29 |
| 321 | 34 |

## Thucydides

| | |
|---|---|
| 2.21 | 74n28 |
| 2.37 | 83n66 |
| 2.53.1 | 73n25 |
| 2.60 | 80n53 |
| 3.37.1—48.2 | 110–11n88 |
| 3.37–48 | 61n97, 61n98 |
| 4.61 | 74n27 |
| 6.39.1–2 | 96 |
| 7.48 | 76 |
| 8.92 | 84–85n74 |

## Xenophon

*Symposium*

| | |
|---|---|
| 2.9–12 | 121 |

## Zeno and Chryssipus

*Stoic. vet. frag.*

| | |
|---|---|
| 111.217.19 | 134 |

# Subject Index

Aalders, Gerhard Jean Daniël, 48n30
Aaron, 76–78, 81–82, 87
Abiram, 75, 86, 87
Aeschines, 121
Aeschylus, 122
Alexander, Loveday, 17
alien residents
   baptism and citizenship of, 139–43
   democracy and, 122–23
   exclusion from citizenship, 49n33, 115, 117
Amador, J. David Hester, 6, 147–48n141, 150
Anderson, Graham, 43, 46n25
apostleship, 158
ἀρχῶν, 107–8
Aristides, Aelius, 33
Aristophanes, 124–27, 146–47
Aristotle
   criticism of democracy, 122, 123
   on logic of exclusion, 118–21, 127, 135
   on place of the mind in democratic discourse, 172–73
assembly. *See ekklēsia*
Athenian council, 44
Athens
   citizenship in, 24, 117–24. *See also* citizenship
   influence in Roman Empire, 3, 14
   as origin of democracy, 187
   *See also* civic *ekklēsia*; democratic *ekklēsia*; Greek educational system
audience
   of classical Greek literature, 74–75
   of Josephus, 73–74n25
   of Paul's rhetoric, 174, 185–86
   *See also ekklēsia* audience

baptismal formula
   Corinthians' understanding of, 12, 112, 116, 138–43, 152, 185–86, 189
   as means of forming Christian *ekklēsia*, 156
   Paul's re-crafting of, 138–40, 155, 159–61, 182
   veiling and, 150
Barrett, C. K., 171
benevolent monarch, 53
Betz, Hanz Dieter
   on Corinthian situation, 168
   on meaning λόγος, 100n42
   on pairing of speech and wisdom, 96n22, 113
   on Paul opening to 1 Corinthians, 90n3, 102n53
   on Paul's use of political terms and *topoi* in 1 Corinthians, 6
body
   Christian *ekklēsia* as, 157, 159
   Greek thought on relationship to head, 133–35
   Paul's use of metaphor in regard to spiritual gifts, 157
   Paul's use of metaphor regarding speech in *ekklēsia*, 135–36
Brooten, Bernadette J., 139n106, 176–77n75, 180–81n82

Campbell, J. Y., 71n8

## Subject Index

Castelli, Elizabeth A., 103, 109
celibacy, 142, 182, 183
Cervin, Richard, 134
Christian *ekklēsia*. See Corinthian *ekklēsia*
citizenship
    Aristotle's logic of exclusion, 118–22
    Athenian values of, 24, 25, 117
    baptismal formula and, 12, 112, 116, 138–43, 152, 155, 159–61, 182, 185–86, 189
    in Christian *ekklēsia*, 114, 154
    defined by exclusions of democracy, 10, 14, 42, 49, 50, 96, 113, 115, 117–24, 178, 185, 188
    democracy blurring boundaries of, 122
    demonstration through rhetoric, 50
    Dio and Plutarch's definition of, 118
    Euripides's definition of, 23–26
    freedom of speech associated with, 10, 48–49
    gendering of in Corinthians, 130–52, 183
    Greek education as preparation for, 10, 15, 19
    link between speech and wisdom, 96–97
    nature of in 1 Corinthians, 12
    Paul's gendering of speech and, 131–32, 185
    responsibility of, 50
    in Roman polity, 12
civic democracy, 40–41, 76. See also democracy
civic discourse, 171–72. See also democratic discourse
civic *ekklēsia*
    authority of elite speakers in, 49
    central to Greek educational system, 15, 40
    democratic interaction in, 94
    Dio and Plutarch's recognition of, 10
    Dio's portrayal of, 41–43
    in first century Greek cities, 8–9, 40–41, 43–45
    interaction between speakers and audience, 45, 48–53
    participants in, 117
    as source of Christian *ekklēsia*, 5
    See also democratic *ekklēsia*; *ekklēsia*
Clement of Alexandria, 148
collective authority, 101
common good
    as citizens' responsibility, 50, 55
    effects of stasis on, 75
    as goal of democratic polity, 35, 37, 84, 88, 168–69
    love as agent of, 161–62, 185
    Moses' commitment to, 84, 86, 88
    Paul and Dio's admonitions to work for, 165
    Praxagora's goal of, 125
    prophesy associated with, 166–67, 168
    self-interest of rhetors vs., 104
    self-limitation of Corinthians in interest of, 144–50, 152, 154–55, 156, 178
    social distinctions for, 159
    speakers claim to, 163
    speech regulation in Christian *ekklēsia* and, 179–80
    spiritual gifts appointed for, 156, 161–65
    use of the mind and, 174
    wisdom equated with concern for, 85
    women as threat to, 180–81
community, 1. See also civic *ekklēsia*; Corinthian *ekklēsia*; *ekklēsia*
Connolly, Joy, 15, 25
Conzelmann, Hans, 103n55, 103n56, 133n67, 150, 163n27
Corinth, 98
Corinthian *ekklēsia*
    authority of, 112, 164–65
    baptism and citizenship in, 12, 112, 116, 139–43
    debate over freedom and leadership, 1, 2, 112
    *ekklēsia* discourse with Paul, 99–100
    gendering of, 166–76
    maintaining order in, 166–76, 178

Paul's demand for women's silence in, 130–52, 149–50, 176–84, 185
Paul's gendering of, 166–76, 178
Paul's gendering of speech in, 13, 115, 130, 133, 143–50, 152, 178, 185
Paul's praise and critique of, 102–3, 110–12
Paul's title for, 11
scholars' view of, 167–68
speech and wisdom of (Paul's view), 106–7, 109, 115, 163–65
speech in, 150–52
spiritual gifts appointed to, 155–66
type of wisdom required for, 109
use of discourse to promote freedom and participation, 9
women's citizenship in, 116
women speaking in, 115–16
*See also ekklēsia*
Corinthians
appreciation for spiritual gifts, 168
awareness of democratic discourse, 99, 185–86
claim to power, 110–11n87
construction of *ekklēsia*, 7–8
debate over freedom and leadership, 1, 2, 112
as *ekklēsia* audience, 110
Paul's praise and critique of, 90, 132–33
socioeconomic make-up of, 105–6
speech and wisdom of (Paul's view), 90
understanding of baptismal transformation, 12, 112, 116, 138–40, 152, 185, 189
understanding of leadership and citizenship, 132
understanding of their identity as *ekklēsia*, 69, 139–43, 152, 189
view of themselves, 102–3, 112, 113, 174, 185–86
Corrington, Gail Patterson, 133n68, 134n78, 135
cosmology, 115, 135–43, 177
creation narratives, 115, 136–43, 177

Cribiore, Raffaella, 16n5, 17n10, 21, 23, 24, 25

*dēmos*
as decision-makers, 49–50
Dio and Pseudo-Xenophon's description of, 57
qualities of good and bad forms, 53
relationship to speakers, 50–52, 110
sovereignty of, 53–57
use of the term, 151n157
wisdom of, 96–97
Dathan, 75, 86, 87
Dautzenberg, Gerhard, 131
debate, 57–66
debaters, 107
decision-making
baptismal transformation and, 141
based on common good, 35
in Corinthian *ekklēsia*, 2, 110
in democratic *ekklēsia*, 48–50, 52, 61–62
effects of tyranny on *demos'* ability, 78–79
in first century Greek cities, 95
of Jews vs. democracy, 76
Moses' view of, 82
through assembly debate, 62–63
declamations, 18, 21, 28–29, 31
Della Corte, M., 17n10
Delobel, Joel, 145n124
democracy
in ancient civic *ekklēsia*, 8–9
ancient critics of, 111, 122–24
Athenian model, 28
baptismal transformation and, 141–43, 161
citizenship defined by exclusions of, 10, 14, 42, 49, 50, 96, 113, 115, 117–24, 178, 185, 188
decision-making institution of, 34, 49
defined, 118
Dio's critique of, 57–58
Euripides and Dio's definition of, 54
fundamental values of, 50

## Subject Index

democracy *(continued)*
  Israelites' assumption of in Josephus' interpretation of Korah's rebellion, 78–80
  Korah's appeal to, 76
  legacy of for first-century Jews, 69
  Libanius' definition and defense of, 30–31
  Lysias' summation of, 50n41
  necessity of diversity, 162–63, 169
  origin in classical Athens, 187
  persistence in first-century, 3–4, 14, 40–41, 43–45
  potential for empowering utter anti-citizens, 122
  reinforcement of in Greek educational system, 9–10
  scholarship on first-century existence of, 2–3, 91–94
  speech as indicator of success of, 109–10
  wisdom required for, 96–97
democratic discourse
  in 1 Corinthians, 90, 110, 113, 152, 188
  baptismal transformation and, 141–43, 161
  connection to Greekness, 187
  Corinthians' deployment of, 99, 185–86
  defining citizenship, 96, 113, 115
  Euripides and, 22
  in first century Greek cities, 14
  fundamental values of, 24, 50, 89, 187
  gendered citizenship, 118–21, 127, 178, 188
  gendered speech and wisdom within, 12, 117–30, 152, 178, 185
  Greek educational system fostering, 15, 17
  Josephus' deployment in portrait of Moses, 68–69, 78–81
  Josephus' deployment in portrayal of Korah, 76–77
  link between speech and wisdom, 96–99, 115
  of Moses (Josephus's interpretation), 81–82
  Ober on, 59
  Paul's gendering Corinthian *ekklēsia* as, 11–12, 168, 178
  Paul's gendering of speech in *ekklēsia* as, 131
  persistence in first century, 43–45, 88, 90, 91–95, 113, 187
  place of the mind in, 172–73
  risk of self-interest, 165
  speech *topos* and, 95–99, 113, 188
  tension between freedom and social unity, 162, 168, 169
  tension between rich and poor men, 31
  tension between tyrant and tyrannicide, 30
  transmission and replication through Greek education, 14–15, 27, 30–31, 95
  *See also* gendering of *ekklēsia*; gendering of speech
democratic *ekklēsia*
  baptismal transformation and, 139–43
  Corinthian Christians as, 110
  Dio's portrayal of, 42–43
  discourse on in Greek education, 15, 32, 35–38, 40
  Greek students' path to understanding, 32, 38
  interaction between speakers and audience, 45, 48–53, 54–55, 56–57, 61–62
  Paul's use of *topoi* from, 11–12
  persistence in first century, 43–45, 94–95
  rebellion of Korah as gathering of, 11
  *See also* civic *ekklēsia*; *ekklēsia*
Democritus, 135n82
Demosthenes
  declamations in imitation of, 18
  place in Greek education, 26, 27, 32–34
  rhetorical ability of, 22
  on rights of citizens, 38–39

Subject Index    219

on safeguard against tyrants, 57
Thersites compared to, 37
view of women, 121
depilation, 148–49
Desideri, Paolo, 48n31
Dickie, M. W., 98n33
Dio Chrysostom
  account of civic *ekklēsia*, 40–45, 48, 66–67
  application of *Phoenissae*, 25–26
  call for harmony, 168–70
  consideration of Roman Empire, 63–66, 88
  critique of democracy, 57–59
  on debate, 62–63
  defense of himself, 54–55
  definition of democracy, 54
  on democratic practices under Roman rule, 10
  on *ekklēsia* debate, 59–60
  exile under Domitian, 46n26
  focus on city as political sphere, 48n31
  on freedom, law, and exile, 48n30
  as Greek citizen and Roman subject, 46–48
  Greek students' study of, 16
  on hair as gender symbol, 148
  involvement in building projects, 47n28
  on leadership through speech, 52
  on place of the mind in democratic discourse, 172, 173–74
  portrayal of *ekklēsia*, 41–43, 45
  portrayal of leadership, 58
  on prevalence of *ekklēsia* discourse, 39
  on self-interests, 165
  on sovereignty of *dēmos*, 53–57
  speeches of, 46n25
  use of discordant instruments *topos*, 168
  use of unskilled speaker *topos*, 105
Diogenes of Apollonia, 135n82
Dionysius Atticus, 46n25
discernment, gift of, 157, 158
discernment of *ekklēsia*, 12, 115–16, 170, 174–75

discourse, 1–2. *See also* democratic discourse; *ekklēsia* discourse
disorder. *See* order
divination, 171–72
divine wisdom, 106–7
Dunn, Francis M., 22n37
Dutch, Robert, 99n37

economic inequality, 31–32
*edah*, 71n9, 78n42
*ekklēsia*
  appearance in Bible, 99–100
  as arena for criticism of leaders, 54
  as arena for student rhetor, 28–29
  as central institution of democracy, 187
  consideration of Roman Empire, 63–66, 67
  Corinthian church as, 91
  course of events in, 35
  Dio's representation of, 52
  effects of stasis, 74–75
  in Greek cities in Roman Empire, 14
  in Greek culture, 3–4
  in Greek educational system, 14–39
  in Greek student reading, 32–35
  interaction between speakers and audience, 45, 48–53, 54–55, 56–57, 61–62, 104–5, 110
  Josephus' description of Israelites in the wilderness, 79–80, 84–86, 87–88
  Josephus' use of the term, 68–69, 71–72, 78–81, 89
  as king/tyrant, 53, 110–11n87
  Moses' response to Korah's rebellion (Joseph's translation of), 72
  opposition to Moses, 78–81
  order in, 166–76
  Paul's construction of ideal and hierarchy of, 13
  Paul's idea of speech within, 13
  persistence in first century, 40–41, 43–45, 94–95
  primary duty of, 35, 67
  qualities of good and bad forms, 53
  reassessment of, 3

*ekklēsia (continued)*
    scholarship on first-century existence of, 2–7, 91–93
    use of the term, 70–72, 92–93, 99–100, 151n157
    wisdom of, 96–97
    women and speech in, 124–27
    in writings of Dio and Plutarch, 40–67
    *See also* civic *ekklēsia*; Corinthian *ekklēsia*; democratic *ekklēsia*; Greek *ekklēsia*
*ekklēsia* audience
    as decision-makers, 49–50
    discernment of, 170, 174–75
    Hebrew congregation as, 87
    interaction with speakers/elite leaders, 45, 48–53, 54–55, 56–57, 61–62, 104–5, 110
    Plutarch's portrayal of, 61–62
    responsibility of, 35
    responsible vs. irresponsible, 84–86
    voice and authority of Hebrews, 83
    wisdom of, 96–97
*ekklēsia* discourse
    in 1 Corinthians, 102–12
    as characteristic of rhetoric in Greek education, 9–10
    in Corinthian *ekklēsia*, 99, 185–86
    defined, 1–2
    dissemination through Greek education, 38
    Euripides' utility in transmitting, 22
    gendering of speech, 115–16, 155
    Josephus' mobilization of, 11, 89
    of Korah, 75–78
    Korah's abilities vs. Moses' abilities, 76
    mapping of in ancient world, 7–9
    of Moses, 79–84, 86–87
    Paul's mobilization of, 97, 103–12, 113, 168
    persistence in first century, 14, 91–95
    replication through Greek education, 33–34
*ekklēsia* rhetoric, 95–99
*ekklēsia* speech, 166–76, 177

elites
    interaction of orators with audience, 45, 48–53, 54–55, 56–57, 61–62, 104–5, 110
    Paul's construction of Corinthians as, 106
    Paul's distancing from, 110
    status defined by rhetoric, 101
    unskilled speaker *topos*, 104–5
    *See also* leadership; speakers
Epictetus, 148
equality
    baptismal transformation and, 116, 139–43
    citizenship and, 117–18
    defined by rhetoric, 101
    Demosthenes on, 34–35
    within the *ekklēsia*, 13
    Euripides's definition of, 24
    as foundational value of Athenian democracy, 24, 50, 89, 187
    in Greek educational system, 15
    of Israelites in the Exodus, 69
    manifestation in political involvement, 49
    Moses' commitment to, 68, 69, 81–82, 86, 87, 88
    people's trust creating, 57
    right of speech as nature of, 48–49, 96, 155
    *stasis* resulting from, 75–76
    as topic of civic discourse, 8–9, 31–32
    veiling and, 149–150
    *See also* citizenship; subordination of women
*Euboicus* (Dio), 40–43, 45, 49–50, 57–58, 59, 66–67
Euripides
    definition of free speech, 49n34
    definitions of freedom, security, and equality, 23–26
    place in Greek education, 16, 17, 22–26, 27, 38
    Plutarch's quotes from, 20
    on role of women, 121, 122
    as spokesman for democratic egalitarianism, 22, 38

## Subject Index   221

on women's veiling and speech, 146
exile, 23

factionalism, 74–75, 103. *See also stasis*
Favorinus, 99
Fee, Gordon
   on 1 Corinthians 11:2, 133n67
   on 1 Corinthians 13, 161–62, 163n27, 164
   dating of 1 Corinthians 4:33b–36, 131
   on Galatians 3:28, 138
   interpretation of 1 Corinthians 11:15, 145n124
   interpretation of "glory," 137, 138n103
Feldman, Louis H., 68n2, 71n12, 73, 75n32, 80, 82n61
Fitzmyer, Joseph, 134
foreigners. *See* alien residents
Foucault, Michel, 1–2, 7–8, 95n21
Foxhall, Lin, 127n46, 129–30
freedom
   common good limiting, 163, 185
   Corinthian debate over, 1
   defined by rhetoric, 101
   democracy as, 31, 187
   Euripides definition of, 23–24
   as foundational value of Athenian democracy, 24, 50, 155, 162
   in Greek educational system, 15
   guarantee of in Athens, 117
   harmony securing under Rome, 51–52, 62, 64–66
   harmony vs., 162, 168, 169
   of Israelites in the Exodus, 69
   love as limiting agent of, 161–62, 185
   manifestation in political involvement, 49
   Moses' championing of, 68
   Paul's attempt to circumscribe, 164–65
   relationship to social unity, 162–63
   Roman threat to, 62–66
   spiritual gifts and, 161–65
   as topic of civic discourse, 8–9
freedom of speech
   baptismal transformation and, 116, 141
   consideration of Roman Empire, 63–66
   definition of citizenship, 12
   as definition of democracy, 54, 122–123, 187
   within the *ekklēsia*, 13, 53
   in *ekklēsia* rhetoric, 95–99
   Euripides's definition of, 23, 24–26, 49n34
   in Greek educational system, 10
   as nature of freedom and equality in Athens, 48–49
   *See also parrhēsia*

Gauthier, Philippe, 44, 94–95n19
Gebhard, Elizabeth R., 98n33
gender differences
   Aristophanes on, 124–27
   Aristotle's view of, 118–21
   hair as indicator, 147–50
   head covering and, 143–50
   Paul's construction of, 132, 135–43
   Plutarch's view of, 127–30
   veiling as indication of, 145
gendering of Christian *ekklēsia*, 166–76, 178–179, 185
gendering of mind, 172–73
gendering of speech
   in 1 Corinthians, 154, 161
   demand for women's silence and, 177–84
   Paul's attempt to reinforce his authority through, 9
   Paul's deployment of cosmology and creation narratives, 13, 115, 132–43, 152, 177
   Paul's deployment of hair and veiling, 115, 143–50, 152, 177
   policing of boundary between citizens and non-citizens, 12, 115, 116, 117–27
   as rhetorical tool for asserting gender difference, 147–50, 185, 189
Georgi, Dieter, 71n8

gifts of speech and wisdom, 154–55. *See also* prophesy; tongues, gift of; word of knowledge; word of wisdom
gifts of the Spirit. *See* prophesy; spiritual gifts; tongues, gift of; word of knowledge; word of wisdom
Glancy, Jennifer, 142–43, 150
Glare, Peter, 134n78
Gleason, Maud, 125
γνῶσις, 100n43
God
  as God of order and peace, 167–68, 178–79
  Moses' reliance on authority of, 79, 81–82, 83, 87–88
  wisdom of, 106–7
Greek culture, 3–4
Greek educational system
  availability of, 15–16n2
  critical function of, 25
  discourse on democratic *ekklēsia*, 15, 32, 38, 40
  dissemination of *ekklēsia* discourse, 38
  *ekklēsia* in student reading, 32–35
  example from *Progymnasmata*, 35–38
  goals of, 15, 19, 29–30, 38
  Greek identity determined by, 20
  Morgan's core and periphery model of, 19
  overview, 15–18
  role of *progymnasmata* exercises, 26–32
  socialization of students into citizenship, 10, 19, 95
  study of Euripides, 22–26
  study of Homer, 19–22
  study of rhetoric, 9–10
  transmission and replication of democratic discourse, 14–15, 27, 30–31, 95
Greek *ekklēsia*, 68–72
Greek literature, 73–74. *See also* Greek educational system; Scripture Index: GREEK TEXTS; *specific Greek writer*

Greekness, 16–25, 38, 90, 187
Greek *paideia*, 10, 19, 20, 25
Grudem, Wayne, 134

hair
  gendering of speech deploying, 115, 147–50
  Paul's naturalization of danger of disorder, 12, 136, 144–50
  as rhetorical tool for asserting gender difference, 125–26
  *See also* veiling
Hansen, Mogens Hermen, 42n7, 54n60, 83n67, 117n4
Harland, Philip A., 94n16
harmony
  democratic debate vs., 66
  disorder vs., 168–69
  freedom vs., 162–63, 168, 169
  love as agent of, 161–62, 185
  prophesy associated with, 168
  as safeguard to rights under Rome, 51–52, 62, 64
  speakers' claim to creation of, 163
  *See also* order
Harris, William V., 15–16n2
head
  definition of, 133–35
  Paul's use of head/body metaphor, 135–37, 177
  *See also* leadership
head covering. *See* veiling
Hedrick, Charles, 115
Hermagoras, 46n25
Herodotus, 171
Homer
  characterization of Thersites, 36
  construction of Greek identity, 20
  importance in declamation, 21
  place in Greek education, 16, 17, 19–22, 26, 27, 38
*homonoia*. *See* harmony
Horrell, David G., 132, 137n93, 138n105, 157n3, 160n17
Horsley, Richard, 91–92
Hurley, James B., 131n64

Iambilicus, 172

*idiōtai*, 104, 106, 108
*isēgoria*, 49
Isocrates
  description of *dēmos*, 58
  on fruits of education, 29
  place in Greek education, 16, 26n53, 27, 33
Israelites, 69–72, 78–79, 83–86

Jervis, L. Ann, 132n66, 137n93, 138, 139, 160n17
Jones, A. H. M., 44, 45n22, 47n27, 59n86, 92n8, 94–95n19
Josephus
  audience of, 73–74n25
  description of tumult of the assembly, 84n74
  engagement with Greek democratic discourse, 89
  mobilization of *ekklēsia* discourse, 11
  portrayal of Moses, 11, 68–69, 73
  reinterpretation of Korah rebellion, 11, 68–69, 75–89
  use of *ekklēsia*, 71–72

Kittredge, Cynthia, 188
Kloppenborg, John S., 94n16
knowledge, 163
Korah, rebellion of
  biblical story of, 75, 86
  Josephus' reinterpretation of, 11, 68–69, 75–89
  Moses' response to (Josephus' interpretation), 11, 68–69, 73, 81–84, 86–87
Kurzinger, J., 138n105
kyriarchal democracy, 141n116

Laks, André, 135n82
law, 31–32, 82, 180–81
leadership
  accountability of, 55–56, 110
  acted out through speech, 48–53, 96
  Aristotle's view of, 119–21, 123
  Corinthian debate over, 1
  in democratic *ekklēsia*, 49
  Dio's portrayal of, 58

  gendered speech and, 115
  Greek examples of, 36–38
  Greek view of, 30–31
  Josephus' ideal of, 76
  limitation of women, 154
  of Moses, 11, 68–69, 73–78
  Moses' view of, 81–82
  Paul's establishment of his leadership, 9, 12, 90, 91, 103–7, 110, 111–12, 115, 132–33, 158, 175–176, 184, 188
  Paul's view of, 103
  shaping students' understanding of, 33–34
  skills and qualities for, 51–52, 60–61, 76–77, 80–81, 87, 89, 97
  *See also* elites
Lévy, I., 2, 43–44, 91–92
Libanius
  encomium for Thersites, 36–39
  exercises on democratic *ekklēsia*, 36
  focus on Demosthenes, 33
  *topos* exercises, 27, 29–31
literacy rate, 15–16n2, 16n3
Livingstone, Niall, 20n24
λόγος, 100
love
  as agent of common good, 161–62, 185
  compared to speech, wisdom, and knowledge, 162, 163–64
Lycugus, 108n84
Lysias, 33, 50n41

Ma, John
  on ideology in narrative description, 50
  on interrogation of democracy by Dio and Plutarch, 59n86
  on persistence of democracy in first-century, 42, 45, 94n19
  on political negotiation in first-century *ekklēsia*, 52
  on standard oligarchic positions, 58
  on tale of the hunter in *Euboicus*, 43
Manville, Philip, 117
Marrou, Henri, 15–16n2

## Subject Index

Martin, Dale, 124n127
  on 1 Corinthians 4:8–13, 110–11n87
  on appropriate speech in Corinthian *ekklēsia*, 171
  identification of scribe, wise man, disputer, 107n80, 108
  pairing of speech and wisdom, 113
  on Paul's direction to prophets, 172
  on Paul's problematizing of rhetoric, 100–101
  on Paul's use of body parts, 157
  on veiling, 145n124, 146
Mason, Steve, 73–74n25, 73n23
McCready, Wayne O., 70n6
McNamara, Jo Ann, 129–30
Meeks, Wayne, 5, 5n13, 93–94, 93n12
Menander, 26n53
metics. *See* alien residents
Millis, Benjamin W., 98n33
*mimesis* of speech in literature, 21
mind
  gendering of, 172–73
  place in Corinthian *ekklēsia*, 171, 172, 174–75, 178
  place in democratic discourse, 172–73
  prophesy and divination and, 171–72
mind-body-soul relationship, 133–36
Mitchell, Margaret
  on 1 Corinthians 13, 161
  drawing parallel between Paul's argument for unity and *homonoia*, 162n22
  on harmony in civic and Christian life, 162n21
  identification of scribe, wise man, disputer, 107n80
  on love, 161
  on Paul's compliments to Corinthians, 102
  on Paul's use of political terms in 1 Corinthians, 6
  on *topos* of discordant instruments, 167, 168
  on use of συζητητής and συζητεῖν, 107n79

Mitchell, Stephen, 44, 45n22, 64n107, 94–95n19, 95n20
Morgan, Teresa
  core and periphery model of Greek education, 19, 26, 36
  on Greek education, 17n10, 18, 25n49
  on Homer as quintessential Greek writer, 20
  work on Greek school papyri, 16nn4–5
Moses
  Korah's accusations against, 76–77
  as persuasive speaker, 80–81
  response to rebellion of Korah (Josephus' interpretation), 11, 68–69, 73, 81–84, 86–87
Munro, Winsome, 131n63
Murphy-O'Connor, Jerome, 131

Nasrallah, Laura, 168
νήπιος, 164

Ober, Josiah
  on diversity in *ekklēsia*, 169
  on effects of democracy, 59
  on *Ekklesuiazusae*, 125
  on elite orators, 104
  on fundamental values of Athenian democracy, 24
  on interaction between speakers and audience, 62n100, 67, 96n24
  on *isēgoria*, 49
  on tension between freedom and social unity, 162–63
  on terms used to describe politicians, 49n35
  on unskilled speaker *topos*, 105
Odysseus, 37–38
Økland, Jorunn, 93n15, 136n92, 137, 145n124, 145n127
Old Oligarch. *See* Pseudo-Xenophon
orators. *See* speakers
order
  in civic *ekklēsia*, 57–66, 84–85
  in Corinthian *ekklēsia*, 166–76, 178–79
  democracy's effect on, 123–24

divine order of households, 136–37, 149
hierarchy of spiritual gifts appealing to, 155
prophesy associated with, 168, 170, 175–76
speech regulation in Christian *ekklēsia* establishing, 179–80
tongues affecting, 167–68, 170, 175
veiling and, 143–44, 149, 179
women's speech affecting, 116, 131, 152, 177–84, 180
*See also* harmony

*paideia*
availability in Corinth, 99
determination of Greek identity, 20
reinforcement of democracy, 187
socialization of students into citizenship, 10, 38
Parker, Holt, 118–19
*parrhēsia*, 23–24, 38, 49, 53, 56–57. *See also* freedom of speech
patriarchalism, 101n49
patriarchal marriage, 140, 142–43, 155, 160–61, 181–82, 183n88
Paul
audience of, 106, 113, 174, 185–86
characterization of Corinthian Christians, 110–11
comparison of love and speech, 162, 163–65
construction of *ekklēsia* as possible vision, 7–8
on Corinthian *ekklēsia*, 90
critique of Corinthians' speech and wisdom, 1, 11, 90, 103, 105–6, 110–12, 115
decentralization of his role, 7
demand for women's silence in *ekklēsia*, 176–84, 185
direction to prophets, 172
discussion of spiritual gifts, 156–67
emphasis on speech linked to wisdom, 96, 97, 106–7, 109, 113
gendering of Christian *ekklēsia*, 166–76, 178, 182–83
gendering of speech in Corinth, 13, 115, 130, 133, 143–50, 152, 178
head/body metaphor, 135–37, 179
hierarchy of spiritual gifts, 158, 166–67, 185
insistence on women's head covering, 143–50
leadership of, 188
on love, 163–65
on practice in the Christian *ekklēsia*, 166–76
praise for Corinthians' speech and wisdom, 90, 102–3, 110
re-crafting of baptismal formula, 138–40, 155, 159–61, 182
scholarship on, 187
self-presentation of, 9, 12, 90, 91, 103–7, 110, 111–12, 115, 132–33, 158, 175–76, 184, 188
title for Corinthian community, 11
on types of wisdom, 106–9, 111, 113
use of democratic discourse, 131, 168, 178
use of *ekklēsia* discourse, 11, 99, 103–13
use of persuasive speech and rhetoric, 7, 9, 99–112
use of term *ekklēsia*, 99–100
use of unskilled speaker *topos*, 103–6, 110
on women's subordinate role, 133–42, 176, 181–83, 185
Penner, Todd, 125, 144, 147–49
persuasive speaking ability
link to wisdom, 97
of Moses in Josephus' account, 11, 68–69, 73, 81–84, 86–87, 88
of Paul, 102–12
Paul's view of, 103, 107
as quality of leadership, 51–52, 60–61, 76–77, 80–81, 89, 97
of tyrants, 76–77
ψηφίζομαι, 76
Philo of Alexandria, 133–34, 135, 172
Philostratus, 33, 46n25
Plato, 20, 133, 135, 172
πλῆθος, 68–72, 78–81. *See also ekklēsia*

## 226   Subject Index

Plutarch
  account of civic *ekklēsia*, 40–41, 66–67
  on active civic assembly, 46n25
  advice to young men entering politics, 60–61, 173
  consideration of Roman Empire, 63–66
  critique of democracy, 59
  on debate, 63
  definition of "head," 134, 135
  on democratic practices under Roman rule, 10
  on *ekklēsia* debate, 59–60
  focus on city as political sphere, 48n31
  as Greek citizen and Roman subject, 46–48
  Greek students' study of, 16
  on interaction between speakers and audience, 45
  on place of the mind in democratic discourse, 172, 173
  political career, 46–47
  on prevalence of *ekklēsia* discourse, 39
  quotes from Homer compared to other writers, 19–20
  on skills and qualities for elite leadership, 51–52
  on sovereignty of *dēmos*, 53, 55–57
  on subordinate role of women, 127–30, 147, 181–82, 183
  use of framework of Greek *polis*, 48n30
  on work, 47n28
Pogoloff, Stephen, 101
*polis*
  definition of in Athens, 117
  Greek educational system and, 17–18
  guarantee of equality in, 82
  as political forum, 47–48
  use of the term, 151n157
politicians, 55–56
politics, 15
poor man
  abilities of, 41
  as character in *progymnasmata* and declamations, 31–32
  Demosthenes' view of, 34
  Moses' view of, 81–82
*porneia*, 142–143
*progymnasmata* exercises, 10, 18, 19, 21n29, 26–32. See also *topos* exercises
prophesy
  common good associated with, 166–67, 168, 174–75
  as key for successful *ekklēsia*, 169–71
  love compared to, 163–65
  order associated with, 167–68, 170, 175
  Paul's regulations for, 178–80
  place in hierarchy of gifts, 157, 158–59
  spirit's control of, 156
  tongues vs., 166, 167, 175
*prosopopoeia*, 28
Pseudo-Xenophon, 57–58, 122–23

*qahal*, 70–71, 78n42, 92

Rajak, Tessa, 73, 73–74n25, 73n23, 74, 87
rhetoric
  as advanced level of education in Greece, 19, 26–27
  defined, 6
  *ekklēsia* as arena for, 28–29
  as goal of Greek educational system, 15, 38
  in Greek educational system, 9–10, 18, 25
  Homer's knowledge of, 21–22
  of Korah, 76
  Moses' response to Korah's rebellion, 68–72, 78–81
  Paul's view of, 103, 107
  of Paul to Corinthians, 91, 102–12, 184–85, 188–89
  as quality of leadership, 81–84
  scholarship on first-century existence of, 91–92, 100–101
  speech *topos* in, 91, 95–99

wisdom linked to, 96–97
rich man. *See* wealthy man
Rogers, Guy MacLean, 95n20
Roman Empire
    classical Athenian influence in, 3
    consideration of in Greek politics, 51–52, 62, 63–66, 67
    democratic practice under, 3–4, 14
    *ekklēsia* in, 2–3
    government of cities in, 95n20
    incorporation of Greek ideas and language, 74
Roman Latin education, 16
rule of law, 82
Russell, Donald A., 28, 41, 47n27

Salmeri, Giovanni, 45, 46, 46n25, 48n31
Saxonhouse, Arlene, 23, 49n35
Schmidt, K. L., 92n10
scholarship
    on Corinth, 98
    on first-century rhetoric, 100–101
    history of, 2–7
    on Paul, 187, 188
    on use of *ekklēsia*, 92–94
    views of Corinthian *ekklēsia*, 167–68
    views of Corinthians, 1
    views of first-century democratic processes, 91–92
Schüssler Fiorenza, Elisabeth
    analysis of Galatians 3:28, 140
    on baptismal self-understanding of Corinthians, 112
    characterization of Paul's rhetoric, 105n73
    characterization of rhetoric, 6–7
    on Corinthian's baptismal understanding, 185
    on *ekklēsia*, 2
    on Greek education, 9n26
    on interpretation of 1 Corinthians, 144n122
    on kyriarchal democracy, 141
    on patriarchal marriage, 160–61
    on Paul's claim to fatherhood of Corinthian church, 112n89
    on Paul's demand for women's silence, 182
    on Paul's gendering of speech, 150, 154
    on private organizations, 5n13, 94n18
scribes, 107, 108
security, 15, 24, 31, 50
self-control
    in Christian *ekklēsia*, 155, 174, 178
    Corinthians' lack of, 90
    of elites, 63
    as guide to *ekklēsia* speech, 13, 63, 115, 176, 180
    love as practice of, 185
    of prophets, 174, 179, 180
    speech regulation in Christian *ekklēsia* and, 179–80
    of tongue speakers, 180
    women portrayed as lacking, 121–22, 126–27, 136, 142, 154, 176, 178, 179, 180, 181, 185
self-interest
    of Korah vs. common good, 84, 86, 88
    Paul and Dio's admonitions to reject, 165
    of rhetors, 104
    as risk in democratic discourse, 165–66
    spiritual gifts and, 161–65
    tongues associated with, 167–68
Septuagint, 5, 70–72
shame
    effeminate men and, 173–74
    woman's uncovered head as, 129, 137, 143–45, 147, 148–49, 150, 157, 176–77, 178, 181
Schrage, Wolfgang, 71, 71n8–9
slavery, 23
slaves
    Aristotle's logic of exclusion, 118–21
    baptism and citizenship of, 139–43
    democracy and, 122–23
    exclusion from citizenship, 13, 49n33, 115, 117, 153, 178
    immature mind of, 172–73

slaves *(continued)*
  options for women slaves, 142–43, 150, 155, 183
social unity. *See* harmony
Socrates, 120, 121, 122
σοφία, 100, 103. *See also* wisdom
Sophistopolis, 28
Spawforth, A. J. S., 98n34
speakers
  as agents of harmony and common good, 163
  authority of in civic *ekklēsia*, 49–50
  interaction with *ekklēsia* audience, 45, 48–53, 54–55, 56–57, 61–62, 104–5, 110
  skills and qualities for, 51–52
  unskilled speaker *topos*, 103–5, 110
  wisdom of, 96–97
  *See also* elites; leadership
speech
  ban on women in *ekklēsia*, 176–84
  baptismal transformation and, 161
  in Christian *ekklēsia*, 150–52, 166–76
  of Corinthians, 90, 99, 102–12, 115, 164
  elements of appropriate for *ekklēsia*, 174
  as essential political tool, 45–53
  gifts of the spirit involving, 157
  as inherent in humans, 118
  love compared to, 162, 163–65
  paired with wisdom in classical period, 109–10, 113, 188
  Paul's emphasis on, 96–99, 113
  Paul's limitation of in Corinthian *ekklēsia*, 166–76
  Plutarch's gendering of women's speech, 127–30
  *topos* in *ekklēsia* rhetoric, 95–99, 113
  veiling and, 143–50
  women and slaves ability and right to, 118–22, 154–55
  *See also* gendering of speech; prophesy; rhetoric; tongues, gift of
spirit, 156
spiritual gifts
  for common good, 156, 161–65
  hierarchy of, 158, 166–67, 185
  *See also* prophesy; tongues, gift of; word of knowledge; word of wisdom
standard oligarchic positions, 58
*stasis*
  as common motif in Josephus' writings, 73
  in Corinthian church, 109, 112
  harmony vs., 168–69
  rebellion of Korah, 68–69, 73–78, 88, 89
  as threat to stability of Israelite *ekklēsia*, 85–86
  tongues associated with, 167–68
Ste Croix, G. E. M. de, 43–44, 91–92, 92n7
Sterling, Gregory G., 68–69nn2–3, 73–74n25
Stichele, Caroline Vander, 125, 144, 147–149, 180n82
Stowers, Stanley K., 102n53
strife. *See stasis*
student rhetor, 28–29
subordination of women, 127–129, 133–142, 176, 180–183
Swain, Simon, 3, 18n11, 62n101, 64n108
*synagōgē*, 70–72

Theissen, Gerd, 138, 139, 145
Theon, Aelius
  citing of Demosthenes, 33
  example from *Progymnasmata*, 35–38
  on introduction of a law, 31–32
  *progymnasmata* exercises, 26–29, 38
  on reading aloud and listening to literature, 32
Thersites's speech, 21, 36–39
thesis, 29
Thomas, Christine, 98
Thompson, Cynthia, 145
Thucydides, 33
tongues, gift of
  disorder associated with, 167–168, 170, 175

employment of spirit not mind, 170, 175
love compared to, 163–165
Paul's regulations for, 178, 179–180
place in hierarchy of gifts, 157, 158–159
prophesy vs., 166, 167, 175
self-interest associated with, 167–168, 169
*topos* exercises, 29–31. *See also progymnasmata* exercises
trust, 56–57
tyrannicide, 30
tyranny, 78–79
tyrant
  agency of *ekklēsia* as safeguard from, 78–79
  Dio's definition of, 54, 55
  distrust as safeguard against, 57
  *ekklēsia* as, 53, 110–11n87
  Korah's description of Moses as, 76–77
  Libanius' *topos* exercise against, 30–31

unskilled speaker *topos*, 103–5, 110
utter anticitizens. *See* alien residents; slaves; women

veiling
  gendering of speech deploying, 115, 132, 133, 143–50, 177, 179
  Paul's naturalization of danger of disorder, 12, 136, 179
  as protection for women, 146
Vernant, Jean-Pierre, 171
violence, 37–38, 39, 76–77

Walters, James, 98, 98n34
wealthy man, 31–32, 34, 81–82
Webb, Ruth, 27–28, 30
Welborn, Lawrence L., 100, 105, 113, 162n21
Whitmarsh, Tim, 18n11
Wire, Antoinette Clark
  on 1 Corinthians 4:8–13, 110–11n87
  on 1 Corinthians 11:11–12, 138, 139
  on 1 Corinthians 11:16, 151n155

on 1 Corinthians 13, 161n19, 162n21, 164n30
on 1 Corinthians 14:33b-36, 176–77n75
on baptismal formula, 139n111, 140n113, 160n17
on Corinthian's view of themselves, 110n86
interpretation of "glory," 137
on Paul's ban on women's speech, 179
on Paul's limitations on women, 182, 183n88
on Paul's re-crafting of baptismal formula, 136n92, 159
on Paul's use of body parts, 157
on speech in Corinthian *ekklēsia*, 175n73–74
on women's celibacy option, 142
wisdom
  of Corinthian *ekklēsia* vs. Paul's, 90, 99, 102–12, 115, 164
  as inherent in humans, 118
  link to speech in 1 Corinthians, 96–99, 113, 155
  link to speech in classical period, 109–10, 113, 115, 188
  love compared to, 162, 163–65
  Paul on types of, 106–9
wise men, 107–8
Witherington, Ben, III, 102n51
Wolin, Sheldon, 118
women
  Aristophanes' view of, 124–27
  Aristotle's logic of exclusion, 118–22, 127
  celibacy option, 142, 182, 183
  connection to divine, 135–37, 141–42, 154, 177, 179
  as dangerous to men/community, 12, 136–37, 144–50, 152, 177
  democracy and, 122–23
  disempowerment of in Greek cities, 23
  exclusion from citizenship, 12–13, 25, 49n33, 115, 117, 153, 154, 178, 185, 188

women *(continued)*
  hair and veiling of, 12, 115, 132, 133, 136, 143–50, 177, 179
  immature mind of, 173
  options for slaves, 142–43, 150, 155, 183
  options for unmarried and celibate women, 142, 182, 183
  Paul's demand for silence in *ekklēsia*, 176–84, 185–86
  Paul's use of head/body metaphor, 135
  Paul's view of speech of, 115, 154, 177, 185
  separation from the divine, 135–37, 177
  speech and discernment in Corinthian *ekklēsia*, 115–16, 152–53, 166, 176–84, 185–86
  speech in Greco-Roman *ekklēsia*, 12–13, 116, 124–27, 178
  subordination of, 127–30, 133–42, 176, 180–81
  *See also* gendering of Christian *ekklēsia*; gendering of mind; gendering of speech
word of knowledge, 156–57, 158–59, 175
word of wisdom, 156–57, 158–59, 175
worldly wisdom, 106, 107

Xenophon, 121, 130

www.ingramcontent.com/pod-product-compliance
Lightning Source LLC
Chambersburg PA
CBHW051638230426
43669CB00013B/2349